Educating English Language Learners: A Synthesis of Research Evidence

The book provides an extensive review of scientific research on the learning outcomes of students with limited or no proficiency in English in U.S. schools. Research on students in kindergarten through grade 12 is reviewed. The primary chapters of the book focus on these students' acquisition of oral language skills in English, their development of literacy (reading and writing) skills in English, instructional issues in teaching literacy, and achievement in academic domains (i.e., mathematics, science, and reading). The reviews and analyses of the research are relatively technical with a focus on research quality, design characteristics, and statistical analyses. The book provides a unique set of summary tables that give details about each study, including full references, characteristics of the students in the research, assessment tools and procedures, and results. A concluding chapter summarizes the major issues discussed and makes recommendations about particular areas that need further research.

Fred Genesee is Professor in the Department of Psychology, McGill University, Montreal. He has conducted extensive research on second language education, including second language immersion programs for majority language students and bilingual education for minority language students. His research on bilingual acquisition focuses on the syntactic and communicative development of bilingual children with typical and impaired patterns of acquisition and addresses issues related to the capacity of the language faculty during the period of primary language development.

Kathryn Lindholm-Leary is Professor of Child and Adolescent Development at San Jose State University where she has taught for seventeen years. Her research interests focus on understanding the cognitive, language, psychosocial, and societal factors that influence student achievement, with a particular emphasis on culturally and linguistically diverse students. Kathryn has worked with dual language education programs for the past twenty years and during that time has evaluated more than thirty programs and helped to establish programs in more than fifty school districts in ten states.

William M. Saunders, Ph.D., is a Senior Research Fellow at CSU, Long Beach, at UCLA, and at LessonLab. He currently directs LessonLab's school-based programs for improving teaching, learning, and schooling. He has directed several research programs including longitudinal studies of the literacy development of English learners, clinical trials of discrete instructional components, and prospective studies of school improvement. Formerly a high school teacher and Director of the Writing Project at the University of Southern California, Saunders has conducted school improvement and professional development programs in the Southern California region for the past twenty years. He is the author of numerous papers and chapters on literacy instruction, school change, assessment, and English language learners.

Donna Christian is President of the Center for Applied Linguistics (CAL) in Washington, DC. She has worked with CAL since 1974, focusing on the role of language in education, including issues of second language learning and dialect diversity. Among her activities, she has directed a program on two-way bilingual immersion, including a study for the National Center for Research on Education, Diversity & Excellence (CREDE), funded by the U.S. Department of Education. She is also a senior advisor to the Heritage Languages Initiative, the Biliteracy Research Program, and the National Literacy Panel on Language Minority Children and Youth.

Educating English Language Learners

A Synthesis of Research Evidence

FRED GENESEE
McGill University

KATHRYN LINDHOLM-LEARY
San Jose State University

WILLIAM M. SAUNDERS
California State University, Long Beach

DONNA CHRISTIAN
Center for Applied Linguistics

CAMBRIDGE
UNIVERSITY PRESS

CAMBRIDGE UNIVERSITY PRESS
Cambridge, New York, Melbourne, Madrid, Cape Town, Singapore,
São Paulo, Delhi, Dubai, Tokyo, Mexico City

Cambridge University Press
32 Avenue of the Americas, New York, NY 10013-2473, USA

www.cambridge.org
Information on this title: www.cambridge.org/9780521676991

First published 2006

A catalog record for this publication is available from the British Library

Library of Congress Cataloging in Publication data

Genesee, Fred.
Educating English language learners : a synthesis of research evidence /
Fred Genesee . . . [et al.].
    p.   cm.
Includes bibliographical references and index.
ISBN 0-521-85975-1 (hardcover) – ISBN 0-521-67699-1 (pbk.)
1. English language – Study and teaching – Foreign speakers.   2. English
language – Study and teaching – United States.   I. Title.
PE1128.A2.G4345   2006
428.0071 – dc22   2005028136

ISBN 978-0-521-85975-2 Hardback
ISBN 978-0-521-67699-1 Paperback

Contents

List of Tables

Preface

This book grew out of the work of the Center for Research on Education, Diversity & Excellence (CREDE). CREDE was a center funded by the U.S. government[1] to conduct research, generate knowledge, and provide services to improve the education of students whose ability to reach their potential is challenged by language or cultural barriers, race, geographic location, or poverty. From 1996 to 2001, CREDE comprised thirty-one research projects around the country that sought to extend knowledge about the education of the diverse students who make up the U.S. school population, from kindergarten through grade 12. These research projects were organized around six themes that are integral to the education of diverse students: language learning and academic achievement; professional development; family, peers, and community; instruction in context; integrated school reform; and assessment. Researchers working on each theme gathered data and tested curriculum models in wide-ranging settings and with diverse student populations – from classrooms with predominantly Zuni-speaking students in New Mexico to inner-city schools in Florida to California elementary schools with large populations of native Spanish-speaking students.

Following the completion of the first phase of research in 2001, CREDE researchers extended the knowledge base that can be used to improve the education of diverse students by carrying out systematic, thorough, and critical reviews of research related to the themes. Seven synthesis teams were created, each involving researchers, practitioners, and policy experts, to survey and critique the available research on a theme and make

[1] This work was supported under the Education Research and Development Program, PR/Award R306A60001, the Center for Research on Education, Diversity & Excellence, as administered by the Institute of Education Sciences (IES) of the U.S. Department of Education. The contents, findings, and opinions expressed in this volume are those of the authors and do not necessarily represent the positions or policies of IES or the U.S. ED.

recommendations for future research agendas. The chapters in this volume report on the work of the team charged with reviewing research on the language and academic development of students who come to school with no proficiency or limited proficiency in English; that is, English language learners (ELLs). The volume reviews and summarizes scientific research on three fundamental aspects of the education of ELL students: their oral language development, their literacy development, and their academic development.

The team members, in addition to the authors, who guided the synthesis work consisted of Diane August (Center for Applied Linguistics), Gil Cuevas (University of Miami), Else Hamayan (Illinois Resource Center), Liliana Minaya-Rowe (University of Connecticut), Mary Ramirez (Pennsylvania Department of Education), Noni Reis (San Jose State University), Charlene Rivera (The George Washington University), Deborah Short (Center for Applied Linguistics), and Sau-Lim Tsang (ARC Associates). We also recognize and appreciate the assistance provided by individuals who co-authored specific chapters of this volume: Graciela Borsato, Gisela O'Brien, and Caroline Riches. Their assistance was critical in the successful completion of this work. Finally, we are grateful for the leadership of Roland Tharp, the director of the Center for Research on Education, Diversity & Excellence (CREDE) for developing and encouraging the synthesis process, and we thank Yolanda Padrón, assistant director of CREDE, for her support during the project.

1

Introduction

Donna Christian

This volume synthesizes research on the relationships among oral language, literacy, and academic achievement for English language learners (ELLs) in the United States, from pre-Kindergarten through Grade 12. It explores how these findings have been applied in school and classroom settings and recommends areas of focus for future studies in order to improve education for these students.

Why is it important to assess what we know about the education of ELLs? The most basic reason, of course, is that we seek to provide, for ALL students, a high quality education that takes into account their individual strengths and needs. The level of academic achievement for students with limited proficiency in English in the United States has lagged significantly behind that of native English speakers. One congressionally mandated study reported that ELLs receive lower grades, are judged by their teachers to have lower academic abilities, and score below their classmates on standardized tests of reading and mathematics (Moss and Puma, 1995). According to a compilation of reports from forty-one state education agencies, only 18.7 percent of students classified as limited English proficient (LEP) met the state norm for reading in English (Kindler, 2002). Furthermore, students from language minority backgrounds have higher dropout rates and are more frequently placed in lower ability groups and academic tracks than language majority students (Bennici and Strang, 1995; President's Advisory Commission on Educational Excellence for Hispanic Americans, 2003; Ruiz-de-Velasco and Fix, 2000).

These educational facts intersect with the demographic facts to strengthen the rationale for this research synthesis. Across the nation, the number of students from non-English-speaking backgrounds has risen dramatically. They represent the fastest growing segment of the student population in the United States by a wide margin. From the 1991–92 school year through 2001–02, the number of identified students with limited English proficiency in public schools (K-12) grew 95 percent while total enrollment

1

increased by only 12 percent. In 2001–02, over 4.7 million school-aged children were identified as LEP (the term used in the survey), almost 10 percent of the K-12 public school student population (National Clearinghouse for English Language Acquisition, 2003). These students speak over 400 languages, but nearly 80 percent are native Spanish speakers. Of the remaining 20 percent, the largest language groups are Vietnamese (2 percent), Hmong (1.6 percent), Cantonese (1 percent), and Korean (1 percent) (Kindler, 2002).

ELL students come to U.S. schools with many resources, including linguistic resources in their native language. However, they enter U.S. schools with a wide range of language proficiencies (in English and in other languages) and of subject-matter knowledge. They differ in educational background, expectations of schooling, socioeconomic status, age of arrival in the United States, and personal experiences coming to and living in the United States.

Among ELLs who are immigrants, some have strong academic preparation. They are at or above equivalent grade levels in the school curricula and are literate in their native language. Other immigrant students enter U.S. schools with limited formal schooling – perhaps due to war or the isolated location of their home. Ruiz-de-Velasco and Fix (2000) found that 20 percent of all ELLs at the high school level and 12 percent of ELLs at the middle school level have missed two or more years of schooling since age six. Among Hispanic students aged 15–17, more than one third are enrolled below grade level (Jamieson, Curry, and Martinez, 2001). These students are not literate in their native language; they have never taken a standardized test. They have significant gaps in their educational backgrounds, lack knowledge in specific subject areas, and often need additional time to become accustomed to school routines and expectations.

Students who have been raised in the United States but speak a language other than English at home may or may not be literate in their home language. Some have strong oral English skills; others do not. Most of the U.S.-born ELLs begin their education in the U.S. public schools. There they must learn basic skills, including initial literacy. They may have some preparation for schooling from participation in pre-school programs, but U.S.-born ELLs have as much diversity in backgrounds as older immigrant students.

Although English language proficiency is a critical factor in educational success in this country, there are many other factors that can put students at risk for educational failure, and a number of these factors tend to co-occur with limited English proficiency (Garcia, 1997; Tharp, 1997). These include economic circumstances, race, educational environment, geographic location, immigration status, health, and many others. Although research on all of those factors is relevant to improving the education of English language learners in general, this synthesis focuses on such factors only as they relate to oral language, literacy, and academic achievement.

The increasing number of students for whom English is an additional language is particularly significant in light of educational reform that calls for high standards and strong accountability for schools and students. Although many states exempt ELLs from state-mandated tests for a period of time, the amount of time may be insufficient for some ELLs to acquire and apply academic English. For example, an immigrant student who enters high school with no English proficiency may be expected to pass tests for graduation in mathematics, biology, English language arts, and other subjects, after three (or fewer) years of U.S. schooling.

Federal programs in the United States have also increased the emphasis on accountability. For example, *No Child Left Behind*, the 2001 reauthorization of the Elementary and Secondary Education Act, calls for annual tests of reading and mathematics for all students in Grades 3–12 (in schools receiving federal funds under the law) and deliberately includes ELLs in state accountability systems. Although schools may exempt ELLs from achievement testing in English for up to three years, they must assess English language proficiency annually (with no exemption period). Improved education is key to improving performance for ELLs on these tests, and research results can inform such improvements.

PROGRAM ALTERNATIVES FOR ELLs

English language learners face the dual challenges of mastering English and acquiring the academic skills and knowledge deemed essential for a sound education and a productive future life. Schools face the challenge of designing programs to help ELLs achieve these goals. As mentioned earlier, ELL students embody diversity at many levels, including their socioeconomic status, the types of neighborhoods in which they live, the varieties of English and/or other languages they speak, and their cultural backgrounds. The challenge is magnified by the fact that these students are entering U.S. schools at every grade level and at various times during the academic year. Students who enter at the elementary level, of course, have the advantage of more time to acquire the language and academic skills they need (compared to ELLs who enter at the secondary level). The availability of time, however, does not lessen the need for appropriate and challenging instruction, from the very beginning, through the first and/or second language.

Genesee (1999) discusses a set of program alternatives that may meet the diverse and complex needs of ELLs (see Table 1.1). Some of them incorporate content instruction in the native language. *Two-way immersion* programs serve ELLs who speak a common native language along with native English speakers (Howard and Christian, 2002). For both groups of students, the goals are to develop high levels of first and second language

TABLE 1.1. *Characteristics of Program Alternatives for English Language Learners (Adapted with permission from Genesee, 1999)*

	Two-Way Immersion	Developmental Bilingual	Transitional Bilingual	Newcomer	ESL	Structured English Immersion	Sheltered Instruction
Language Goals	Bilingualism	Bilingualism	English proficiency	English proficiency	English proficiency	English proficiency	Proficiency in academic English
Cultural Goals	Integrate into mainstream American culture & maintain/ appreciate ELL home culture	Integrate into mainstream American culture & maintain/ appreciate ELL home culture	Integrate into mainstream American culture	Integrate into mainstream American culture	Integrate into mainstream American culture	Integrate into mainstream American culture	Integrate into mainstream American culture
Language(s) of Instruction	L1 of ELLs and English	L1 of ELLs and English	L1 of ELLs and English	English (some programs use L1)	English	English	English
Students	Both native & non-native (with same L1) speakers of English	Non-native speakers of English with same L1; varied cultural backgrounds	Non-native speakers of English with same L1; varied cultural backgrounds	No/limited English Low level literacy Recent arrivals; varied L1 & cultural backgrounds	Non-native English speakers with various levels of Eng proficiency; varied L1 & cultural backgrounds	No/limited English; varied L1 & cultural backgrounds	Non-native speakers of English; varied L1 & cultural backgrounds
Grades Served	K-12	Primarily elementary	Primarily elementary	K-12; many at middle & high school levels	K-12	Primarily elementary	K-12
Typical Length of Participation	5–12 years	5–12 years	2–4 years	1–3 semesters	1–3 years	1 year	1–3 years

proficiency, academic development, and crosscultural understanding. All students experience an additive bilingual environment (one in which both languages are valued and developed), and academic content is learned through two languages. These are typically full K-6 or K-12 instructional programs.

Developmental bilingual programs provide a similar additive bilingual environment, with a goal of high levels of proficiency in two languages, but the students served are primarily or solely ELLs. This model, also referred to as "late-exit" or maintenance bilingual education, uses both English and the students' native language for academic instruction and promotes sustained development of the first language as well as English. Students generally participate in these programs for five to six years.

In *transitional bilingual* programs (also known as "early-exit" bilingual education), academic instruction in the students' native language is provided while they learn English (to varying extents and for varying lengths of time) through ESL classes. As their English proficiency develops, students are exited from the program and placed in all English, mainstream classes, typically after one to three years.

Newcomer programs are specially designed programs for recent arrivals to the United States, who have no or low English proficiency and often limited literacy in their native language (Short and Boyson, 2004). The goal is to accelerate their acquisition of language and academic skills and to orient them to the United States and U.S. schools. Students typically participate in such programs for one to one and one-half years. Although newcomer programs exist in elementary schools, they are more prevalent at the secondary level. Some programs follow a bilingual approach; others focus on sheltered instruction in English (see the later discussion of sheltered instruction).

Other program models offer primarily English instruction to ELLs. This choice is often made when ELLs in a school come from many different language backgrounds. In *English as a Second Language (ESL)* programs (also known as English language development [ELD] programs), carefully articulated, developmentally appropriate English language instruction is designed to meet the needs of students at various levels of English proficiency. ELLs may receive content instruction from other sources while they participate in the ESL program, or they may be in self-contained classrooms. Students generally participate in ESL programs for one to five years, depending on their initial level of proficiency and rate of progress. Students often benefit greatly when programs provide various kinds of support after they have moved fully into English mainstream classes, to give targeted assistance as needed. *Structured English immersion* is a form of ESL program taught in self-contained classrooms where most instruction is provided in English, though use of the student's native language is possible.

The core curriculum includes English language development (ELD), and content area instruction is taught using special techniques for second language learners (Baker, 1998). This program type has become most well known as the approach prescribed by state referenda (e.g., Proposition 227 in California) that restrict the use of bilingual education programs.

Another ESL-oriented program model is *sheltered instruction*, which is often found in school systems with ELLs from multiple language backgrounds. Sheltered programs offer ELLs a comprehensive, articulated program where the regular grade-level, core content courses are taught in English through instructional strategies that make the content concepts accessible to ELLs and that promote the development of academic English (Short and Echevarria, 1999). Sheltered instruction teachers should have ESL or bilingual education training in addition to training in the content area, and they often form a school team or learning community. Most sheltered instruction programs are designed to meet all the requirements for credit toward grade-level promotion or graduation. Students remain in them for two to three years. The term *sheltered instruction* may also be used to describe pedagogy rather than a program design. Sheltered instruction practices and individual sheltered instruction courses can be and often are implemented in conjunction with other program alternatives.

These program models differ in certain dimensions. Some set a goal of bilingualism for language development (two-way immersion, developmental bilingual), while others emphasize proficiency in English (ESL, sheltered instruction). The characteristics of the appropriate student population vary, particularly in terms of the homogeneity of native language backgrounds. The typical length of student participation also differs, with some programs being intended as short-term or transitional (one to four years) and others longer in duration (six or more years). The resources required vary from model to model, in terms of teacher qualifications (language skills and professional preparation), curricula and materials (how extensive bilingual offerings need to be), and so on.

METHODOLOGY FOR THE REVIEW

Our synthesis is based on a systematic review of the research literature. The goal was to be as comprehensive as possible in terms of the student population, to include ELLs from pre-Kindergarten through Grade 12 of diverse language backgrounds in educational programs in the United States. Given the demographic characteristics of the United States, however, most of the published research on ELLs focuses on low-income native Spanish speakers, and the largest number of studies involve elementary school-aged students. This will undoubtedly limit the generalizability of the results to other language and age groups, but it also highlights areas where future research is clearly needed.

We convened a thirteen-member team of researchers knowledgeable about the education of ELLs to conduct the synthesis of research in this area (see Preface for a list of team members). The team met three times during the two-year project period to set the parameters for the synthesis, review the findings of literature searches, and review drafts of sections of the synthesis.

The synthesis was conducted in three phases, parallel to the team meetings. In the first phase, the team defined the scope of the synthesis and the research to be reviewed. In the second phase, we conducted searches of the literature according to the defined parameters and evaluated the documents identified in the searches for relevance and quality. Finally, in the third phase, we synthesized the relevant research that met basic quality criteria and formulated our conclusions.

Phase 1: Inclusion Parameters

As mentioned previously, the focus of the research synthesis is the development of oral language, literacy, and academic achievement for ELLs in a variety of alternative programs, including English mainstream classrooms. The synthesis examined only English learners and did not consider research on ethnic minority or immigrant students except as the samples and results specifically address ELLs. For the searches of the literature, the following parameters were set to define which research studies to include:

• Empirical
• Conducted in the United States
• Published in English
• Focused on oral language development, literacy, and academic achievement among ELLs, with outcome measures in English
• Focused on pre-K through Grade 12
• Published in the last 20 years (may include seminal works conducted earlier)
• Published as peer-reviewed journal articles and selected technical reports (no books, book chapters, or dissertations)
• In the case of literacy, included reading, writing, or reading- or writing-related outcomes

Phase 2: Literature Searches and Quality Indicators

The synthesis was divided into three parts: oral language, literacy, and academic achievement. A subgroup of the team reviewed the literature in each area, considered which articles to include in the synthesis, and compiled the research. The subgroups conducted several types of searches. First, we searched three large databases of language and education materials using specific key terms – the Education Resources Information Center (ERIC), Linguistics and Language Behavior Abstracts (LLBA), and PsycInfo. The key terms for the searches included *limited English speaking, academic achievement (and math, science, social studies), English second language, bilingual education, literacy, reading,* and *oral language proficiency*. In addition, team members searched a number of education journals by hand (see Appendix for list of journals searched) and reviewed technical reports from several federally funded research centers (see Appendix for list). As a result of the computer and hand searches, over four thousand articles and reports were considered (at least by title, but most often by abstract).

To facilitate the processing and synthesizing of studies, we developed a coding system to record pertinent information for each study into a database. Each entry included the bibliographic citation, type of study, analytic methods, research questions addressed, information about the methodology, information about the sample, and the domain of the synthesis that the study addresses (oral language, literacy, and/or academic achievement).

We reviewed each of the abstracts obtained from the computerized searches for relevance to the topic and entered those that met the criteria into a database along with the articles and technical reports identified through hand searching. About five hundred articles and reports were reviewed at this level. In several instances, articles and reports were relevant to two subtopics. For instance, some studies fit into both literacy and academic achievement because student outcomes on both reading and mathematics were reported. Each subgroup reviewed all the studies relevant to their domain, so some studies were reviewed by more than one subgroup. We then obtained full texts of the articles, and reviewed their bibliographies to identify additional resources. When we found relevant articles in those bibliographies, they were added to the database as well. Each article was read and annotated, according to a coding framework for entries into the database. Based on this coding, articles that did not qualify for inclusion for relevance or quality reasons (discussed next) were rejected and not included in the synthesis. If two or more articles contained the same analyses based on the same data, only the more complete one was included.

The guiding principles for scientific research in education identified in the National Research Council report on *Scientific Research in Education* (Shavelson and Towne, 2001) formed the basis for the quality indicators used to examine the articles under consideration. The team looked for (a) appropriate research design to answer the questions being posed; (b) research that was well carried out and clearly described; and

(c) conclusions that were supported by the evidence presented. Some particular qualifiers were:

- Careful description of study participants (including age, language and ethnic background, socioeconomic status, other relevant characteristics);
- Sufficient detail in description of study interventions (including length and type of treatment) to allow for replicability;
- Description of study methods sufficient to allow judgments about how instructional fidelity was ensured, where appropriate;
- Full description of testing instruments, data-collection procedures, outcome measures, and data analytic techniques (all of which are appropriate for the goals of the study);
- Empirical outcomes reported;
- Study conclusions and implications clearly and reasonably linked to data.

The result was a set of articles that could be included in the synthesis for each topic. The final corpus included in the synthesis contained approximately two hundred articles and reports.

During the search and evaluation process, studies were coded according to information given by the authors of the research reports. Each of the following chapters includes tables summarizing relevant characteristics of the studies being synthesized in a given section (e.g., sample characteristics, outcome measures). The descriptions in these tables reflect the terms used by the authors of the articles, in order to avoid making any inferences about the characteristics (e.g., description of the sample students as "Hispanic," "Mexican American," or "Latino/a"). In addition, the categories of information provided in the tables vary in some cases across domains (the chapter topics) in order to suit the research represented (e.g., the tables in Chapter 4 include the category "instructional methods" while others do not). Definitions of abbreviations used in these tables are provided in Appendix A at the end of the book.

Phase 3: Synthesis of Research

As we reviewed the research studies for relevance and quality, we also sorted them by themes that captured the features of the research base. Within each domain (oral language, literacy, and academic achievement), we grouped together studies that addressed topics like instructional factors, home/community factors, assessment, and so on. At first, we planned to examine the research on each domain according to a common set of dimensions. However, it became clear that studies in each domain clustered in different ways, and we allowed those clusters to emerge from the research base. Thus, we developed a framework for characterizing the corpus of studies for each domain. In some cases, that corpus of studies was very eclectic and some subthemes clustered better than others. When we found several studies that addressed the same questions, we could draw stronger generalizations. When we found only one or two studies that looked at an issue, we could not generalize. In the discussion, we provide different levels of detail on different studies, depending on how well they fit with a group of studies to address certain questions. As a result, we may only briefly mention some studies in the database because they do not fit well into a cluster with other studies.

Once we identified the themes for each topic area, we reviewed the studies in each theme as a group and synthesized them. Various team members took the lead in drafting the synthesis chapters and then the entire team reviewed them. At the final meeting, team members revisited and revised the themes within domains to better fit the research base that was found, and they identified strengths and gaps in the research base. As the team finalized the syntheses of research by domain, it developed recommendations on future directions for research in this area.

ORGANIZATION OF THE VOLUME

The organization of the research synthesis parallels the major research areas that we explored: oral language, literacy, and academic achievement. Literacy is divided into two chapters, one dealing with crosslinguistic and crossmodal issues in literacy development and one on instructional issues. Different members of the team developed these sections, as authorship indicates, but worked closely together to ensure comparable methods and complementary scope. The full team reviewed all the sections. As mentioned earlier, the scopes of the three domains overlap, so some studies appear in more than one chapter. The final chapter offers conclusions that may be derived from the synthesis as well as recommendations for future research.

Before moving on to the synthesis itself, a note about terminology and labels may be useful. This is an area of considerable complexity in studies that involve students who come from homes where a language other than English is spoken. Research in the field suffers from inconsistency in definitions of categories into which the students may be grouped and inconsistent application of definitions to student populations by researchers and practitioners.

In this volume, "English language learner (ELL)" is used as the term for students who first learn a language other than English in their home and community (U.S.-born or immigrant) and then learn English as a new language. When they enter school in the United States, they may or may not have some knowledge of English, but they are not yet fully proficient.

In the past, a more common label for these students was "limited English proficient" or "LEP." This term has a legislative history in the federal government and remains the one in use in federal-policy contexts. Detailed legal definitions are provided in such legislation as the *No Child Left Behind Act* of 2001 in order to specify terms for eligibility for services and applicability of various requirements. Other terms often used include non-native English speaker, language minority student, ESL student, or bilingual student. In reporting the results of studies here, our best attempts were made to determine how the subject populations were characterized; however, this remains an area of concern in interpreting the research.

For native speakers of English (who may be compared with ELLs), the label "English-only" ("EO") is often used, signifying the monolingual language skills possessed by these students. Another convention that will be maintained in the chapters that follow is the use of "L1" to refer to an individual's native or home language and "L2" for the second (or later) language. Thus, a native Spanish-speaking student who is learning English could be described as having Spanish L1 and English L2.

References

Baker, K. 1998. Structured English immersion: Breakthrough in teaching limited-English-proficient students, *Phi Delta Kappan* (November).

Bennici, F. J., and Strang, E. W. 1995. *An analysis of language minority and limited English proficient students from NELS 1988*. Report to the Office of Bilingual Education and Minority Languages Affairs, U.S. Department of Education, August 1995.

Garcia, G. N. 1997. Placing a face on every child and youth. *Talking Leaves* 2(1): 3, 7. Fall, 1997. (Newsletter of the Center for Research on Education, Diversity & Excellence.)

Genesee, F. (ed.). 1999. *Program alternatives for linguistically diverse students*. Educational Practice Report No. 1. Santa Cruz, CA, and Washington, DC: Center for Research on Education, Diversity & Excellence. Available: http://www.cal.org/crede/pubs/edpractice/EPR1.htm.

Howard, E., and Christian, D. 2002. *Two-way immersion 101: Designing and implementing a two-way immersion program at the elementary level*. Educational Practice Report No. 9. Santa Cruz, CA, and Washington, DC: Center for Research on Education, Diversity & Excellence.

Jamieson, A., Curry, A., and Martinez, G. 2001. School enrollment in the United States – Social and economic characteristics of students. *Current Population Reports*, P20–533. Washington, DC: U.S. Government Printing Office. Available: http://www.census.gov/prod/www/abs/school.html.

Kindler, A. L. 2002. *Survey of the states' limited English proficient students and available educational programs and services: 2000–2001 summary report*. Washington, DC: National Clearinghouse for English Language Acquisition & Language Instruction Educational Programs.

Moss, M., and Puma, M. 1995. *Prospects: The congressionally mandated study of educational growth and opportunity. First year report on language minority and limited English proficient students.* Washington, DC: National Clearinghouse for Bilingual Education.

National Clearinghouse for English Language Acquisition. 2003. *The growing numbers of limited English proficient students 1991–92–2001–02.* Retrieved July 31, 2003, from http://www.ncela.gwu.edu/states/stateposter.pdf.

President's Advisory Commission on Educational Excellence for Hispanic Americans. 2003. *From risk to opportunity: Fulfilling the educational needs of Hispanic Americans in the 21st century.* Washington, DC.

Ruiz-de-Velasco, J., and Fix, M. 2000. *Overlooked & underserved: Immigrant students in U.S. secondary schools.* Washington, DC: The Urban Institute.

Shavelson, R. J., and Towne, L. (eds.). 2001. *Scientific research in education.* Washington, DC: National Academy Press.

Short, D. J., and Boyson, B. 2004. *Creating access: Language and academic programs for secondary school newcomers.* McHenry, IL, and Washington, DC: Delta Systems and Center for Applied Linguistics.

Short, D. J., and Echevarria, J. 1999. *The Sheltered Instruction Observation Protocol: A tool for teacher-researcher collaboration and professional development.* Educational Practice Report No. 3. Santa Cruz, CA, and Washington, DC: Center for Research on Education, Diversity & Excellence.

Tharp, R. 1997. *From at-risk to excellence: Research, theory, and principles for practice.* Research Report No. 1. Santa Cruz, CA, and Washington, DC: Center for Research on Education, Diversity & Excellence.

APPENDIX TO CHAPTER 1

Journals Searched

Annual Review of Applied Linguistics
Applied Linguistics
Applied Psycholinguistics
Bilingual Research Journal
Educational Researcher
Elementary School Journal
Harvard Education Review
International Journal of Bilingual Education and Bilingualism
Journal of Education
Journal of Education of Students Placed at Risk
Journal of Educational Issues of Language Minority Students
Journal of Learning Disabilities
Journal of Reading Behavior
Language and Education
Language Learning
Modern Language Journal

NABE Journal
Peabody Journal of Education
Phi Delta Kappan
Studies in Second Language Acquisition
TESOL Quarterly

Federal Research Centers Technical Reports Searched

Center for Research on Education, Diversity & Excellence
National Center for Research on Cultural Diversity and Second Language Learning
Center for Language Education and Research
Center for Research on the Education of Students Placed At Risk
Center for Research on Evaluation, Standards, and Student Testing

2

Oral Language

William M. Saunders and Gisela O'Brien

INTRODUCTION

For English Language Learners (ELLs) in U.S. schools, developing proficiency in oral English is essential for academic and future professional and personal success. Developing proficiency in oral English involves acquiring vocabulary, gaining control over grammar, and developing an understanding of the subtle semantics of English. At the same time, acquiring proficiency in English involves learning how to use the language to interact successfully with other speakers of the language. Oral interactions can vary considerably from exchanging greetings to initiating and sustaining conversations to negotiating collaborative tasks to giving and/or receiving directions to telling or listening to stories to delivering or comprehending lectures.

While the design of programs for ELLs varies in terms of the use of L1, many programs (that is, ESL pull-out, English immersion, transitional bilingual, developmental bilingual, and two-way immersion) recommend daily oral English language instruction until students achieve at least a minimum level of proficiency in English (see Genesee, 1999, for a description of alternative programs). Moreover, while there are different theoretical views about the minimum level of English oral proficiency necessary for successful participation in classrooms with English reading, writing, and content area instruction (Baker, 1998; Cummins, 1979; Fitzgerald, 1995; Krashen, 1996), there is no controversy about the fundamental importance of English oral language development as part of the larger enterprise of educating ELLs.

Despite the centrality afforded English oral language development in both theory and practice, the empirical literature on oral language development in ELLs is small. Our search for studies on the English oral language development of ELLs turned up approximately one fourth of the number of studies recovered for literacy. Of the approximately 150 studies on oral language development, fewer than two thirds reported actual oral language outcomes, and fewer than one third reported oral language outcomes and also met criteria for relevance and methodological adequacy. Moreover, the studies that were retained vary considerably; some measured general oral language proficiency; others measured discrete elements of oral language proficiency (e.g., vocabulary); and yet others measured language choice and use. Such variation makes synthesis and generalizability difficult.

We clustered studies that met our criteria topically. In some topic clusters, we found a sufficient number of studies to warrant firm conclusions. For most topics, however, the small number of studies allows for only qualified conclusions that best serve as hypotheses for future research. We thoroughly reviewed and analyzed the studies that were retained, looking for every opportunity to utilize data, datasets, and findings to address relevant topics. Given the paucity of research on oral language development, we thought it best to retain a topic, even if it was addressed by only two or three studies, in order to encourage and inform future research on that topic. The following review is organized according to these topics:

1. Language Development
2. School Factors
3. Non-school Factors
4. Assessment

LANGUAGE DEVELOPMENT

In this section, we synthesize research findings that establish some of the major characteristics of English oral language development among ELLs in U.S. schools (see Table A.2.1 for studies reviewed in this section). Topics include (1) Specific Features of L2 Oral Language Development, (2) Language Learning Strategies, and (3) Personality and Social Factors.

Specific Features of L2 Oral Language Development

Research on L1 oral language development has focused on the acquisition of specific aspects of the language, such as vocabulary, specific grammatical forms, or pragmatic patterns. Our search of the L2 oral language development literature revealed surprisingly few studies of this type. Thus, we have a very limited understanding of specific aspects of L2 oral language development and, thus, little empirical basis for planning educational interventions that would promote language development in specific ways. In light of evidence reviewed in Chapter 3 that specific aspects of oral language proficiency are linked to literacy and academic development, this gap in our knowledge is of concern. Notwithstanding the overall lack of research of this sort, two domains of L2 oral language acquisition have received some attention; namely, question formation and vocabulary. One of the major themes that runs through these studies concerns the nature and development of more academic uses of oral language. In an attempt to investigate that theme further, this subsection concludes with a review of results drawn from several studies in the corpus that report correlations between L2 oral and L2 reading.

Findings from research on question formation suggest that the acquisition of question forms in ELLs is similar to that observed among monolingual English-speaking children. In addition, more proficient ELLs demonstrate a wider repertoire of question forms than less proficient ELLs, but even less proficient ELLs demonstrate some command over English question forms and show considerable growth over relatively short periods of time (six months to a year). Support for this trend comes from research by Lindholm (1987) and Rodriguez-Brown (1987).

Lindholm (1987) carried out longitudinal and cross-sectional analyses of natural language samples from young fluent and limited English proficient (LEP) Spanish-speakers. She found (a) increasing sophistication in ELLs' questions over a one-year period, (b) question use even among students with limited oral language proficiency, and (c) significant differences in the kinds of questions used by limited and fluent English proficient students, indicating that, with greater proficiency, ELLs acquire increasing command over more sophisticated question types.

Rodriguez-Brown (1987) found essentially the same pattern of results as Lindholm among Grade 3 ELLs from bilingual homes who were participating in a two-way immersion program. While some students were fluent-Spanish but LEP and others were fluent-English but limited-Spanish proficient, the kinds of questions used by these two groups were similar in their stronger and weaker languages. These results suggest that question forms might develop similarly for L2 learners (i.e., regardless of whether their L1 is Spanish and their L2 is English, or vice versa), at least for languages that belong to the Indo-European family. Additionally, students showed equal facility with almost all question types but used a wider variety of question types in their stronger language. Finally, students with low levels of proficiency could transact requests for information and yes/no questions, suggesting that question use emerges early in L2 development.

Studies on vocabulary development indicate that ELLs demonstrate greater capacity to define words as they become more proficient. Initially, ELLs are more likely to define words through simple associations, termed *informal definitions* (e.g., cat: "My aunt has one and it's all furry and has a long tail."), and then at higher levels of proficiency through explication, termed *formal definitions* (e.g., cat: "A cat is a domesticated mammal which is related to the lion."). This line of research, initiated by Snow et al. (1987;

the source for the examples listed previously) is particularly relevant because it is one, if not the only, attempt in this corpus to operationalize and examine empirically the nature of oral language use for academic purposes. The protocol used by Snow and her colleagues involves asking students in a one-on-one administration what relatively common words mean. Their definitions are coded as informal or formal and are rated for quality. The most effective responses – high quality formal definitions – do not presume shared knowledge with the interlocutor, do not necessitate or attempt to elicit interactive support from the interlocutor, and involve more sophisticated vocabulary and syntax. All three of these elements are, according to Snow and her colleagues, hallmarks of language that is appropriate for interpersonally decontextualized, academic usage.

Snow et al. (1987) found that among middle-class 2nd through 5th graders, some of whom were ELLs and others native English speakers learning French, there was a significant correlation between L2 proficiency and the quality of students' formal definitions. Moreover, the strength of the correlation increased over grades: $r = 0.16$, 0.45, and 0.50 in Grades 2, 4, and 5, respectively. Finally, they found that ELLs with high levels of L2 proficiency scored as well as native English speakers.

Carlisle et al. (1999) corroborated most of Snow et al.'s findings in a study of low SES Spanish-speaking children in Grades 1, 2, and 3. Carlisle et al. also helped ground empirically the distinction between formal and informal definitions. They found a stronger relationship between informal definitions and receptive vocabulary in both Spanish and English ($r = 0.67$ in English and $r = 0.79$ in Spanish) than between formal definitions and receptive vocabulary ($r = 0.36$ in English and $r = 0.43$ in Spanish). These data fit well with Snow et al.'s original formulation. Both receptive vocabulary (correctly associating words with picture stimuli) and informal definitions measure less formal aspects of oral language proficiency. In contrast, formal definitions measure more formal and academic aspects of language proficiency. That the pairs of correlations vary substantially (almost 2 to 1: 0.67 and 0.79; 0.36 and 0.43) suggests that being familiar with words (including receptive vocabulary and informal definitions) is one aspect of language proficiency, whereas explicating their meaning (formal definitions) is qualitatively different.

Several studies report correlations between L2 oral proficiency and L2 reading achievement. Table 2.1 organizes all correlations by study and grade level. Among the twenty-eight correlations, significant relationships were more evident among oral measures that are linked to more academic aspects of language proficiency: specifically, vocabulary (Saville-Troike, 1984), formal definitions (Carlisle et al., 1999; Snow et al., 1987), and story-retell content (Goldstein, Harris, and Klein, 1993). Goldstein et al.'s story-retell correlations provide a good illustration. A significant correlation emerged with their measure of the quality of the content of the retells, as

TABLE 2.1. *Correlations Between L2 Oral and L2 Reading Measures*

Studies, n and Mixed Grade Levels	Oral English Measure	English Reading Measure	Grade Levels							
			Mixed	1st	2nd	3rd	4th	5th	6th	≥7th
• Saville-Troike (1984) n = 19; 2nd–5th	Interview: Vocabulary	CTBS	0.63[a]							
	Interview: Verbosity		0.40							
	Interview: Syntax		0.29							
	NSST		0.29							
	BSM		0.26							
	FLS		0.14							
	Interview: T-Unit Length		0.11							
	Interview: Grammar		0.03							
• Carlisle et al. (1999) n = 57; 1st–3rd	PPVT	CAT	0.42[a]							
	Informal Definitions		0.43[a]							
	Formal Definitions		0.33[a]							
• Snow et al. (1987) n = 136	Formal Definitions	CAT			0.16[a]		0.45[a]	0.50[a]		
• Ulibarri et al. (1981) n = 165–207	LAS-O	CAT, CTBS, SAT		0.48[b]		0.29[b]		0.31[b]		
	BSM			0.26[b]		0.25[b]		0.16[b]		
	BINL			0.11[b]		0.15[b]		0.27[b]		
• Royer and Carlo (1991), n = 29	SVT: Listening	SVT: Reading						0.23	0.17	
• Goldstein et al. (1993) n = 31; 7th–9th SE	Story Retell: Content	PIAT								0.40[a]
• Garcia-Vázquez et al. (1997) n = 100; 6th–12th	Story Retell: Language	ITBS								0.12
	WLPB									0.70[a]

Notes: [a]Statistically significant (p < 0.05); [b]Ulibarri et al. did not report significance levels (zero-order correlations within a multiple regression analysis). Abbreviations: BINL: Basic Inventory of Natural Language; BSM: Bilingual Syntax Measure; CAT: California Achievement Test; CTBS: California Test of Basic Skills; FLS: Functional Language Survey; ITBS: Iowa Test of Basic Skills; NSST: Northwest Syntax Screening Test; LAS-O: Oral portion of Language Assessment Scales; PIAT: Peabody Individual Achievement Test; PPVT: Peabody Picture Vocabulary Test; SAT: Stanford Achievement Test; SVT: Sentence Verification Technique; WLPB: Woodcock Language Proficiency Battery. Goldstein et al. (1993) includes Special Education students (SE).

measured by the inclusion of details about the plot, setting, and characters' intentions, for example (r = 0.40), but not with their measure of the quality of language used to retell the stories, as measured, for example, by the use of complete sentences and correct syntax (r = 0.12). This same finding holds for results elicited using language proficiency test batteries (Garcia-Vázquez et al., 1997; Ulibarri, Spencer, and Rivas, 1981). More specifically, broader, more academically oriented batteries like the Woodcock Language Proficiency Battery (WLPB; r = 0.70) and the Language Assessment Scales-Oral component (LAS-O; r = 0.29 to 0.48) correlated more strongly with reading outcomes than assessments like the Bilingual Syntax Measure and the Basic Inventory of Natural Language (r = 0.11 to 0.27) that have a narrower, less academic focus.

In a related vein, there is some evidence that the relationship between reading achievement and measures of English oral proficiency that have an academic focus becomes stronger in advancing grades, arguably because both are similarly influenced by schooling and both are indicative of academic success. More specifically, Snow et al. (1987) found significant, increasingly large correlations between reading achievement and quality of formal definitions across Grades 2, 4, and 5: r = 0.16, 0.45, and 0.50, respectively. Garcia-Vázquez et al. (1997) found a correlation of 0.70 between WLPB and reading achievement for bilingual Hispanic students in Grades 6 to 12, the oldest sample represented and the strongest correlation reported in Table 2.1.

The relationship between L2 oral proficiency that is linked to academic uses and academic achievement deserves further research attention, particularly in the higher grades. As discussed later in this chapter, there is virtually no U.S. research on how classroom instruction might best promote more academic aspects of oral language development, and there is very little research on oral language proficiency beyond the elementary grades.

Language Learning Strategies

An added dimension of L2 acquisition is the use of strategies for acquiring language. The use of explicit strategies often characterizes L2 acquisition because ELLs are typically older and more mature than L1 learners, and they already have competence in an L1. Thus, L2 acquisition does not call on exclusively implicit processes but can also entail conscious or explicit strategies. In this regard, Chesterfield and Chesterfield (1985a) provide a comprehensive study of the strategies used by preschool and early elementary age Spanish-speaking ELLs from Mexican-American families. The study incorporated strategies that appear to be directly linked to the acquisition of the target language (language-learning strategies), as well as strategies that serve L2 acquisition indirectly through communication with target language speakers (communicative strategies).

Chesterfield and Chesterfield found a hierarchical relationship among twelve communicative and language-learning strategies, in ascending order: repetition, memorization, formulaic expressions, verbal attention getters, answer in unison, talk to self, elaboration, anticipatory answer, monitoring, appeal for assistance, request for clarification, and role play. Strategies at the lower end of the scale (e.g., repetition and memorization) do not necessarily elicit further interaction and tend to be more receptive. Those at the middle range of the scale (e.g., verbal attention getters, elaboration, and anticipatory answers) serve to initiate and maintain interaction with interlocutors. The higher end of the scale includes strategies that involve a heightened awareness of language and communication: monitoring, appeal for assistance, and request for clarification. It follows from the results of this implicational scale analysis that regular use of any particular strategy implies use of all other strategies lower in the hierarchy.

Chesterfield and Chesterfield (1985a) also found that (a) a substantial proportion of ELLs' interactions involved language-learning strategies; (b) strategies emerged over time in the same relative order, although at different rates and times, for ELLs who began pre-school with more and less English proficiency; and (c) students' repertoires of language-learning strategies developed along with increasing English proficiency. Overall, this study contributes to our understanding of language learning by establishing a relationship among learner strategies that had been studied separately in prior research (i.e., communicative and language-learning strategies). It also documents the use of strategies among young ELLs and thereby confirms some degree of intentionality in their language learning.

One limitation to the Chesterfield and Chesterfield research, and studies that preceded it, however, is that data were collected almost exclusively through recordings or observations of students' interactions with others. Thus, the strategies that ELLs might use when they are not interacting with others were not examined. Indeed, Saville-Troike (1988) found that ELLs use language-learning strategies even during the silent period, when many ELLs (six of nine in her study) engage in few, if any, interactions with other ELLs or English speakers. Saville-Troike's findings with respect to the use of language-learning strategies during the silent period help explain at least one mechanism by which some ELLs successfully acquire English, in some cases at rates and with outcomes that surpass those of more social and communicative ELLs, despite lengthy periods of little or no interpersonal communication with English speakers.

We conclude this subsection with discussion of two studies that focused on the use of learning strategies by high school ELLs (O'Malley et al., 1985a, provide a summary of both studies; see O'Malley et al., 1985b, for a more detailed explanation of the first of the two studies). The first study identified through the use of small group interviews the strategies students used in different discrete and integrated listening and speaking tasks; discrete tasks included practicing pronouncing words and learning vocabulary words, for example; and the integrated tasks included listening to a lecture and preparing and making an oral presentation. Following previous L1 research, strategies were classified as metacognitive (e.g., selective attention), cognitive (e.g., note-taking), and socioaffective (e.g., collaborating with others). O'Malley et al. found that students reported using cognitive strategies more often than metacognitive strategies, and they were more likely to report using strategies with less demanding discrete tasks than with more demanding integrative tasks.

Based on these findings, O'Malley et al. conducted a second study designed to test the effects of an eight-day (50 minutes per day) intervention designed to train students to use metacognitive and cognitive strategies in the context of integrative tasks: listening to lectures and making oral presentations. Students were randomly assigned to one of three groups – metacognitive + cognitive strategies, cognitive strategies only, and control. Students were pre- and post-tested on both listening to lectures and making oral presentations. Analysis of covariance (controlling for pretest variation among the groups) found no significant differences on the listening task but significant differences favoring the metacognitive + cognitive strategies group on the speaking task. In fact, O'Malley et al.'s analyses of the strengths and weaknesses of their training modules suggest that with refined curricula and delivery, listening outcomes could be improved.

The O'Malley et al. studies are unique in at least two respects. First, like other studies reviewed in this subsection, their first study demonstrates that ELLs use explicit and conscious strategies to acquire language and to accomplish listening and speaking tasks. Second, their second study demonstrates that ELLs, at least teenage ELLs, might benefit from instruction and training in the use of strategies. The first study determined that students were less likely to apply strategies, particularly meta-cognitive strategies, to more challenging integrative tasks, and the second study demonstrated that this weakness or need was amenable to instruction and training. It is difficult to generalize based on the results of one study, but the evidence recommends further research. We note this particularly in light of the fact that this was the only study we located that systematically examined the effects of instruction and training on oral language outcomes. We include discussion of O'Malley et al. in this section because of its relationship to language learning strategies. With its focus on instruction and training, it could also have been discussed in the School Factors section.

Personality and Social Factors

Research on personality and social factors has been motivated by interest in the individual differences that account for variation in L2 proficiency. Arguably, evidence for such influences could be useful in educational settings to the extent that teachers could modify instruction to better match individual learners' learning styles or personal characteristics. Researchers often postulate that children who are disposed to social interaction might possess language-learning advantages on the assumption that such children seek out more interactions with fluent English speakers and will thereby engender more English input, interactive experiences and, consequentially, language acquisition opportunities. Wong-Fillmore (1976, cited in Strong, 1983) added a sociocultural dimension to this hypothesis. Among the Spanish-speaking ELLs she studied, the strongest language learners were more willing to engage with L2 speakers in order to gain access and acceptance from that group.

Research by Strong (1983) has expanded our understanding of the complexities of the relationship posited by Wong-Fillmore. More specifically, Strong analyzed the "natural communicative language" (NCL) of thirteen Spanish-speaking ELLs in one bilingual kindergarten class comprised of ELLs, fluent English proficient students (FEPs), and monolingual English speakers. NCL was elicited during interviews and observed during play activities. Audio recordings of these activities were transcribed and analyzed for sentence structure, vocabulary, and pronunciation. Strong found that NCL measures were unrelated to some social styles but strongly related to others: talkativeness (initiations toward others in Spanish), responsiveness (responses to others in Spanish), and gregariousness (number of interlocutors in Spanish and/or English). He also found that the frequency with which ELLs interacted with native English speakers was associated with some aspects of language proficiency (viz., vocabulary) but not others (viz., sentence structure and pronunciation). Drawing on the strong and significant correlations between NCLs and talkativeness and responsiveness ($r = 0.65-0.82$), Strong argued that the most successful language learners maintain interaction more effectively than less successful language learners because they are equally capable of initiating interaction and responding to others' initiations. Strong argued further that mere exposure to English speakers is probably not as important as the nature of the interactions that ensue between ELLs and native English speakers.

In a separate study, Strong (1984) examined another social/personality factor – namely, integrative motivation – defined as the willingness of the learner to associate with members of the target language group. Strong found evidence of a significant, positive relationship between integrative motivation (indexed by number of nominations of English-speaker playmates) and language proficiency among ELLs who began school with relatively high levels of English. However, he found no evidence of such a relationship among ELLs who began the year with low levels of English proficiency. Strong proposed that associations with members of the target language group might result from high levels of proficiency in that language, rather than the other way around. In fact, when a number of playmate nominations was plotted across the year, as students' English developed, there was an increasing tendency to nominate monolingual English speakers. These findings suggest that ELLs may need some minimum level of English proficiency before they are likely to begin associating with monolingual English speakers.

SCHOOL FACTORS

Perhaps no topic speaks more directly to the education of ELLs than schooling. One might have expected to find a fairly large body of research that examined the effects of different types of programs and instructional models on ELLs' oral language development. In fact, no such body of research exists. For the most part, research on the effects of programs and instructional models ignores oral language outcomes in favor of literacy outcomes (see Chapter 4) or academic achievement outcomes (see Chapter 5). Notwithstanding this significant gap in the literature, studies were identified that speak to issues related to school and classroom learning contexts (see Table A.2.2 for summaries of these studies). More specifically, in this section we review research on two topics: (1) Rates of Oral Language Proficiency Development, and (2) Language Use and L2 Oral Development.

Rates of Oral Language Proficiency Development

The rates at which ELLs achieve oral language proficiency is of considerable interest at least in part because of the long-standing policy debate about how long ELLs should receive federally funded services. Estimates of proficiency attainment typically focus on literacy (see Collier, 1987). With one exception (Hakuta, Butler, and Witt, 2000), no U.S. study published within the last twenty years has explicitly addressed the rates of oral English language proficiency attainment. However, our search identified a small number of studies that report longitudinal or cross-sectional oral language outcomes, providing the opportunity to begin to look at rates of development of oral proficiency over years of instruction and schooling.

Table 2.2 displays results reported in six different studies. Studies are organized by their research designs: one-year and multiple grades, longitudinal, quasilongitudinal, and cross-sectional. For each study, Table 2.2 lists the program students participated in (see table notes for explanation of abbreviations), the oral language assessment instrument, sample or subsamples of students, language of testing, and number of students. Mean scores are arranged by grade level, from Kindergarten to Grade 5. With one exception (Hakuta et al., 2000, Sample B), all results are reported in terms of mean proficiency levels based on a five-point scale (see table notes for the conversions we performed on some datasets). In general, Level 5 is

TABLE 2.2. *Results of Longitudinal and Cross-Sectional Studies of Oral Language Outcomes*

Study	Design	Program	Instrument	Sample or Subsamples	Test Lang	N	Oral Language Mean Results by Grade						Overall Gain	Per Year
							K	1	2	3	4	5		
Weslander & Stephany (1983)	1-year multiple grades	ESL	BSM Levels 1–5	ELLs	Eng	577							0.43	0.43
Medina & Escamilla (1992)	Longitudinal	DBE	LAS-O Levels 1–5	Span-spkrs	Eng	298	1.86		3.70				1.84	0.61
		DBE		Limited Span-spkr	Span	187	1.45		2.42				0.97	0.32
Howard et al. (2003)	Longitudinal	TWI	Proj. dev. Levels 1–5	Span-spkrs	Eng	125				4.35		4.86	0.51	0.26
		TWI		Eng-spkrs	Span	115				3.58		4.14	0.56	0.28
Thomas & Collier (2002)	Quasi-longitudinal	TWI 50/50	SOLOM Levels 1–5	Span-spkrs	Eng	238		2.72	3.28	3.44	3.49	4.02	1.30	0.33
		TWI 50/50		Eng-spkrs	Span	279		1.57	1.61	2.06	2.73	2.87	1.30	0.33
Lindholm-Leary (2001) Sample H	Cross-sectional	TWI 90-10	SOLOM Levels 1–5	Span-spkrs	Eng	1,816	2.82	3.32	3.70	3.74	4.28	4.82	2.00	0.40
		TWI 90-10		Eng-spkrs	Span	1,008	2.88	3.50	3.80	4.04	4.40	4.80	1.92	0.38
Lindholm-Leary (2001) Sample L	Cross-sectional	TWI 90-10	SOLOM Levels 1–5	Span-spkrs	Eng	1,122	2.64	3.12	3.54	3.88	3.96	4.48	1.70	0.34
		TWI 90-10		Eng-spkrs	Span	707	2.52	3.36	3.72	4.04	3.96	4.14	1.62	0.32
Hakuta et al. (2000) Sample A	Cross-sectional	All-Eng	IPT Levels 1–5	ELLs	Eng	1,872		1.75	3.40	4.35	4.60	4.80	3.05	0.76
Hakuta et al. (2000) Sample B	Cross-sectional	Varied	WLPB-R Age Equiv.	ELLs	Eng	122		4.4		5.8		7.5	3.1	0.78
				Eng-spkr norms	Eng			7.0		9.0		11.0	4.0	1.0

Notes: Program designations are ESL: English as a Second Language; DBE: Developmental Bilingual Education program; TWI: Two-way Immersion program (% Sp instruction in K/% English instruction in K); All-English: no primary language instruction. The following conversions were calculated by chapter authors: BSM results were converted from a 6- to a 5-point scale; SOLOM raw means were converted to mean levels; IPT means, originally expressed on a scale from 0 to 1.0, were converted to a 5-level scale (IPT is based on a 6-level scale). Thomas and Collier's results are based on years in program (1–5, quasilongitudinal); K-6 elementary school, Northwest, U.S. Lindholm's Sample H includes students from schools with high ethnic density and high SES need, and Sample L includes students from schools with low ethnic density and SES need. Hakuta el al.'s Sample B includes students from both bilingual and all-English programs; the study found no significant differences between the two groups and collapsed them into one sample.

interpreted as native-like proficiency, and Level 4 is viewed as sufficient for participation in mainstream English instruction – that is, proficient but not yet native-like. Expressing results on a common scale allows us to compare results across studies, samples, and subsamples. Overall and per year gains were calculated and are displayed in the far left-hand columns of the table. Results for Sample B from Hakuta et al. (2000) are explained at the end of this subsection.

Three studies (Howard, Christian, and Genesee, 2003; Lindholm-Leary, 2001; Thomas and Collier, 2002) include both Spanish-speaking ELLs and native or fluent English speakers involved in two-way or dual language immersion programs, wherein both ELLs and native-English speaking students learn a second language. Each study reported L2 oral language outcomes for all students: English for Spanish-speaking ELLs and Spanish for native or fluent English speakers. Results for these two subsamples allow for comparisons across different L2s: Spanish and English.

The data reported in these studies vary in terms of the number of data points, design, sample characteristics, programs under investigation, and the instruments used to assess oral proficiency, including criterion-referenced assessments (Bilingual Syntax Measure – BSM, Language Assessment Scales-Oral – LAS-O, Howard et al.'s experimenter-developed instrument, and the Idea Oral Language Proficiency Test – IPT), a teacher rating scale (Student Oral Language Observation Matrix – SOLOM), and a norm-referenced test (Woodcock Language Proficiency Battery-Revised – WLPB-R). Thus, caution must be exercised in interpreting the following patterns. Nevertheless, the results compiled in Table 2.2 represent, to the best of our knowledge, the first attempt to synthesize results across studies and examine patterns in the rates at which ELLs attain oral language proficiency.

A number of noteworthy trends emerge from analysis of these data. First, it seems that ELLs, on average, require several years to develop oral English proficiency. More specifically, the results in Table 2.2 show that means of 4.00 or higher (generally proficient but not yet native-like) do not emerge before Grade 3 and do not appear consistently across studies until Grade 5. Even in the dataset that includes students from all-English programs (Hakuta et al., Sample A), where presumably students receive maximum exposure to English, means of 4.00 or better do not appear until Grade 3. Moreover, none of the datasets include means that begin to approach 5.00 (native-like) until Grade 5. This holds regardless of whether students participated in bilingual (Lindholm-Leary, Howard et al., Thomas and Collier) or all-English programs (Hakuta et al., Sample A). Second, and in a related vein, ELLs, on average, tend to make more rapid progress from lower to middle levels of proficiency (i.e., from Levels 1 through 3; see especially Medina and Escamilla, and Hakuta et al., Sample A) and slower progress as they move beyond Level 3. By the end of Grade 3, means are typically at or around 4.00, but it takes until Grade 5 before means begin approaching 5.00 (Hakuta et al., Sample A; Lindholm-Leary, Sample H; Howard et al.).

Third, despite varied measures, samples, programs, and even languages, rates of L2 oral language progress appear to be strikingly consistent. In most cases, datasets with K or Grade 1 means below 2.00 show larger per-year gains (Medina and Escamilla: 0.61; Hakuta et al., Sample A: 0.76), and datasets with K and Grade 1 means above 2.00 show smaller per-year gains (Thomas and Collier: 0.33; Lindholm-Leary, Sample H: 0.40). However, notwithstanding these differences, the range in rates of development is generally small. Of greatest interest in terms of consistency are the results from two-way bilingual studies that show virtually identical average per-year gains among Spanish-speakers tested in English and English-speakers tested in Spanish: respectively, 0.26 and 0.28 per year (Howard et al., 2003), 0.33 and 0.33 (Thomas and Collier, 2002), 0.40 and 0.38 (Lindholm-Leary, Sample H), 0.34 and 0.32 (Lindholm-Leary, Sample L). Even the average per-year gain of an intensive ESL program (Weslander and Stephany, 1983) is within approximately the same range as the other programs: 0.43. The same holds for the all-English program (Hakuta et al., Sample A), when the large increase from Grade 1 to 2 (1.75 to 3.40) is isolated and the per-year gain is recalculated based on means from Grades 2 through 5: 0.47 per year.

Identifying and analyzing reliable estimates of per-year gains no doubt require more systematic sampling of programs and grade levels, more consistent forms of measurement, and more discerning statistical analyses. Notwithstanding these cautions, at least two hypotheses might account for the apparent consistency in per-year gains evident in the existing data: (a) on average, L2 oral language development proceeds at a fairly constant rate independent of program; or (b) on average, school contexts, independent of program, exert a fairly constant or homogenizing effect on oral language development.

Hakuta et al. (2000; Sample B), the final dataset listed in Table 2.2, makes a unique contribution to this discussion of rates of L2 oral development. Hakuta et al. report cross-sectional proficiency data (age equivalents) for randomly selected Grades 1, 3, and 5 ELLs based on the WLPB-R. These data differ significantly from the other data reported in Table 2.2 for two reasons. First, WLPB-R is generally viewed as more academically oriented than most available oral proficiency instruments. Second, WLPB-R is a norm-referenced assessment with norms based on the performance of native English-speaking children. As Hakuta et al. explain, "[WLPB-R] was selected because it was felt to be the best measure available to indicate the student's academic competitiveness with English-speaking peers" (p. 6). Indeed, Hakuta et al.'s Sample B results stand in sharp contrast to other results in Table 2.2 that show ELLs at or close to proficient by the end of Grade 5. Despite gains from 1st to 3rd to 5th Grade, Hakuta et al.'s results show ELLs performing substantially below English-speaker norms at all grades, and the gap between ELLs and English-speakers actually widens from 1st to 5th Grade. By Grade 5, ELLs are performing 3.5 years below native-English speaker norms. We cannot rule out the possibility that the below-norm results are simply unique to Hakuta et al.'s sample. In the meantime, the question remains: Do the criterion-referenced measures and teacher rating scales commonly used in research and at school sites underestimate or establish a low ceiling for proficiency, one that falls far below native English-speaker norms?

Language Use and L2 Oral Development

Several studies in the corpus examined ELLs' language use in the classroom. Based on the assumption that language use contributes to language development, researchers have investigated ELLs' language choices, the nature and outcomes of peer interactions involving ELLs and fluent English speakers, and the relationship between L2 use and L2 proficiency. All of the studies to be discussed focused on language use during interactive classroom activities, including paired activities, cooperative groups, and independent work time when students are allowed to converse and assist one another. During these activities, ELLs were free to choose to use either L1 or L2.

In general, the evidence suggests that ELLs' language choices tend to align with the dominant language of instruction. Chesterfield, Chesterfield, Hayes-Latimer, and Chávez (1983) investigated the language choices of Spanish-speaking ELLs in bilingual pre-school classes. In classes where teachers tended to use more English throughout instruction, ELLs tended to use more English with their peers. In classes where teachers tended to use more Spanish, ELLs tended to use more Spanish. Chesterfield and Chesterfield (1985b) also report language use data for Grade 1 Mexican-American ELLs, half of whom were enrolled in "English" classes and half of whom were enrolled in Spanish bilingual classes. In the English classes, ELLs used English during peer interactions a majority of the time. ELLs in the bilingual classes used Spanish a majority of the time. Among Grade 2 ELLs in Spanish bilingual programs where at least a majority of instruction was delivered in Spanish, both Milk (1982) and Malave (1989) found that ELLs were more likely to use Spanish during peer interactions; in fact, Malave found students using Spanish over English by a ratio of 6 to 1. Finally, among Grade 4 ELLs who had participated in Spanish bilingual classrooms through Grade 3 and were then placed in an "English-only" class, Pease-Alvarez and Winsler (1994) found a substantial increase from the beginning to the end of the year in students' use of English in their classroom interactions (53 to 83 percent).

While the studies reviewed thus far focused on language choice during classroom interactions, another topic represented in the corpus examines explicit attempts to cultivate interaction between ELLs and native or fluent

English speakers. Most programs for ELLs incorporate some provision for the integration or mixing of ELLs and native or fluent English speakers (see Genesee, 1999). The assumption is that such integration, aside from its potential social benefits, provides ELLs with worthwhile language learning opportunities. The corpus of peer-interaction studies, however, suggests that creating such opportunities and producing positive oral language outcomes involve more than simply pairing ELLs with native or fluent English speakers.

Several studies suggest that pairing native or fluent English speakers and ELLs, in and of itself, may not yield language-learning opportunities. For example, in a study of naturally occurring interactions among kindergartners during play situations, Cathcart-Strong (1986) found that the response patterns of native English-speaking peers did not dependably provide interactions that would be expected to contribute to ELLs' language development. She concluded that such interactions might only come from adult interlocutors or in response to more carefully structured tasks. In a related vein, Platt and Troudi (1997) describe the case of a Grebo-speaking girl enrolled in a mainstream English classroom where the teacher relied almost exclusively on native-English-speaking students to support ELLs' classroom participation. In fact, the ELL child's interaction with her native-English-speaking partners rarely provided language learning opportunities, primarily because class assignments were well beyond her language and knowledge, and her English-speaking peers were at a loss as to how to assist her. Similarly, Jacob et al. (1996), in a study of cooperative learning groups comprised of Grade 6 ELLs and native English speakers, found few instances that served as language learning opportunities for ELLs. The researchers concluded that interaction in cooperative groups is heavily influenced by the nature of the tasks and by the students' interpretations of the tasks. In this class, ELLs and native English speakers tended to cut short their interactions in order to complete assigned tasks in the allotted time: "Just write that down. Who cares? Let's finish up" (Jacob et al., p. 270).

Other studies (August, 1987; Peck, 1987) confirm the important role of tasks and also the training required of native English speakers to help them become language-learning facilitators. However, they also suggest that there is probably a minimum level of oral proficiency ELLs require in order for them to benefit from structured paired activities, at least in terms of verbal participation. August (1987) employed specific tasks to guide interaction between six- to ten-year-old ELLs and fluent English speakers and found a significant relationship between the frequency of verbal interactions and L2 proficiency. ELLs with relatively high levels of proficiency in contrast to ELLs with lower levels of proficiency interacted more frequently and extensively with fluent English peers. Similarly, Peck (1987) carefully selected and then trained a Grade 2 native English speaker to teach games to nine Kindergarten Spanish-speaking ELLs of varying proficiency levels.

Language outputs correlated with proficiency levels such that high- and middle-level students, in comparison to low proficiency students, spoke significantly more and displayed more sophisticated vocabulary.

Johnson (1983) tested the effects of a program (Inter-ethnolinguistic Peer Tutoring, IEPT) that incorporated specific tasks and training designed to promote more extensive interaction between ELLs and fluent English speakers (FESs). The study was conducted over a five-week period. Matched pairs of ELLs and matched pairs of FESs (16 ELLs and 18 FESs; 5–9 years old) were randomly assigned to either the treatment or control group. Interactions before, during, and after the five-week treatment were observed and coded. Data were analyzed for group differences over time and at the end of the treatment period. Results favored the treatment group but also revealed an interesting pattern that emerged over time. By the end of the five-week period, ELLs and FESs in the treatment group were inter-acting significantly more than ELLs and FESs in the control group. How-ever, the difference emerged over time because verbal interactions between ELLs and FESs increased slightly for students in the treatment group but declined considerably for students in the control group. At least in this case, the treatment seemed to help ELLs and FESs maintain interactions that – to the extent the control group is representative – typically taper off over time.

A corollary issue concerning language use is whether increased L2 use results in increased L2 oral language proficiency, on the one hand, and enhanced academic achievement on the other. Two of the studies already discussed also analyzed L2 oral outcomes associated with L2 use (Chesterfield et al., 1983; Johnson, 1983), and another study examined rela-tionships among L2 use, oral outcomes, and reading achievement (Saville-Troike, 1984). The findings of these studies are suggestive but by no means conclusive. Findings from the Chesterfield et al. and Saville-Troike stud-ies, in particular, help unpack and also qualify the potential effects of L2 use.

Johnson (1983) administered three oral language proficiency assess-ments to ELLs prior to and immediately following the five-week IEPT treatment: Language Assessment Scales (LAS), Peabody Picture Vocabu-lary Test (PPVT), and the Child-Child Communication Test (CCCT). To investigate the relationship between the amount of interaction in English and growth in English proficiency, Johnson calculated partial correlations (controlling for pre-test) between post-test proficiency scores and mea-sures of the frequency of ELLs' interactions with FEPs. None of the partial correlations, however, was statistically significant. Johnson also compared pre- to post-test gains of the treatment and control ELLs on the PPVT and the LAS. A significant difference favoring the treatment group was found on the PPVT but not on the LAS. Thus, IEPT contributed to vocabulary growth, but within the five-week period there was no identifiable relation-ship between individual students' L2 use and their gains in L2 proficiency.

In contrast, among pre-school ELLs and over a longer duration of time, Chesterfield et al. (1983) found significant and positive rank-order correlations between increased L2 use and increased L2 oral proficiency. However, results suggest that while there may be a positive relationship between English use and oral gains, ELLs (particularly young ELLs) might benefit differentially from teacher and peer interlocutors depending on their level of L2 proficiency. Among relatively less proficient students, gains in L2 proficiency (mean length of utterances) correlated significantly with increased interactions with the teacher (rho = 0.93). Among relatively more proficient students, gains in proficiency were significantly correlated with increased interactions with peers (rho = 0.83).

Saville-Troike (1984) found positive and significant rank-order correlations between English use and oral proficiency among nineteen ELLs ranging in age from 7 to 12 (Grades 2–6). Students' parents were participating in a one-year graduate program for foreign students. The year of the study represented the first year of L2 exposure and instruction for all nineteen ELLs. The overall amount of students' English verbal interactions (percentage of English interactions sampled across an entire 5.5 hour day) correlated significantly with their end of year language proficiency rankings on the Northwest Syntax Screening Test (r = 0.69) and with their mean length of T-units determined through interviews (r = 0.50).

However, while Saville-Troike found that L2 oral language proficiency was associated with overall L2 use, there was little evidence among her first-year ELLs of any relationship between use or proficiency and academic achievement. Specifically, none of the study's measures of English language use correlated significantly with standardized measures of English reading (CTBS): total interactions (r = 0.19), interactions with child (r = −0.06), and interactions with adults (r = 0.13). With one exception, moreover, none of the study's measures of language proficiency correlated significantly with CTBS reading: NSST (r = 0.29), Functional Language Survey (r = 0.14), Bilingual Syntax Measure (r = 0.26), interview-based measures of verbosity (r = 0.40), mean length of T-unit (r = 0.11), and grammatical accuracy (r = 0.03). Only vocabulary (the number of different vocabulary items students used during interviews) correlated significantly with CTBS reading: r = 0.63.

Saville-Troike herself identifies a number of possible reasons for the failure to find a link between L2 oral language use and achievement. First, the oral language proficiency instruments in her study may not have captured the kind of language proficiencies that are implicated by academic tasks and tests (like CTBS reading). Second, interpersonal communication, despite or perhaps because of its social/contextual nature, may not be a particularly fruitful means of promoting oral language proficiency in the service of academic achievement, at least not for students who are just beginning to learn L2. In many cases, students' interpersonal communication with each other and with native English-speaking peers, as well as with teachers, could be successfully negotiated with gestures and single words, providing little opportunity for academic language development. Third, among the students who most quickly began initiating and carrying out interactions with peers in English, not one was in the group that scored highest on the CTBS. To the contrary, the five students who scored highest on the CTBS at the end of the year used little or no English at all in their interactions with peers throughout the whole first half of the year. In fact, three of these five students relied exclusively on their L1 to clarify and discuss academic assignments during the first half of the year. Saville-Troike speculates that, at least with this population of first-year ELLs, access to other L1 speaking peers and adults might make a stronger contribution to academic achievement than opportunities to engage in interpersonal communication in English.

NON-SCHOOL FACTORS

The most extensively documented non-school factor related to oral language development is language use outside of school, specifically at home with family and also among peers. The research investigates the relationship among oral English language proficiency, out-of school English language use, and L1 maintenance. Although the number of studies reviewed is small (see Table A.2.3 for a summary of studies), they yield a fairly straightforward finding – English language use outside of school is positively associated with ELL's oral English development. At the same time, the corpus of studies also begins to unpack the very complex relationship or tension between learning English on the one hand and maintaining L1 on the other.

Pease-Alvarez (1993) collected self-reports on immigration history and language use from the parents of fifty-five Grade 3 ELLs of Mexican descent. Four groups were established ranging from "child and parents born in Mexico/speak mostly Spanish in the home" (Group 1) to "child and at least one parent born in United States/speak mostly English in the home" (Group 4). Oral English proficiency results based on the English Peabody Picture Vocabulary Test (EPPVT) were closely associated with immigration history and home language use, with means increasing successively from Groups 1 to 4: means = 52, 62, 85, and 90, respectively.

Umbel and Oller (1994) examined samples of thirty-four children at each of Grades 1, 3, and 6 matched for SES (middle class), parental education (high school grad or better), and parental occupation (3 or 4 on four-point scale, where 3 = sales and clerical workers, and 4 = professionals and managers). The parents of all students in the sample spoke both Spanish and English and introduced their children to both languages at birth (simultaneous bilinguals). Across the sample, students whose parents reported using Spanish and English equally at home averaged about 0.4 standard deviations higher on the EPPVT than students whose parents reported using more Spanish than English (mean for Spanish-English equally is 97; for more Spanish than English is 90; sample standard deviation, 0.16). This sample is unusual in that the children are simultaneous bilinguals who had exposure to both languages in the home since birth. That is not necessarily typical of the ELL population at large. Nevertheless, it is noteworthy that an association between English use and proficiency emerged in such a population.

Hansen (1989) examined the learning rates of 117 Spanish-speaking ELLs in Grades 2 to 5 in bilingual classrooms over a one-year period using English auditory vocabulary (Stanford Diagnostic Reading Tests, SDRT) as an outcome measure. Students were assessed in the fall, spring, and again the following fall. Using regression analyses, Hansen found that the proportion of English and Spanish used in the home (1 = exclusively English and 7 = exclusively Spanish) was the best second-order predictor of subsequent English vocabulary achievement, better than language use with peers or language use in the classroom. Prior English vocabulary scores accounted for 65 percent and home language use accounted for an additional 10 percent of the variance in subsequent English vocabulary scores.

While all three of the studies described herein present evidence of a positive relationship between English use outside school and oral English proficiency, there are at least three qualifiers that need to be taken into account. First, although the development of L2 oral proficiency is likely aided by L2 use outside of school, it is not necessarily impeded by continued development and use of L1. Second, at higher levels of language and literacy development, English use outside of school may not be as critical as English use in school. Finally, L1 and English use in the home are interrelated, and the nature of the relationship and the impact on children's L1 and English proficiency are likely mediated by sociocultural factors.

Regarding continued development and use of L1, while Umbel and Oller (1994) found significant mean differences in English vocabulary attributable to differences in English-Spanish use at home, they also found that students with better Spanish vocabularies tended to have strong English vocabularies. The results of regression analyses indicated that Spanish vocabulary, followed by grade level, and then home language use, accounted for, successively, 27, 33, and 36 percent of the variance in total English vocabulary scores.

Regarding the limits of English use outside school, while Hansen (1989) found that English use at home contributed to English receptive vocabulary, he found a more complex relationship between various language use variables and reading comprehension. While the proportion of English and Spanish used in the home remained a significant predictor in some analyses, classroom language use and task-oriented peer language use also proved to be significant and, in some cases, superior predictors of

L2 reading comprehension. Hansen concluded that while home language use makes a critical contribution to oral language development in general, language use at school probably plays a more critical role in supporting higher levels of language and literacy development.

With regard to the possible role of sociocultural factors on L1 use in the home, we revisit Pease-Alvarez (1993) and Umbel and Oller (1994). Among working-class families of Mexican descent that varied in terms of immigration history and Spanish-English use in the home, Pease-Alvarez found an inverse relationship between English use and proficiency on the one hand, and Spanish use and proficiency on the other hand. Across four groups that ranged from "child and parents born in Mexico/speak mostly Spanish in the home" to "child and at least one parent born in United States/speak mostly English in the home," Pease-Alvarez found an increasing progression in English vocabulary scores (from 52 to 62 to 85 to 90 for Groups 1–4, respectively) and a decreasing progression in Spanish vocabulary scores (from 71 to 61 to 52 to 46 for Groups 1–4, respectively).

In contrast, among middle-class, bilingual families of Cuban descent who began introducing their children to Spanish and English at birth, Umbel and Oller found no relationship between English and Spanish use and proficiency. Half the sample reported using English and Spanish equally and the other half reported using more Spanish than English at home. Children from the former group demonstrated higher levels of English proficiency, but there was no difference between groups in terms of Spanish proficiency. Means were identical and virtually at norm (i.e., 96 with a norm of 100) for this sample of simultaneous bilinguals.

The contrasting findings of Pease-Alvarez (1993) and Umbel and Oller (1994) suggest that the relationship between L1 and English use and its impact on L1 and English proficiency might be mediated by cultural or class variables insofar as their respective samples varied along those lines – working-class families of Mexican descent and middle-class families of Cuban descent. We located no studies that shed light on the potential cultural differences in this matter. However, we found one study that provides self-report data indicating that attitudes toward L1 maintenance can vary across classes within the same culture. Lambert and Taylor (1996) found differences between middle- and working-class Cuban-born mothers living in Miami in their perceptions of the importance of their children learning English and Spanish. While mothers in both samples reported strong overall support for learning English and maintaining Spanish, working-class mothers tended to place greater emphasis on learning English, and middle-class mothers tended to place greater emphasis on maintaining Spanish. Working-class mothers tended to associate learning English with improving one's economic status; their ratings of their children's English fluency correlated positively and significantly with their own perceived economic status. No such correlation emerged among middle-class mothers. Rather, middle-class mothers tended to associate maintaining Spanish with maintaining the family's cultural identity; their ratings of their children's Spanish fluency correlated positively and significantly with their own sense of self-respect. No such correlation emerged among working-class mothers.

The small number of studies reviewed in the section limit the generalizability of the findings. However, it seems quite clear that the relationship among L2 development, L1 maintenance, and language use is quite complex. (See also Schecter & Bayley, 1997, for a case study analysis.)

ASSESSMENT

The assessment of oral English language proficiency is commonplace in U.S. school districts that serve ELLs. In a survey of ninety-three randomly selected school districts from the ten states with the highest numbers of ELLs, Cardoza (1996) found that virtually all districts assessed oral English proficiency at both program entry and exit. For those students whose parents indicated upon enrollment that a language other than English was spoken in the home, 90 percent of the school districts administered an English oral language proficiency assessment to determine students' language classification and program placement. Eighty-eight percent of the districts also reported using an English oral language assessment as part of their procedures for reclassifying students as fluent English proficient (FEP) and determining whether or not to place students in mainstream English programs. The vast majority of districts also reported using an English reading assessment at both entry (72 percent) and exit (93 percent), and most said they assessed L1 oral language proficiency at entry (64 percent). Only 34 percent of the districts, however, reported assessing L1 oral language at exit. The most commonly used instruments are the Language Assessment Scales (LAS), Bilingual Syntax Measure (BSM), and the Language Assessment Battery (LAB). More than 80 percent of the districts reported using one or more of these three instruments for entry and/or exit assessments. Other instruments mentioned, though with substantially less frequency, included the Basic Inventory of Natural Language (BINL) and the Individualized Developmental English Activities Placement Test (IDEA).

While the assessment of oral language proficiency is commonplace, research on the validity and reliability of commonly used oral language assessments is not. Our search identified six studies, most of which focus on issues related to validity. In this section, we examine validity from the following perspectives: technical information provided by test developers, intertest correlations, predictive validity, classifications of students, use of monolingual test norms, and monolingual versus bilingual assessments. The section closes with a discussion of one study that illustrates the challenges involved in developing reliable and valid oral language measures. A summary of the studies reviewed in the section is presented in Table A.2.4.

One should not assume that the technical qualities of commonly used oral language assessments have been rigorously or successfully evaluated and documented. Merino and Spencer (1983) evaluated the technical manuals for the English versions of several oral language assessments: LAS, BSM, LAB, BINL, and the Bahia Bay Area Oral Language Test (BOLT). Nine items were evaluated for each assessment: Classifications, Criterion-Validity, Content-Validity, Construct-Validity, Test-retest Reliability, Inter-scorer Reliability, Internal Consistency, Inter-examiner-Reliability, and, finally, Norms. The quality of documentation on the tests was evaluated on a four-point scale: no information provided, information provided but inadequate, information provided but not thorough, and information thorough and adequate. The BINL and LAB provided information on only three of the items. The BOLT had information on almost all items, but none were judged satisfactory. The BSM and LAS provided information on at least six of the nine items, but neither received consistent satisfactory marks: BSM I received satisfactory marks on five of nine, BSM II on three of nine, LAS I on four of nine, and LAS II on only one of nine. Based on this review, Merino and Spencer concluded that schools should use none of the assessments to gauge students' proficiency in English. It is possible that the technical information provided with current editions of these assessments is more complete and adequate on a wider range of criteria. However, we know of no recent and similarly comprehensive study of these or other currently used oral language instruments.

The validity of tests is often established by examining their correlations with similar instruments reputed to assess the same skill or skills. Oral English language measures typically used to evaluate ELLs do in fact correlate with one another, despite the fact that they often emphasize different elements of oral language. For example, based on assessments of ELLs in Grades 1, 3, and 5, Ulibarri et al. (1981) found significant moderate to strong positive correlations (r = 0.76, 0.74, and 0.58 at Grades 1, 3, and 5, respectively) between the oral subtest scores of LAS, which evaluates vocabulary, syntax, and story retelling, and BSM, which focuses exclusively on syntax. Based on assessments of Kindergarten and Grade 2 ELLs, Schrank, Fletcher, and Alvarado (1996) found significant and positive correlations (r = 0.75 to 0.91) among the oral subtest scores of LAS (and Pre-LAS for K), the WLPB-R, and the IPT-I. The highest correlations all involved WLPB-R: 0.91 with Pre-LAS among kindergartners, and 0.81 with LAS and IPT-I for second-graders.

Another way to examine the validity of assessments is to evaluate the consistency with which they classify students into specific levels of performance. Significant positive correlations mean that different assessments rank-order students from low to high similarly. However, most oral language assessments come with recommended cutoff points for different levels of proficiency (e.g., non-proficient, limited-proficient, fluent-English speaking: NES, LES, FES). Thus, when states, districts, schools, and/or researchers choose a particular oral language instrument, they simultaneously choose a set of criteria and cutoff points for classifying ELLs. Ulibarri et al. (1981) found dramatic differences in the classifications produced by LAS and BSM. Despite their moderate to strong positive correlations, the two assessment instruments utilized substantially different cutoff points. Indeed, across more than one thousand ELLs in Grades 1, 3, and 5, LAS and BSM produced the exact same classification (NES, LES, and FES) for only 32 percent of the students: 51 percent of the sample was classified as "fluent" by LAS but "limited-proficient" by BSM; 17 percent of the sample was classified as non-proficient by LAS but limited-proficient by BSM.

MacSwan, Rolstad, and Glass (2002) conducted an evaluation that focused specifically on the validity of "non" proficient classifications. When ELLs are assessed in English upon entry to school, non-proficient classifications are quite common. However, MacSwan et al. analyzed the Pre-LAS results of Spanish-speaking Pre-K and Kindergarten ELLs who were classified as non-proficient in Spanish (n = 6,118 of a total of 38,000; 15 percent). Among other things, the study found that most of the non-proficient classifications were attributable to students' difficulty with the last two portions of the test (sentence completion and story retell). Sixty-seven percent of the students classified as non-proficient scored 80 percent or higher on parts 1–3, and 51 percent scored 80 percent or higher on parts 1–4 (acting out commands, naming items in pictures, identifying pictures that correspond to uttered phrases, and repeating sentences). Space does not allow for a full explication of their discussion of weighting, scoring, and administration issues that also contributed to non-proficient classifications. However, MacSwan et al. provide sufficient evidence to recommend cautious interpretation of non-proficient classifications. That this study focuses on misclassifications in L1 (possibly 50–67 percent false negatives) brings the problem of misclassification into sharp relief. Undoubtedly, similar misclassifications occur with English assessments as well.

Predictive validity refers to the accuracy with which a test predicts performance on other target measures. For example, do oral language measures predict success in mainstream English classrooms? Results from both Schrank et al. (1996) and Ulibarri et al. (1981) suggest that more academically oriented instruments and instruments that sample a broad range of oral language skills produce stronger correlations with estimates of mainstream success than less academic instruments with a narrower focus. Schrank et al. (1996) used teachers' ratings of students' academic language proficiency as an estimate of success in mainstream classrooms and correlated those ratings with students' scores on WLPB-R, LAS (and Pre-LAS for K), and IPT. WLPB-R, typically viewed as a more academically oriented instrument, yielded the highest correlations with teachers' ratings (r = 0.80), and IPT-I, typically viewed as less academically oriented, yielded the lowest (r = 0.68).

Ulibarri et al. (1981) conducted two separate analyses to gauge the predictive power of LAS and BSM. The former provides a broader assessment of oral proficiency, focusing on vocabulary, syntax, and story retelling, while the latter is narrower, focusing on syntax only. Based on classifications produced by each measure, Ulibarri et al. conducted analyses of variance with standardized measures of English reading and math for each of Grades 1, 3, and 5. LAS classifications produced significant results in the expected direction for both reading and math at each of the three grade levels: NES, LES, FES. BSM produced significant differences only between the FES and LES groups and only in four of the six analyses. Ulibarri et al. then conducted stepwise regression analyses designed to predict reading and math achievement at each grade level, using as predictors teachers' ratings of student achievement and preparedness for mainstream and an oral language measure (either LAS or BSM). For every regression analysis (Grades 1, 3, and 5 for each of reading and math), teachers' ratings proved to be a better single predictor than either LAS or BSM. However, along with teachers' ratings, LAS results added significantly to the prediction in four of six analyses (overall R-squares ranged from 0.34 to 0.56; LAS contributed from 0.03 to 0.08 to the overall R-square). BSM did not add anything significant over and above teacher ratings. Taken together, both studies suggest that mainstream placement decisions are likely best served by a combination of informed teacher judgments and oral measures that are academically oriented and broad in scope.

Some oral language proficiency assessments publish norms, which allow test users to compare students' results to that of the norming group. At least one study suggests that comparing the oral language results of ELLs to norms derived from monolingual samples can be problematic. Fernandez et al. (1992) report two important findings based on their analysis of Spanish and English receptive vocabulary results (Peabody Picture Vocabulary Test-Revised, PPVT-R, and the Test de Vocabulario en Imágenes Peabody-Adaptación Hispanoamericana, TVIP-H). Their sample consisted of 396 Spanish-speaking preschoolers from Miami, two thirds of whom were of Cuban descent. First, the Cuban American students in the study sample responded differently to the list of Spanish words on the TVIP-H than the Mexican and Puerto Rican children who comprised the norming sample. Some words that were difficult for the study sample were easy for the norming sample; other words that were easy for the study sample were difficult for the norming sample. Although both groups were native Spanish speakers, the Spanish lexicon acquired by students in Mexico and Puerto Rico and that acquired by the students in Miami varied, making comparisons between the study sample and the norm group problematic. The implication here is that practitioners or researchers would not want to interpret norm-referenced results, either for tests of L1 or L2 oral language without some knowledge about the composition of the norm group and its relative comparability to the students being tested.

Second, Fernández et al. also postulate that independent L1 and L2 receptive vocabulary assessments of young bilingual students (here, Spanish-English bilinguals) likely underestimate total vocabulary in cases where a child knows particular words in one language but not the other. Citing data from another study (Umbel et al., 1992), Fernandez and her colleagues estimate that approximately 75 percent of a young bilingual child's vocabulary might be constituted by pairs (e.g., English and Spanish versions of the same concept), and as much as 25 percent in each of L1 and L2 might be comprised of singlets (concepts lexicalized in one language but not the other). L1 assessments fail to capture the concepts lexicalized only in L2, and L2 assessments fail to capture the concepts lexicalized only in L1. The authors argue that a more comprehensive assessment of the linguistic development of bilingual children should account for vocabulary across both languages and employ norms based on a bilingual population, not monolingual samples from each language.

A final topic related to oral language assessments concerns how oral language is measured. All of the assessments discussed thus far consist of tasks designed to elicit and evaluate samples of language use under on-demand conditions. In general, this is no different than most other assessments used in schools to measure reading, writing, mathematics, or any other domain of knowledge and skill. Like most other assessments used in schools, most oral language assessments should be recognized for their limitations: They do not capture and measure the breath of natural language use both in and outside of school, and the evaluative information they provide about students should not be overinterpreted. Commins and Miramontes (1989) provide a good demonstration of this in their detailed ethnographic study of the oral Spanish and English language use of four 5th and 6th Grade native Spanish speakers. Based on general classroom observations and assessment results, students were judged by their teachers to be lacking conceptual knowledge and full language proficiency in both languages. In fact, the authors' qualitative data analyses (200 hours of classroom observations and 50 hours of observations outside of school) revealed that students were more proficient in both Spanish and English than their teachers had been able to determine. Moreover, students showed higher levels of proficiency in their language use outside of school than they did in classroom settings. These results were arrived at through far more extensive and intensive observations and evaluations than classroom teachers can ever be expected to complete, yet the study offers a cautionary tale: even the best oral language assessments and teacher observations likely sample a small set of language skills from a narrow range of language tasks and contexts. (See also Gonzalez, Bauerle, and Felix-Holt, 1996.)

Before ending this section, it is important to point out that while it is easy to criticize oral language assessments on a variety of grounds, developing better assessments, especially ones that try to capture students' day-to-day language abilities, represents a substantial challenge. Work by Gomez et al. (1996) illustrates this point. Gomez et al. provide a detailed account of their unsuccessful efforts to develop and validate a language observation scale. The research team tested their scale against several measurement criteria including interrater reliability, stability over time, internal consistency, criterion-related validity, and also efficiency. None of the five widely used observational scales Gomez et al. reviewed prior to their own development work met any of these criteria, and none had been evaluated for any more than two of them. Among the several findings they report, Gomez et al. found that few of the attributes of language use prescribed in the theoretical literature could be successfully operationalized (seven of twenty-three). Of the seven attributes that were successfully operationalized, only four could be observed and evaluated reliably by the research team. In addition, the research team found it extremely difficult to produce stable scores over time. Gomez et al. estimate that one would need to collect and analyze a minimum of six 30-minute language observations over a two- to three-week period in order to achieve appropriate levels of stability. As the authors note, such extensive observations are impractical for school personnel.

CONCLUSIONS

Studies of language development suggest that question forms develop in L2 following the same progression observed among monolingual English children. With increasing proficiency, ELLs demonstrate a wider repertoire of question forms, but even less proficient, young ELLs demonstrate some command over English questions and show considerable growth over relatively short periods of time (six months to a year). Similarly, with increasing proficiency, ELLs also demonstrate greater capacity to explicate what words mean through formal definitions; however, even beginning-level ELLs, as early as first grade, are able to articulate word meanings through simple associations or informal definitions. This capacity to explicate word meaning is an example of academic language use. Existing evidence suggests that the academic uses of language are associated with higher levels of oral language proficiency and with literacy achievement. Clearly, however, much more needs to be done to clarify the precise nature of academic oral language proficiency, independent of literacy and, at the same time, in relationship to traditional constructs of literacy.

More proficient ELLs also demonstrate a wider repertoire of language-learning strategies. Those strategies, observable in ELLs as young as four to five years old, appear to be hierarchical and emerge in the same relative order, from receptive strategies to interactive strategies to language and communication monitoring strategies. At least one study suggests that explicitly teaching ELLs how to use strategies effectively, especially metacognitive strategies, might be beneficial, at least for older ELLs. While it is not possible to generalize based on one study, strategy instruction has a reasonably strong basis of support in other domains (see Chapter 4). Thus, it would be important to establish the effects and nature of strategy instruction as applied to listening and speaking, in particular for ELLs of different ages and at different levels of proficiency.

Studies of social and personality factors indicate that ELLs can develop L2 skills without a predisposition to associate with English speakers. In fact, some level of English proficiency may be necessary before ELLs are likely to begin associating with English speakers. Moreover, exposure to English speakers is probably not as critical to language acquisition as the use of that exposure and the interactions that ensue.

A small set of studies suggests that ELLs require several years of schooling to attain L2 oral proficiency. Progress from beginning to middle levels of proficiency is relatively rapid, but progress from middle to upper levels of proficiency is slower. Moreover, rates of growth, at least based on existing studies, appear to be similar for English-speakers learning Spanish and Spanish-speakers learning English, and more similar than one might expect for ELLs in programs that vary in terms of their relative emphasis on English and L1 usage (all-English, two-way, and developmental bilingual). This finding might be idiosyncratic to this small sample of studies, or it might be indicative of a reliably constant rate of oral proficiency development. Alternatively, it might reflect a general lack of instructional attention to oral language development once students advance to middle levels of proficiency.

Clearly, additional research is needed that documents rates of oral proficiency development. Some may take objection to this proposal insofar as rates of development or proficiency attainment tend to gloss over considerable individual variation. Nevertheless, with schools under considerable pressure to establish criteria for adequate yearly progress for ELLs, such data are critical. States, districts, and schools throughout the country are trying to define criteria for adequate yearly progress, essentially, without the aid of any empirically derived estimates.

There is also a clear need for research that examines systematically the relationship between L2 oral language development and instruction. We simply do not know empirically the extent to which the rates at which ELLs achieve oral proficiency can be accelerated. We do not know empirically the extent to which oral language development is amenable to instruction, whether defined in terms of direct instruction, natural language approaches, and/or content-based approaches, all of which are discussed in the ELL literature and none of which, apparently, has been systematically investigated in terms of oral outcomes. Given this gap in research, it is not surprising that teachers tend to express confusion about how best to support the English oral language development of ELL students (see Gersten and Baker, 2000).

The majority of studies clustered together under the topic of school factors focused on ELLs' classroom language use. These studies suggest that ELLs are most likely to use the language used to deliver instruction in their interactions with peers and teachers. Interactive activities that pair ELLs with native or fluent English speakers can provide language learning opportunities for ELLs, but careful consideration must be given to the design of the task, the training of non-ELLs, and the language proficiency of the ELLs. It also appears that increased L2 use is associated with improved L2 proficiency. At the same time, several studies imply that while use and exposure are necessary conditions for language learning, they may not be sufficient conditions, especially when it comes to achieving higher levels of proficiency involving more academic uses of language. The content and quality of L2 exposure and use are probably of equal if not greater, importance than L2 exposure and use per se. Morever, at least one study (Saville-Troike, 1984) reminds us that classroom language use is a vehicle for both language and academic development. While the use of L2 may contribute to L2 proficiency, for students just beginning to acquire English, the use of L1 may make a stronger contribution to academic development.

According to the research reviewed on non-school factors, there is a positive relationship between English language use outside of school and oral English proficiency. However, this finding is qualified by three other findings. First, although the development of L2 oral proficiency is likely aided by L2 use outside of school, it is not necessarily impeded by continued development and use of L1. Second, at advanced levels of English language and literacy development, English use outside of school may not be as critical as English use in school. Third, the relationship between L1 and L2 use outside school may be mediated by sociocultural factors: The emphasis families place on maintaining L1 relative to learning L2 may vary across cultural and/or SES groups. Unfortunately, these findings on non-school factors are limited by the small sample of studies on which they are based. It should be noted, however, that our sample is small primarily because among the many studies that focus on non-school factors, very few include measures of oral language development. It seems important that future research attempt to incorporate such measures in order to establish empirical links among home, school, and community factors and the language development of ELLs.

Regarding assessment, most schools in the United States with at least moderate numbers of ELLs assess oral English language proficiency upon entry to school and to inform program exit decisions. However, most oral language instruments are imperfect and produce results that should be interpreted cautiously. Most tests in use have not been subjected to rigorous evaluation; classification cutoffs for proficiency levels can vary from one test to the next; normative results can be problematic depending on the match between examinees and the norming group; and non-proficient classifications can be inaccurate. In short, all oral language assessment results should be viewed as a sampling of students' overall oral proficiency. Predicting success in mainstream classrooms – typically, the process of determining whether or not to reclassify ELLs as FEP – should involve multiple sources of information and is likely best served by oral language instruments that are more academically oriented and broad rather than narrow in scope. A significant qualifier to these findings, however, is the datedness of some of the studies that support them (e.g., Merino & Spencer, 1983; Ulibarri et al., 1981). However, our search located no recent studies that evaluated the validity and reliability of more current generations of oral language assessments. This represents a critical area of needed research.

As a closing remark, this chapter shines a spotlight on an area of the curriculum – oral language – that typically remains in the shadows. This has been consistently noted by researchers of L2 development (see Fillmore and Valadez, 1986), by researchers of L1 development (Loban, 1976), and by scholars who document the history of the English Language Arts (Squire, 1991). Loban (1976) places blame partly on the fact that oral language is impervious to paper and pencil assessment and, therefore, has not been incorporated into the high-stakes testing system that greatly influences curriculum and research in the United States. The results of our review confirm what seems to be a continuing neglect of oral-language research. For the most part, English oral language development for ELLs has over the last twenty years continued to remain in the shadows of literacy and mathematics, the mainstays of high-stakes testing.

References

August, D. 1987. Effects of peer tutoring on the second language acquisition of Mexican-American children in elementary school. *TESOL Quarterly* 21(3), 717–36.

Baker, K. 1998. Structured English immersion: Breakthrough in teaching limited-English-proficient students. *Phi Delta Kappan* 79, 199–203.

Cardoza, D. 1996. The identification and reclassification of limited-English-proficient students: A study of entry and exit classification procedures. *NABE Journal* 11(1), 21–45.

Carlisle, J., Beeman, M., Davis, L., and Spharim, G. 1999. Relationship of metalinguistic capabilities and reading achievement for children who are becoming bilingual. *Applied Psycholinguistics* 20, 459–78.

Cathcart-Strong, R. L. 1986. Input generation by young second language learners. *TESOL Quarterly* 20(3), 515–29.

Chesterfield, R. A., and Chesterfield, K. B. 1985a. Natural order in children's use of second language learning strategies. *Applied Linguistics* 6(1), 45–59.

1985b. "Hoja's with the H": Spontaneous peer teaching in bilingual classrooms. *Bilingual Review* 12(3), 198–208.

Chesterfield, R. A., Chesterfield, K. B., Hayes-Latimer, K., and Chavez, R. 1983. The influence of teachers and peers on second language acquisition in bilingual preschool programs. *TESOL Quarterly* 17(3), 401–19.

Collier, V. P. 1987. Age and rate of acquisition of second language for academic purposes. *TESOL Quarterly* 21(4), 617–41.

Commins, N., and Miramontes, O. 1989. Perceived and actual linguistic competence: A descriptive study of four low-achieving Hispanic bilingual students. *American Educational Research Journal* 26(4), 443–72.

Cummins, J. 1979. Linguistic interdependence and the educational development of bilingual children. *Review of Educational Research* 49, 222–51.

Fernandez, M., Pearson, B., Umbel, V., Oller, D., and Molinet-Molina, M. 1992. Bilingual receptive vocabulary in Hispanic preschool children. *Hispanic Journal of Behavioral Sciences* 14(2), 268–76.

Fillmore, L. W., and Valadez, C. 1986. Teaching bilingual learners. In M. Wittrock (ed.), *Handbook of Research on Teaching* (pp. 648–85). New York: MacMillan.

Fitzgerald, J. 1995. English-as-a-second-language learners' cognitive reading processes: A review of research in the United States. *Review of Educational Research* 65(2), 145–90.

Garcia-Vázquez, E., Vasquez, L. A., Lopez, I. C., and Ward, W. 1997. Language proficiency and academic success: Relationships between proficiency in two languages and achievement among Mexican-American students. *Bilingual Research Journal* 21(4), 395–408.

Genesee, F. (ed.). 1999. Program alternatives for linguistically diverse students (Educational Practice Report 1). Santa Cruz, CA, and Washington, DC: Center for Research on Education, Diversity, and Excellence.

Gersten, R., and Baker, S. 2000. The professional knowledge base on instructional practices that support cognitive growth for English-language learners. In R. Gersten, E. Schiller, and S. Vaughn (eds.), *Contemporary Special Education Research: Syntheses of the Knowledge Base on Critical Instructional Issues* (pp. 31–79). Mahwah, NJ: Lawrence Erlbaum Associates.

Goldstein, B., Harris, K., and Klein, M. D. 1993. Assessment of oral storytelling abilities of Latino junior high school students with learning handicaps. *Journal of Learning Disabilities* 26(2), 138–43.

Gomez, L., Parker, R., Lara-Alecio, R., Ochoa, S. H., and Gomez, R. 1996. Naturalistic language assessment of LEP students in classroom interactions. *The Bilingual Research Journal* 20(1), 69–92.

Gonzalez, V., Bauerle, P., and Felix-Holt, M. 1996. Theoretical and practical implications of assessing cognitive and language development in bilingual children with qualitative methods. *The Bilingual Research Journal* 20(1), 93–131.

Hakuta, K., Butler, Y. G., and Witt, D. 2000. How long does it take English learners to attain proficiency? Linguistic Minority Research Institute (ERIC Document Reproduction Service No. FL 026 180). (Available at LMRI website: http://www.lmri.ucsb.edu/resdiss/pdf files/hakuta.pdf).

Hansen, D. A. 1989. Locating learning: Second language gains and language use in family, peer and classroom contexts. *NABE Journal, 13,* 161–79.

Howard, E. R., Christian, D., and Genesee, F. 2003. *The development of bilingualism and biliteracy from grade 3 to 5: A summary of findings from the Cal/CREDE study of two-way immersion education.* Santa Cruz, CA, and Washington, DC: Center for Research on Education, Diversity, and Excellence.

Jacob, E., Rottenberg, L., Patrick, S., and Wheeler, E. 1996. Cooperative learning: Context and opportunities for acquiring academic English. *TESOL Quarterly* 30(2), 253–80.

Johnson, D. M. 1983. Natural language learning by design: A classroom experiment in social interaction and second language acquisition. *TESOL Quarterly* 17(1), 55–68.

Krashen, S. 1996. A gradual exit, variable threshold model for limited-English-proficient children. *NABE News* 19(7), pages 1 and 15–17.

Lambert, W. E., and Taylor, D. M. 1996. Language in the lives of ethnic minorities: Cuban-American families in Miami. *Applied Linguistics 17,* 478–500.

Lindholm, K. J. 1987. English question use in Spanish-speaking ESL children: Changes with English language proficiency. *Research in the Teaching of English* 21(1), 64–91.

Lindholm-Leary, K. J. 2001. *Dual Language Education.* Clevedon, UK: Multilingual Matters.

Loban, W. 1976. *Language development: Kindergarten through grade twelve* (Research Report No. 18). Urbana, IL: National Council of Teachers of English.

MacSwan, J., Rolstad, K., and Glass, G. 2002. Do some school-age children have no language? Some problems of construct validity in the Pre-LAS Español. *Bilingual Research Journal* 26(2), 395–419.

Malave, L. 1989. Contextual elements in a bilingual cooperative setting: The experiences of early childhood LEP learners. *NABE Journal 13,* 96–122.

Medina, M., and Escamilla, K. 1992. English acquisition by fluent- and limited-Spanish-proficient Mexican-Americans in a 3-year maintenance bilingual program. *Hispanic Journal of Behavioral Sciences 14*(2), 252–67.

Merino, B., and Spencer, M. 1983. The comparability of English and Spanish versions of oral language proficiency instruments. *NABE Journal 7*(2), 1–31.

Milk, R. D. 1982. Language use in bilingual classrooms: Two case studies. In M. Hines and W. Rutherford (eds.), *On TESOL '81* (pp. 181–91). Washington, DC: TESOL.

O'Malley, J. M., Chamot, A. U., Stewner-Manzanares, G., Kupper, L., and Russo, R. P. 1985a. Learning strategies used by beginning and intermediate ESL students. *Language Learning 35*(1), 21–46.

O'Malley, J. M., Chamot, A. U., Stewner-Manzanares, G., Russo, R., and Kupper, L. 1985b. Learning strategy applications with students of English as a second language. *TESOL Quarterly 19*(3), 557–84.

Pease-Alvarez, L. 1993. *Moving in and out of bilingualism: Investigating native language maintenance and shift in Mexican-descent children* (Research Report No. 6). Santa Cruz, CA: University of California, National Center for Research on Cultural Diversity and Second Language Learning.

Pease-Alvarez, L., and Winsler, A. 1994. Cuando el maestro no habla Espanol: Children's bilingual language practices in the classroom. *TESOL Quarterly* *28*(3), 507–35.

Peck, S. 1987. Signs of learning: Child nonnative speakers in tutoring sessions with a child native speaker. *Language Learning 37*(4), 545–71.

Platt, E., and Troudi, S. 1997. Mary and her teachers: A Grebo-speaking child's place in the mainstream classroom. *The Modern Language Journal 81*, 28–49.

Rodriguez-Brown, F. V. 1987. Questioning patterns and language proficiency in bilingual students. *NABE Journal 13*(3), 217–33.

Royer, J. M., and Carlo, M. S. 1991. Assessing the language acquisition progress of limited English proficient students: Problems and a new alternative. *Applied Measurement in Education 4*(2), 85–113.

Saville-Troike, M. 1984. What *really* matters in second language learning for academic achievement? *TESOL Quarterly 18*(2), 199–219.

1988. Private speech: Evidence for second language learning strategies during the "silent" period. *Journal of Child Language 15*(3), 567–90.

Schecter, S., and Bayley, R. 1997. Language socialization practices and cultural identity: Case studies of Mexican-descent families in California and Texas. *TESOL Quarterly 31*(3), 513–41.

Schrank, F., Fletcher, T. V., and Alvarado, C. G. 1996. Comparative validity of three English oral language proficiency tests. *The Bilingual Research Journal 20*(1), 55–68.

Snow, C. E., Cancino, H., Gonzalez, P., and Sriberg, E. 1987. *Second language learners' formal definitions: An oral language correlate of school literacy* (Tech. Rep. No. 5). Los Angeles: University of California, Center for Language Education and Research.

Squire, J. 1991. The history of the profession. In J. Flood, J. Jensen, D. Lapp, and J. Squire (eds.), *Handbook of research on teaching the English language arts* (pp. 3–17). New York: Macmillan.

Strong, M. 1983. Social styles and the second language acquisition of Spanish-speaking kindergartners. *TESOL Quarterly 17*(2), 241–58.

1984. Integrative motivation: Cause or result of successful second language acquisition? *Language Learning 34*(3), 1–13.

Thomas, W., and Collier, V. 2002. *A national study of school effectiveness for language minority students' long-term academic achievement final report: Project 1.1* Santa Cruz, CA, and Washington, DC: Center for Research on Education, Diversity, and Excellence.

Ulibarri, D. M., Spencer, M. L., and Rivas, G. A. 1981. Language proficiency and academic achievement: A study of language proficiency tests and their relationship to school ratings as predictors of academic achievement. *NABE Journal 5*(3), 47–79.

Umbel, V. M., and Oller, D. K. 1994. Developmental changes in receptive vocabulary in Hispanic bilingual school children. *Language Learning 44*(2), 221–42.

Umbel, V., Pearson, B., Fernandez, M., and Oller, D. 1992. Measuring bilingual children's receptive vocabularies. *Child Development 63*(4), 1012–20.

Weslander, D., and Stephany, G. V. 1983. Evaluation of English as a second language program for Southeast Asian students. *TESOL Quarterly 17*(3), 473–80.

TABLE A.2.1. *Summary of Studies on Language Development*

Authors	Sample Characteristics	Grades	Instructional Method or Program	Design	Outcome Measures	Results
Carlisle et al. (1999)	Mexican-American ELLs, low SES, low achieving	1, 2, 3	English-only parochial school	Within group: Correlational – n = 57	– PPVT: Spanish and English receptive vocabulary – Formal and informal definitions	– Significant correlation only for Spanish-English formal definitions
Chesterfield and Chesterfield (1985a)	Mexican-American ELLs from Spanish-speaking homes in a border Texas city	Pre-K-1	Bilingual program	Within group: Longitudinal – n = 14	– Observed use of 12 language learning strategies	– Strategies hierarchically organized – Higher levels of L2 oral proficiency associated with more varied strategies
García-Vázquez et al. (1997)	Bilingual Hispanic students	6–12	Not reported	Within group: Correlational – n = 100	– WLPB: English oral proficiency – ITBS: English reading achievement	– Significant correlation between English oral proficiency and reading
Goldstein, Harris, and Klein (1993)	Mexican-American, fluent English proficient, previously ELL	7–9	L1 instruction through Grade 3	Within group: Correlational – n = 31	– English story retell scored for lang and content scores (adapted from LAS-O) – PIAT: English reading	– Moderate, sign correlation for retell content and reading – No sign correlation for lang and reading

Study	Population	Level	Focus	Design	Measures	Results
Lindholm (1987)	Mexican-American from Spanish-English bilingual families	K, 2	Varying involvement in bilingual program	Between-group: longitudinal – Limited English prof (n = 2) – Fluent English prof (n = 2) – One K and one 2nd in each pair	– Question forms in English observed during home visits over one-year period	– All children showed growth in question use over one-year period – Fluent English prof students showed command of wider array of question forms
O'Malley, Chamot, Stewner-Manzanares, Kupper and Russo (1985a)	Spanish- and Vietnamese-speaking ELLs, in intermediate level ESL classes	High school	Listening and speaking strategy training	Random assignment to: – TR1: metacog + cognitive strategies (n = 27) – TR2: cognitive strategies (n = 26) – CO: no strategy training (n = 22)	Pre- and post-testing: – Listening to lecture followed by comprehension test – Oral presentation, videotaped and scored by research team	– TR2 > CO on post-test speaking (oral presentation) – No sign difference on listening

(continued)

TABLE A.2.1 (*continued*)

Authors	Sample Characteristics	Grades	Instructional Method or Program	Design	Outcome Measures	Results
O'Malley, Chamot, Stewner-Manzanares, Russo, and Kupper (1985b)	Spanish- and Vietnamese-speaking ELLs, in beginning or intermediate level ESL classes	High school	Beginning or intermediate ESL	Within group: Numerical results, no stat analysis – n = 70	– Self-reported use of language learning strategies	– Metacognitive, cognitive, and social strategies identified – Students tended to use more cog than metacog strategies – More likely to use cog strategies on less rather than more demanding tasks
Rodriguez-Brown (1987)	Hispanic, fluent Spanish-limited English speakers and fluent English-limited Spanish speakers	3	Two-way immersion	Between group: English and Spanish speakers; some stronger in Spanish, some stronger in English – numeric results, no stat analysis – n = 6	– Question forms in English and Spanish observed in and out of school	– Students showed command of wider array of question forms in their stronger language

Study	Population	Grade	Program	Design	Measures	Findings
Royer and Carlo (1991)	Puerto Rican-American ELLs, transitioning from Spanish to English instruction	5–6	Transitional bilingual program	Within group: Longitudinal – n = 49	– Sentence verification technique: English listening and reading comp	– No significant correlation between English listening and reading at either grade 5 or 6
Saville-Troike (1984)	L1 and ethnicity varied, first year in United States, parents in graduate program for foreign students	2–5	English-only with ESL; 30 min/day of L1	Within group: Correlational – n = 19	– English reading – Several measures of oral English proficiency – Classroom language use	– Moderate, significant correlation with reading only for measure of vocabulary
Saville-Troike (1988)	Chinese, Japanese, Korean speakers, first year in United States, parents in graduate program for foreign students	Pre-K–3	English-only programs	Ethnographic description and transcript excerpts – n = 9	– Intrapersonal learning strategies exhibited in private speech	– Six of nine experienced "silent period;" all six evidenced strategies

(continued)

TABLE A.2.1 (*continued*)

Authors	Sample Characteristics	Grades	Instructional Method or Program	Design	Outcome Measures	Results
Snow et al. (1987)	Mid SES ELLs and English speakers learning French	2, 3, 4, 5	ESL for ELLs; French for English speakers	Between group comparisons: – Quality of definitions by low and high English prof – Correlations by grade level – n = 137	– Quality of informal and formal definitions of common words	– Quality of formal def. varied by prof – Sign correlation between formal def and reading – Magnitude of correlation stronger in grades 4 and 5 than in grade 2
Strong (1983)	Span-speaking ELLs enrolled in one classroom, small industrial community in California	K	Bilingual class with ELLs, and native and fluent English speakers	Within group: correlational – Between group comparisons: more and less successful L2 learners – n = 13	– Natural communicative lang: English voc, syntax, pronunciation; social styles (e.g., talkativeness); contacts with English speakers	– Some social styles correlated w/ some lang measures – Successful ELLs made good use of contact with English speakers

Strong (1984)	Span-speaking ELLs	K	Bilingual class with ELLs, and native and fluent English speakers	Within group: Correlational - Between gp comparisons: low and high English prof - n = 19	- Nominations of English speaker playmates - English voc, syntax, pronunciation	- High English prof more likely to nominate English speakers as playmates - Low English prof increased English speaker as their prof increased
Ulibarri, Spencer, and Rivas (1981)	1,110 Hispanic students representing four major regions of California: Bay Area, Central Valley, Los Angeles, San Diego	1, 3, 5	Not reported	Between group: Correlational - grade 1 (n = 165) - grade 3 (n = 196) - grade 5 (n = 207)	- LASO, BSM, BINL: Oral L2 language use - Standard scores from either CAT, CTBS, or SAT (district's chosen assessment): reading	- Stronger correlations with reading at all grades for broader, more academic measures of oral prof-LAS-O

TABLE A.2.2. *Summary of Studies on School Factors*

Authors	Sample Characteristics	Grades	Instructional Method or Program	Design	Outcome Measures	Results
August (1987)	Mexican-American ELLs from Spanish-speaking homes, low SES, multiethnic community	1–5	6-week peer-tutoring training	Btwn grp: Matched pairs, random assign – group diff – correlations – n = 12	– Observations of quantity and type of verbal interactions – PPVT: vocab – LAS-O: oral prof – Pre- and post-measures	– TR sign > CO in frequency of use of English – Sign correlation between amount of English and PPVT and also with some LAS-O subtests
Cathcart-Strong (1986)	Spanish-speaking ELLs and English-speakers at one school in suburb of San Francisco	K	ELLs in a bilingual program	Within group: descriptive – n = 4 ELLs	– Response pattern among English-speakers to ELLs in play situations	– English-speakers did not provide worthwhile interaction to ELLs
Chesterfield and Chesterfield (1985b)	Mexican-American, Spanish-speaking ELLs from 11 classrooms in California and Texas	1	All-English and Spanish-English bilingual programs	Btwn group: chi squares – All-English classes (n = 10) – Bilingual classes (n = 10)	– Language use during peer interactions and oral proficiency	– ELLs in all-English used sign more English than Spanish; – ELLs in bilingual used sign more Spanish than English

Study	Population	Grade	Program	Design	Measures	Findings
Chesterfield et al. (1983)	Spanish-speaking ELLs from low-income families in Texas and Wisconsin	Pre-K	Bilingual program	Within group: Correlational – n = 11	– ELLs use of English and Spanish – Oral English proficiency (mean length of utterance) measured via observations at beginning and end of year	– Significant positive rank-order correlations between increase in English use and increases in L2 oral proficiency
Hakuta, Butler, and Witt (2000) Sample A	ELLs of various L1s enrolled in same district since K, classified as ELL in K, Northern California	1, 2, 3, 4, 5	English-only program from one district	Cross-sectional: oral prof across grades – All ELLs with available data included – n = 1,872	– IPT: Oral English proficiency	– Almost all English proficient by grade 5 – Largest gain from grades 1 to 2
Hakuta, Butler, and Witt (2000) Sample B	Spanish-speaking ELLs from high-poverty schools enrolled in same district since K, classified as ELL in K, Northern California	1, 3, 5	Some from bilingual, some English-only	Cross-sectional: Oral prof across grades – About 40 ELLs randomly selected per grade – n = 122	– Oral English proficiency (WLPB-R)	– Gains evident from grades 1 to 5 – 3 + years behind native English speaker norms at grade 5

(continued)

TABLE A.2.2 (continued)

Authors	Sample Characteristics	Grades	Instructional Method or Program	Design	Outcome Measures	Results
Howard, Christian, and Genesee (2003)	Low SES Hispanic Spanish-speaking ELLs & mid SES English-speakers	3–5	Two-way immersion program	Longitudinal: Oral prof across grades - Spanish-speakers (n = approx. 125) - English-speakers (n = 115)	- Parallel, study-developed measures of oral Spanish & English proficiency	- Almost all English proficient by grade 5 - Similar rates of L2 oral prof growth for native Spanish and native English speakers
Jacob et al. (1996)	Limited and fluent proficient ELLs in one ethnically mixed classroom, working class Eastern United States	6	Coop. learning; mainstream Social Studies class	Within group: - Numeric results, no stat analysis - Transcript excerpts - n = 7	- Observed instances of potential language learning opportunities	- Few language learning opportunities - Most (54%) involved clarifying pronunciation during oral reading

Study	Grade	Program	Design/Sample	Measures	Findings
Johnson (1983)	K-4	5-week training: Inter-ethno-linguistic Peer Tutoring (IEPT)	Mexican-American ELLs from Spanish-speaking homes participating in a summer school program at Stanford experimental school	Btwn gp: matched pairs, random assign: – TR: IEPT – CO: No training, – ELLs (n = 16) – Fluent English-speaking tutors (n = 18)	– Observations of quantity and type of verbal interactions – PPVT: Vocab – LAS – O: Oral prof – Child-Child Communication Test (CCCT) – Pre- and post-measures	– TR sign > CO at post on quantity of interaction with fluent English tutors – TR sign > CO at post on PPVT, but not LAS-O or CCCT
Lindholm-Leary (2001)	K, 1, 2, 3, 4, 5	Dual language (two-way) immersion program, 90/10 model	Hispanic, Spanish-speaking ELLs, Hispanic-, European-, African-, and Asian-American English-speakers, high and low ethnic density and SES	Cross-sectional: Oral prof across grades – Spanish-speakers (n = 2,938) – English-speakers (n = 1,715)	– Student Oral Language Observation Matrix (SOLOM): Teacher ratings of students' oral language proficiency	– Almost all English proficient by grade 5 – Similar rates of L2 oral prof growth for native Spanish and native English speakers

(continued)

TABLE A.2.2 (*continued*)

Authors	Sample Characteristics	Grades	Instructional Method or Program	Design	Outcome Measures	Results
Malave (1989)	Hispanic, Spanish-speaking ELLs with mid-level English prof, low-mid SES, western New York	2	Bilingual program	Within group: Numeric results, no stat analysis – n = 5	– Observed verbal behaviors and language choice during small group activities	– Although mid-level English prof, on average, ELLs used Spanish 87% of time
Milk (1982)	Spanish-speaking ELLs from Spanish-speaking homes, both Spanish-dominant and balanced bilinguals	2	"Model" maintenance bilingual program	Between groups: Numeric results, no stat analysis – Spanish dom (n = 8) – Balanced bil (n = 8) – English dom (n = 8)	– Observed speech acts and language choice during small group activities	– Spanish dominant and balanced bilinguals rarely used English
Medina and Escamilla (1992)	Spanish-speaking ELLs from 24 schools in Arizona school district	K-2	Developmental (maintenance) bilingual program	– Longitudinal: Oral prof at K and grade 2 – ELLs (n = 298, of whom 187 limited Spanish prof)	– LAS-O in English and Spanish: English and Spanish oral proficiency	– Stronger oral gains for all ELLs in English than among limited Spanish prof in Spanish

Study	Grade	Population	Context	Design	Data source	Findings
Pease-Alvarez and Winsler (1994)	4	U.S.-born Mexican-American, Spanish-speaking ELLs, immigrant, working-class parents	Bilingual program and transitioning from Spanish to English instruction	Case study: Multi subject, numeric results, no stat analysis – n = 3	– Spanish and English use at school with teacher, peers, self	– Significant shift over year from Spanish to English use for all three ELLs
Peck (1987)	K	Mexican and Mexican-American Spanish-speaking ELLs from three classrooms at one school in LA area	ELLs tutored by trained Grade 2 English speaker	Between groups: Chi-squares – hi (n = 3) – med (n = 3) – low (n = 3) – Selected based on obs to max L2 variation	– ELL language output observed during tutoring sessions	– Language outputs consistent with proficiency levels: H & M > L
Platt & Troudi (1997)	3	Liberian, Grebo-speaking girl, first year in United States	English mainstream classroom	Single subject case study: descriptive – n = 1	– Daily, year-long observations of child's interactions, and language proficiency	– Assistance from English-speakers not sufficient to meet ELL's needs – minimal lang growth

(continued)

TABLE A.2.2 (*continued*)

Authors	Sample Characteristics	Grades	Instructional Method or Program	Design	Outcome Measures	Results
Saville-Troike (1984)	Ethnicity, L1 varied, 1st year in United States, parents in grad program for foreign students	2, 3, 4, 5	English-only with ESL; 30 min/day L1	Within group: correlational – n = 19	– English reading – Several measures of oral Eng proficiency – Classroom language use	– Significant correlation between L2 use and L2 prof – No correlation between use and rdg
Thomas & Collier (2002)	Mostly Hispanic, low SES, Spanish L1, and English L1, Northwest United States	1, 2, 3, 4, 5	Two-way dual language immersion	– Quasi longitudinal (Data avail for multi grades for most students) – Spanish-speakers (n = 238) – English-speakers (n = 279)	-SOLOM: Teacher's ratings of students Eng and Span oral proficiency	– Almost all English proficient by grade 5 – Similar rates of L2 oral prof growth for native Spanish and native English speakers
Weslander & Stephany (1983)	Southeast Asians, in United States for 2–68 months, Des Moines, Iowa	2–10	District developed ESL program for recent immigrants	Within group: pre/post test – n = 577	– BSM: Oral proficiency measure -Taken in fall and spring	– Average 1-year gain about half a proficiency level

TABLE A.2.3. *Summary of Studies on Non-School Factors*

Authors	Sample Characteristics	Grades	Instructional Program	Design	Outcome Measures	Results
Hansen (1989)	Mexican-Am ELLs, Spanish dominant homes, San Francisco area	2, 5	Bilingual programs	Within group: correlational (regression) – n = 117	– Stanford Diagnostic Reading Test: Auditory vocabulary	– Positive relationship between English use at home and English vocabulary
Lambert and Taylor (1996)	Cuban-American mothers living in Miami with middle-school-age children	Not applicable	Not reported	Between group: middle- and working-class mothers – n = 108 (56 per gp)	– Mothers' self-reports: language use, attitudes toward Spanish and English, ratings of child's proficiency	– Working-class mothers tend to emphasize English – middle-class mothers tend to emphasize maintenance of Spanish
Pease-Alvarez (1993)	Mexican-American ELLs and their families living in California	3	Bilingual programs	Between group: 4 gps ranging from born in Mexico/ use mostly Spanish at home to born in United States/use mostly English at home – n = 55 (n varies per gp)	– PPVT, TVIP-H: Spanish and English oral vocabulary – Parents self-reports of language use in home	– Positive relationship between English use at home and English vocab – Negative relationship between English use at home and Spanish vocab

(continued)

TABLE A.2.3 (continued)

Authors	Sample Characteristics	Grades	Instructional Program	Design	Outcome Measures	Results
Schecter and Bayley (1997)	Mexican-American families living in California and Texas	Varies, but all children elementary school age	Not reported	Case study of each family – n = 4 families	– Parents' descriptions of efforts to support English and maintain Spanish	– Maintaining Spanish tied to cultural identity – Maintenance strategies varied across families
Umbel and Oller (1994)	Cuban-American, bilingual parents, children introduced to English and Spanish since birth (simultaneous bilinguals)	1, 3, 6	English immersion programs	Between group: 2 gps – more Spanish than English and Spanish-English used equally at home – n = 102 (44 per gp)	– PPVT, TVIP-H: Spanish and English oral vocabulary	– Equal Spanish-English at home grp scored higher on English vocab than more Spanish than English gp – No gp diffs on Spanish vocab – Spanish vocab sign 1st order predictor of English vocab

TABLE A.2.4. *Summary of Studies on Assessment*

Authors	Sample Characteristics	Grades	Instructional Program	Design	Outcome Measures	Results
Cardoza (1996)	School districts from 10 states with highest number of ELLs	Pre-K-12	75% of districts offered some form of bilingual programming	Survey: Districts selected from target states randomly – n = 93	– Survey responses: what does the district assess for ELLs, when do they do it, and with what instruments?	– Most schools assess ELLs' oral Eng prof at entry and exit – Most common: LAS, BSM, LAB
Commins & Mira-montes (1989)	Underachieving ELLs in innovative program, presumed to be limited Span and Eng proficiency	5, 6	Bilingual program designed for underachievers	Case study: descriptive – n = 4	– Researcher observations of students' Span and Eng use across school and non-school settings	– Students demonstrated greater proficiency than school had presumed, and higher levels of proficiency in non-school settings than in classroom settings
Fernandez et al. (1992)	– Study sample: Mid-level SES bilingual Hisp, in Miami – Norm group: mid-level SES monolingual Hisp, in Puerto Rico and Mexico	Preschool	Not reported	Between group: Study sample and norm group – n = 396 (study sample)	– PPVT and TVIP-H: Eng and Span receptive vocabulary	– Order of difficulty of words on Span measure for study sample differed from that of the norm group

(continued)

61

TABLE A.2.4 (*continued*)

Authors	Sample Characteristics	Grades	Instructional Program	Design	Outcome Measures	Results
Gomez et al. (1996)	Bilingual Hisp students in summer program	Pre-K – 6	Students had been enrolled in either bilingual or ESL program	Validity and reliability study: Naturalist lang observational scale – n = 24	– Social language proficiency (e.g., topic development, understandability, absence of hesitations)	– Scale failed to meet most measurement criteria and did not meet efficiency criteria
Gonzalez, Bauerle, and Felix-Holt (1996)	1st, 2nd, & 3rd generation Mexican-American, mostly Span-speaking	K	Either bilingual or English program	Validity and reliability study: Qualitative scale for identifying gifted bilingual children – n = 17	– Qualitative Use of English and Spanish Tasks (QUEST), includes verbal (Span & Eng) and nonverbal classification tasks	– Gifted best identified via multiple verbal and nonverbal measures in both L1 and L2
MacSwan, Rolstad, and Glass (2002)	Span-speaking ELLs in a large metropolitan school district classified as non-Spanish-proficient (non-Spanish-speaking; NSS)	Pre-K, K	Not reported	Critical validity study of Pre-LAS (Language Assessment Scales) – n = 6,118	– Pre-LAS subtests: acting out commands, naming items in pictures, matching pictures to phrases, sentence repetition, sentence completion, story retell	– Classifications weighted heavily on last two components – At least 51% likely misclassified as non-Spanish-proficient (all passed components 1–4)
Merino and Spencer (1983)	Not applicable	Not applicable	Not applicable	Critical review of technical information reported by test publishers	– LAS, BSM, LAB, BINL, and BOLT: oral language assessment	– None of the assessments provided adequate technical information

Study	Sample	Grade		Design	Measures	Findings
Schrank, Fletcher, and Alvarado (1996)	Span-Eng bilingual children from Arizona and Texas	K, 2	Not reported	Validity study of oral language assessments – n = 196	– 3 assessments: IPT-I, LAS (Pre-LAS & LAS-O), & WLPB-R – Teacher ratings of students' academic language proficiency (Houston school district rating scale)	– Strong inter-test correlations among all assessments – WLPB-R correlated most strongly with teachers' ratings of academic language proficiency
Ulibarri, Spencer, and Rivas (1981)	Hispanic students representing four major regions of California: Bay Area, Central Valley, Los Angeles, San Diego	1, 3, 5	Not reported	Validity study of oral language assessments – n = 1,000	– LAS-O, BSM, BINL: Oral language assessment – Standard scores for reading & math from CTBS, CAT, SAT (depending on district): achievement – Teacher ratings of achievement, language proficiency, likelihood of success in mainstream program	– Assessments did not classify students consistently ANOVA: sign diffs in achievement based on LAS-O classifications, not for BSM or BINL Stepwise Regression: – Teacher ratings the best 1st-order predictor of achievement, but LAS-O was a sign 2nd- or 3rd-order predictor – BSM and BINL were not

3

Literacy

Crosslinguistic and Crossmodal Issues

Caroline Riches and Fred Genesee

Crosslinguistic relationships between the L1 and the L2 as well as cross-modal relationships between oral and written language provide a basis for discussing research on the reading and writing development of ELLs. There are two fundamental and inescapable reasons why this is so. First of all, the learners under consideration, by definition, are acquiring literacy in English as a second language and have an ongoing developmental history in their first language. As a result, the relationship between their L1 and their L2 figures prominently in much of the research on reading and writing development in ELLs. In fact, relatively little research looks at L2 literacy development in ELLs without reference to their L1. Second, since reading and writing in any language implicate both oral and written modes of language, the relationship between oral and written language in the L1 and L2 of ELLs has also been a primary theme in much of the research reviewed here. The questions are: What is the relationship between oral and written language development? Is it the same for native English speakers and ELLs? The following specific relationships are examined in the sections that follow:

1. L1 oral proficiency and the development of L2 literacy,
2. L2 oral proficiency and the development of L2 literacy,
3. Specific component skills or abilities related to oral and written language and the development of L2 literacy, and
4. L1 literacy and the development of L2 literacy.

The crosslinguistic and crossmodal relationships identified herein are complex and interwoven. Consequently, a number of the studies reviewed focused on more than one of these issues. For example, Lanauze and Snow (1989) and Langer, Barolome, and Vasquez (1990) examined the relationship between L1 and L2 literacy development and considered aspects of both L1 and L2 oral proficiency. Studies such as these are discussed in all of the relevant subsections.

THEORETICAL BACKGROUND

A number of theoretical perspectives have served as the impetus or starting point for many of the studies reviewed here and these warrant some consideration before proceeding with our synopsis. The developmental interdependence hypothesis (Cummins 1981, 1991) recurs frequently in many studies (see MacSwan and Rolstad, 2003, for a critique of Cummins's hypothesis). This hypothesis defines the nature of the relationship between the L1 and the L2 of ELLs and in so doing distinguishes different types of language proficiency. On the one hand, some language skills are fundamentally interpersonal in nature and characterize everyday social conversations and usage. These skills are thought to be language specific. Interpersonal communication is usually embedded in meaningful and immediate contexts so that the meanings participants seek to convey are supported by shared context and, moreover, the participants are able to actively negotiate meaning directly through feedback to one another. Context may be shared by virtue of common past experiences or by the immediate setting in which communication is taking place. A face-to-face conversation about a movie that two people have seen is an example of context-embedded communication. The speakers have the shared experience of seeing the movie that they can draw on when discussing it. Talking about a football game that both speakers are watching is another example of context-embedded communication. These language skills are often implicated in oral uses of language, although not necessarily, and are acquired relatively quickly in the first language of all normal children.

On the other hand, other language skills serve more complex cognitive or academic purposes and are characteristically used in decontextualized ways, such as during educational instruction. Decontextualized language skills are often associated with written forms of language (e.g., reading a history textbook), but not necessarily since they can also occur during oral language use – such as during a lecture on history. Because the conversation takes place without an immediate or explicit context, care must be taken to provide context and details that will make the message meaningful. Returning to our movie example, if the conversational partners are talking about a movie that they have not both seen, then background information or "framing" is required on the part of the person who has seen it to make sure that his or her meaning is clear and to explicate personal views about the movie because the participants have little recourse to immediate contextual cues or shared experiences to draw on. As Cummins notes (2000, pp. 68–9): "the essential aspect of <u>academic language proficiency</u> [underlining added by authors] is the ability to make complex meanings explicit . . . by means of language itself rather than by means of contextual support or paralinguistic cues (e.g., gestures, intonation etc.)." Indeed, success in school in the long run ultimately depends critically on students' ability to read about or express abstract, complex ideas without the benefit of past experience or concurrent contextual cues.

Academic language proficiency is posited to be part of "a common underlying proficiency" made up of knowledge and abilities that once acquired in one language are potentially available for the development of another (Lanauze and Snow, 1989; Royer and Carlo, 1991). Literacy-related abilities fall into this latter category. When one has learned to read, then there are many components of reading that can be used in learning to read another language. While interpersonal communication skills and the language abilities that underlie the use of language in contextualized situations are often acquired relatively rapidly in a second language, research suggests that more time is needed to acquire proficiency in an L2 for academic and decontextualized uses – it is reported that five years or more may be required for ELLs to develop proficiency in English as a second language for academic purposes that is comparable to that of same-age native speakers (Collier, 1987; Cummins, 1981, 1992; Lindholm and Aclan, 1991).

An additional related theoretical construct that has been addressed in this corpus is the threshold hypothesis (Cummins, 1979, 1981; Toukomaa and Skutnabb-Kangas, 1977; for example, Lindholm and Aclan, 1991, examined in this issue). The threshold hypothesis posits that both language and cognitive development are enhanced if certain levels and types of proficiency are attained in either or both the L1 and the L2. In contrast, linguistic and cognitive enhancement are less like to occur if learners acquire limited competence in one or both languages. Together, the interdependence and threshold hypotheses raise a number of theoretically and pedagogically important developmental issues concerning the crosslinguistic and crossmodal aspects of language and their crisscrossing effects on bi- and multilingual development. These issues continue to be at the forefront of research into the development of literacy in bilingual settings (Cummins, 1997).

Echoing a contrastive analysis framework (Lado, 1957), some studies in this corpus have examined differences and similarities between ELLs' L1 and L2 and their effects on the development of reading and writing abilities by ELLs. According to the Contrastive Analysis Hypothesis, learners will have difficulty acquiring aspects of a second language that differ from their first language, but their acquisition of a second language will be facilitated by similarities between their first and second languages. A contrastive analysis perspective is evident, for example, in studies that have examined similarities and differences in sound – letter correspondences in the L1 and the L2 and their effects on L2 writing development (e.g., Fashola et al.,

1996; Zutell and Allen, 1988) and the effect of crosslinguistic cognates on vocabulary development (e.g., Hancin-Bhatt and Nagy, 1994; Nagy, Garcia, Durgunoglu and Hancin-Bhatt, 1993). These effects are commonly referred to as positive and negative transfer. A number of studies in this review have sought to identify instances of positive and negative transfer from the L1 during L2 literacy development.

Other articles in this corpus are based on interlanguage principles (e.g., Cronnell, 1985; Tompkins, Abramson, and Pritchard, 1999). Interlanguage theory postulates that second-language acquisition is dynamic and characterized by a series of intermediary stages, from early to advanced, that reflect influences from the L1 and from developmental processes associated with the target L2. For example, Tompkins, Abramson, and Pritchard (1999) identified patterns of L2 development that were similar to those of English L1 learners. Such effects are commonly referred to as developmental because they reflect developmental patterns that characterize native speakers of the language in question. Interlanguage theory is one of a group of contemporary theories that emphasize cognitive strategies in L2 acquisition (see Chapter 3 in Ellis, 1986, for an overview).

We now turn to a review of research related to each of these developmental conceptualizations. We have included tables highlighting pertinent details of the studies at the end of the chapter.

L1 ORAL PROFICIENCY AND L2 LITERACY

Much contemporary theory on literacy education emphasizes the need to draw on students' sociocultural experiences (e.g., Heath, 1983; Hudelson, 1994; Maguire and Graves, 2001) and their preexisting knowledge about reading and writing, including emergent literacy (e.g., Sulzby and Teale, 1991) as a basis for the development of initial literacy abilities in school. The same arguments have been made for students learning to read and write in their second language. According to this perspective, the critical early literacy-related and sociocultural experiences that ELLs have developed in their L1 can be used to advantage during L2 literacy development. From a pedagogical perspective, this could involve direct instruction in the L1 (as in forms of bilingual education) or in English-only programs with some kind of pedagogical recognition of the existing resources that ELLs have already developed in the L1 (e.g., use of folktales that are familiar to ELLs). In contrast, others have argued that promotion of ELLs' L1 oral proficiency detracts from their L2 development and especially the development of L2 literacy because it deprives these learners of valuable learning time in the L2 (Porter, 1990; Rossell and Baker, 1996). This is sometimes referred to as the "time-on-task" argument. This view assumes a sequential and *mono-linguistic* relationship between oral language proficiency and literacy development in a given language. Inherent in such a view is the notion that L2 reading and writing development proceeds autonomously from L1 proficiency. The studies reviewed in this section (see Table A.3.1 for a summary of these studies) examine the effects of L1 oral proficiency on L2 literacy with respect to general aspects of L1 ability and with respect to more specific aspects of L1 ability. We begin with the former.

The role that L1 oral proficiency plays in the development of L2 literacy has been examined in global ways in terms of the extent of L1 use outside of the school setting. A number of these studies used national data sources and multivariate research designs and found that use of a language other than English at home had no or only a weak or indirect relationship with literacy achievement in school (Buriel and Cardoza, 1998; Fernandez and Nielsen, 1986; Kennedy and Park, 1994; Nielsen and Lerner, 1986). There are a number of exceptions to this general trend, but even the effects reported in these studies are circumscribed. More specifically, Buriel and Cardoza (1998) compared three generations of Hispanic ELLs and found a significant negative relationship between L1 oral proficiency and L2 reading development in the third generation cohort, but found no relationship between L1 proficiency and L2 reading development in the first and second generation cohorts. Kennedy and Park (1994), comparing Hispanic and Asian background ELLs, found that speaking a language other than English at home had a negative relationship with standardized reading test scores in English for ELLs with Asian backgrounds but not with other measures of reading achievement. Moreover, no such effects were reported for the Hispanic cohort. It is particularly noteworthy that, notwithstanding these exceptions, all of the large-scale studies cited found that other factors, such as socioeconomic status, sense of control, aspirations, and amount of homework, were more significant predictors of reading achievement than was L1 use outside of school. In other words, L1 language use was generally less predictive of subsequent L2 reading development than other psychosocial factors. The link between L1 use and other factors outside of school and L2 literacy development in school is discussed more comprehensively in the "Language of Instruction" section in the following chapter.

Generally speaking, studies that have examined the link between more specific aspects of L1 oral ability or usage (e.g., emergent literacy, being read to at home) and L2 reading and writing development in school report "that early literacy experiences support subsequent literacy development, **regardless of language** [emphasis added]; and time spent on literacy activity in the native language – whether it takes place at home or at school – is not time lost with respect to English reading acquisition, at least through middle school" (Reese et al., 2000, p. 633). More specifically, Reese et al. (2000) found that family literacy practices, regardless of which language they occurred in, and L1 emergent literacy were significant predictors of L2 reading achievement in later grades. Following from this, a number of studies found that ELLs can draw on L1 experiences and abilities to the benefit of their performance on L2 literacy tasks, especially when given explicit opportunities to do so. Langer et al. (1990), using rigorous qualitative analyses, found that ELLs successfully made use of competencies in their L1 to make sense of L2 reading tasks. For example, they found that ELLs drew on words and ideas in their L1 especially when reading in the L2 was difficult. Lanauze and Snow (1989) found that students who were orally proficient in their L1 but not their L2 as well as students who were proficient in both their L1 and L2 exhibited similar levels of complexity, sophistication, and semantic content in their L2 writing. Lanauze and Snow note that writing performance in the L2 can surpass oral proficiency in the L2 in some cases. Accordingly, they go on, if proficiency is developed in the L1 (Spanish), those skills can transfer easily to the L2. In further support of the recruitment of the L1 in L2 reading, Saville-Troike (1984) reports (albeit descriptively) that the majority of top achievers on measures of L2 reading made use of their L1 during problem solving.

In summary, the findings outlined in this section suggest that, with some exceptions, measures of general L1 language proficiency or usage outside of school have not been found to relate consistently to the L2 literacy development of ELLs in school. Viewed differently, use of the L1 does not seem to detract from ELLs' L2 literacy development. Furthermore, it would appear that more specific measures of L1 oral proficiency or usage – and, in particular, those that are related to literacy – have a more significant and positive developmental relationship with L2 literacy than do general oral language proficiency measures. For example, ELLs with early L1 emergent literacy experiences and skills appeared to be able to utilize these experiences in the continued development of literacy abilities in the L2. In addition, ELLs were able to draw on existing L1 oral abilities, either in the absence of similar abilities in the L2 or in addition to similar abilities, in the service of L2 literacy tasks.

The role that L1 oral proficiency plays in L2 literacy should be considered in future research in more systematic ways, particularly with more direct measures of L1 oral proficiency. In the majority of studies reviewed here, L1 oral proficiency was assessed very generally, using self-report or global indicators, or was simply assumed. Since much of the research reviewed here suggests that certain levels and aspects of L1 oral proficiency are related to L2 literacy development than others, more attention to the precise nature of this relationship is needed if these relationships are to be explicated clearly.

L2 ORAL PROFICIENCY AND L2 LITERACY

Although a certain minimum level of general oral language proficiency in L2 is undoubtedly necessary for L2 literacy development, the relationship between L2 oral and L2 literacy development appears to be more complex than the relationship between L1 oral language and L1 literacy. As discussed in the previous section, L2 literacy often draws on knowledge and experiences linked to the L1; thus, L2 oral proficiency is likely to play a different role in the L2 literacy development of ELLs. In other words, the contribution that L2 oral proficiency makes to L2 literacy development in the case of ELLs may be composed of specific aspects of L2 oral proficiency that work in a complementary fashion with L1 oral proficiency (Peregoy and Boyle, 1991). Research reviewed in this section (see Table A.3.2) supports the notion that the development of L2 literacy can proceed with limited L2 oral proficiency if students have sufficiently developed abilities in their L1 (e.g., Lanauze & Snow, 1989; Reese et al., 2000). In such cases, it appears that L1 oral proficiency and emergent literacy in the L1 can fill gaps in L2 oral proficiency as it develops. This does not mean that L2 oral proficiency does not contribute to L2 literacy development since, as Reese et al. (2000) have noted, ELLs who begin school with well-developed L2 oral abilities achieve greater success in English reading than children with less well-developed L2 oral language abilities. However, the findings from these studies underline the important contribution that L1 abilities can make to L2 literacy development when dealing with students with limited L2 oral proficiency. Furthermore, a consideration of the differential roles that L1 and L2 oral proficiency might play in relation to L2 literacy development could help to define more clearly a number of important constructs that are often used when investigating these issues; specifically, the constructs of developmental interdependence, common underlying proficiency, and the thresholds of oral proficiency necessary to promote L2 literacy development discussed earlier.

Lindholm and Aclan (1991) sought to identify whether or not there is a threshold level of bilingual proficiency that results in enhanced levels of L2 reading achievement, as proposed by the threshold hypothesis (Cummins, 1991). More specifically, they examined the relationship among high, medium, and low levels of bilingual proficiency and English L2 reading achievement among Grades 1 to 4 elementary school ELLs. Since the students' levels of bilingual proficiency varied primarily with respect to level of L2 proficiency (with L1 oral proficiency assumed), their study permits us to examine the link between L2 oral proficiency and L2 literacy. The authors report that although there was a trend for scores on English reading measures to increase in accordance with increasing levels of bilingual proficiency, there was no significant difference between proficiency groups on reading measures in Grades 1 and 2. However, by Grade 3, the same year in which English reading instruction was introduced, differential effects of bilingual proficiency were evident with high levels of bilingual proficiency being significantly related to high levels of L2 reading ability. By implication, these results suggest that high levels of L2 oral proficiency can enhance L2 literacy development to a significant extent. In support of the threshold hypothesis, they also found that only the highly proficient bilingual students reached grade-level norms in English by Grade 4. In concluding, Lindholm and Aclan (1991) emphasize the need to evaluate student achievement in bilingual education programs from a long-term developmental perspective in order to determine the true effects of bilingualism on L2 literacy development (see also Cummins, 1992).

The remaining studies reviewed in this section focused on discrete aspects of L2 oral proficiency, to identify those specific features of L2 oral proficiency that contribute significantly to L2 literacy development. Studies that have addressed this issue have identified a differential relationship between L2 literacy achievement, on the one hand, and specific facets of L2 oral language proficiency on the other hand, with L2 oral abilities that are linked to academic tasks being more highly related to L2 literacy development than general L2 oral proficiency. Saville-Troike (1984) found that diversity of L2 vocabulary was significantly related to reading achievement, whereas general oral proficiency and verbosity were not. In a multiple-case study, Peregoy (1989) compared the L2 reading abilities of high, intermediate, and low L2 oral proficiency groups. She found a general correspondence between levels of L2 oral proficiency and L2 reading comprehension, and evidence for differential effects of specific components of oral proficiency at different proficiency levels. Lack of vocabulary knowledge resulted in reading miscomprehension at all levels, but it was particularly detrimental for low-level students, where lack of syntactic knowledge also impeded reading comprehension. Perez (1981) found that direct instruction in aspects of L2 oral competence specifically related to literacy (e.g., multiple word meanings, sentence patterns) resulted in significant improvements to the L2 reading scores of third-grade ELLs. In a study by Royer and Carlo (1991), L2 listening comprehension, as measured by performance on a sentence verification task, was a significant predictor of L2 reading performance, second in importance only to L1 or L2 reading scores.

Goldstein, Harris, and Klein (1993) and Peregoy and Boyle (1991) both examined the relationship between L2 reading comprehension and L2 oral proficiency as measured by knowledge of surface structure elements (e.g., grammatical complexity) versus deep structure elements (e.g., informativeness of responses). Goldstein, Harris, and Klein (1993) used a story-retelling task as a measure of L2 oral proficiency. The students' oral retellings were scored in two different manners, first for surface structure features and understanding and second for underlying story structure and in-depth understanding. They found that the results from the deep structure analyses were more highly related to L2 reading comprehension than were the results for the surface structure features. Peregoy and Boyle (1991) compared high, medium, and low level reading proficiency groups on four oral proficiency measures, two that reflected relatively surface level linguistic abilities and two that reflected deeper cognitive-linguistic abilities. Their results provide some evidence for the differential effects of deep versus surface structure features insofar as the intermediate and high groups differed significantly on two of the four measures, including the deep structure feature of "informativeness."

These studies considered together provide evidence that certain features of L2 oral proficiency are more directly related to L2 literacy than others. However, since the specific aspects that have been examined are diverse, it is difficult to draw definitive conclusions about which specific features are consistently related to improvements in L2 reading and writing performance. Clearly, more research is needed to clearly identify those aspects of L2 oral proficiency that contribute more directly and reliably to L2 literacy development.

In sum, findings from research in this and the preceding section on the link between L1 and L2 oral proficiency and L2 literacy development provide evidence for both crosslinguistic and crossmodal effects. It appears that aspects of both L1 and L2 oral proficiency are linked to L2 literacy development and that the relationship between oral and literacy development in ELLs is more specific and complex than might have previously been thought. The link between L2 oral proficiency and L2 literacy that is revealed by extant research points to a nuanced role for L2 oral language development, with academic- and literacy-related L2 oral proficiency being more important than general communicative competence in the L2. At the same time, the contribution of specific L2 oral language abilities to L2 literacy development needs to be considered with reference to the linguistic knowledge and real-world experiences that ELLs acquire through the medium of their L1. That is to say, it would appear that L1 oral language experiences and knowledge are critical developmental factors in ELLs' L2 literacy development, and that L2 oral proficiency may contribute in a complementary and specific manner. Furthermore, the relationship of oral proficiency in both the L1 and L2 needs to be considered more specifically in terms of how they might contribute to a common underlying proficiency.

In the following section, we review research that focuses on discrete aspects of L2 literacy development, often referred to as component skills or abilities, such as phonological awareness and vocabulary development. Because these components are, arguably, more easily definable and measurable than other, more complex aspects of reading and writing development, they have yielded relatively clear results and might serve as a basis for conducting further research on aspects of L2 literacy development that are more complex in nature.

COMPONENTS OF LITERACY DEVELOPMENT

The studies reviewed in this section (see Table A.3.3) are diverse in their focus and approaches but are considered together because all look at specific components of reading and writing. At issue is the extent to which L2 literacy development is influenced by common underlying language-related abilities that apply to virtually any language, as in studies dealing with phonological awareness or, conversely, by language-specific abilities that emanate from the L1 or the L2, as in studies dealing with spelling or cognate vocabulary.

Phonological Awareness

Research on L1 reading has established that phonological awareness is a significant correlate of successful beginning reading development (Adams, 1990). Phonological awareness is the ability to analyze and manipulate the sounds that make up oral and written language and can be assessed using a variety of tasks: *rhyme detection* – what two words sound the same at the end: pat, pan, cat?; *phoneme deletion* – what sound is left if the sound "k" is removed from the word "cat"; *blending* – what word do you get if the sound "s" is added to the word "top." The causal relationship between reading and phonological awareness has been shown to be bidirectional, with certain aspects of phonological awareness playing a fundamental role in facilitating early reading acquisition, while reading acquisition itself facilitates the emergence of yet other, more sophisticated aspects of phonological awareness (Adams, 1990; Snow, Burns, and Griffin, 1998). The causal role of phonological awareness in reading acquisition is also supported by intervention studies that show that children with difficulty learning to read exhibit statistically significant gains in reading ability following training in phonological awareness (Torgesen et al., 2001) and also by research that shows that poor and good L1 readers differ significantly from one another on tasks that tap phonological awareness, suggesting that phonological awareness is a decisive factor (Wagner and Torgesen, 1987).

The research reviewed in this section examines phonological awareness in L1 and L2 and its relationship to L2 reading. A critical question at the heart of this research is whether phonological awareness and its relationship to reading acquisition is tied to a particular language or whether it is a meta- or common underlying linguistic ability that has crosslinguistic repercussions, as noted by Durgunoglu, Nagy, and Hancin-Bhatt (1993, p. 454): "The ability to hear small components of spoken language may be highly correlated between languages." The corpus of research reviewed here is small since our literature search was limited to studies that examined the link between phonological awareness and reading directly; that is to say, the study had to have measures of reading to be included. Although few in number and diverse in focus, the studies reviewed here all point toward the same general conclusion; namely, that phonological awareness is a common underlying ability that is linked to oral language development and is shared crosslinguistically – phonological awareness in one language (e.g., L1) supports phonological awareness in an additional language (e.g., L2) and, in turn, reading acquisition in that language. The results from instructional studies also suggest that phonological awareness in the L2 can be developed through direct intervention, even if L2 oral development is itself somewhat limited, adding further evidence that phonological awareness is a metalinguistic or common underlying proficiency.

That L2 phonological awareness is significantly related to L2 reading development, as L1 phonological awareness is linked to L1 reading development, is evidenced in research by Carlisle et al. (1999). They found that English L2 phonological awareness contributed to English L2 reading comprehension. Durgunoglu, Nagy, and Hancin-Bhatt (1993) point to phonological awareness as fundamentally crosslinguistic in nature based on their finding that Spanish L1 phonological awareness was a significant predictor of English L2 word recognition. The crosslinguistic interdependence of phonological awareness is supported further in an interesting study by Roberts and Corbett (1997) that showed that instruction in English L2 phonological awareness significantly improved Hmong L1 phonological awareness. Evidence for the trainability of L2 phonological awareness comes from Roberts and Corbett (1997) and Terrasi (2000), who found that direct instruction in phonological awareness in L2 English significantly enhanced phonological awareness in that language. That phonological awareness can be promoted independently of general L2 oral proficiency is supported by Durgunoglu at al. (1993), who found that L1 phonological awareness was a more significant predictor of L2 word reading ability than were either L1 or L2 oral proficiency.

Orthographic Knowledge

While the findings from studies of phonological awareness argue for crosslinguistic influences that are common in learning any language, studies that have examined sound-letter correspondences and spelling report evidence for both language-specific and common developmental influences. Thus, on the one hand, it appears that L2 spelling is subject to contrastive L1–L2 effects in line with a contrastive analysis perspective – that is to say, differences in sound-letter correspondence in the L1 and L2 can result in negative transfer from the L1. On the other hand, ELLs' English spelling patterns have been shown to reflect developmental processes that are also exhibited by native English speakers.

Evidence of negative transfer in spelling comes from studies by Fashola et al. (1996) and Zutell and Allen (1988), who found that Hispanic ELLs erroneously applied Spanish L1 phonological and orthographic rules when asked to write selected words with contrastive English/Spanish spelling patterns. In a descriptive analysis of writing samples, Cronnell (1985) also identified L1 influences in L2 errors. In contrast, Tompkins, Abramson, and Pritchard (1999) failed to find such negative transfer when they examined naturally occurring spelling errors in the writing journals of ELLs from different language backgrounds and English L1 children; the authors suggest that the ELLs may have avoided using words with contrastive patterns in order to avoid errors. The only errors differentiating the ELLs and English L1 students in the Tompkins et al. study were those involving inflectional endings, a finding also reported by Cronnell (1985). The students exhibited largely developmental patterns in their English spelling, patterns that were also exhibited by native English speakers. Such target-like error patterns argue for developmental language learning processes that characterize both native speakers and L2 language learners of the same language.

Research by Hsia (1992) that used both phonological and spelling measures to examine L1 transfer effects on L2 development suggests that such effects may be more likely in the early or beginning stages of development when learners lack knowledge of more appropriate, target-like features of the new language. More specifically, Hsia examined the influence of Chinese-background ELLs' knowledge of L1 Mandarin syllable segmentation patterns on their phoneme and syllable segmentation abilities in English and found that, although there was an initial Mandarin L1 effect, English native-like phonological constraints were subsequently and quickly acquired.

Cognate Vocabulary

Research on ELLs' recognition and use of cognate relationships between L1 and L2 vocabulary has shown that ELLs can make use of L1 vocabulary knowledge to determine the meaning of cognate vocabulary in L2 text. All of the research on this issue has examined ELLs of Hispanic background. More specifically, Nagy et al. (1993) and Jimenez, Garcia, and Pearson (1996) found that more successful L2 readers were better able than less successful L2 readers to explicitly recognize Spanish-English cognates and to make use of their knowledge of cognates during reading. These researchers, as well as Hancin-Bhatt and Nagy (1994), also found that the ability to translate cognates from L2 to L1 was linked to individual students' preference to speak Spanish and their level of bilingualism and, in particular, their knowledge of Spanish vocabulary, arguing, once again, that ELLs' L1 need not be a distracting but rather a facilitating factor in L2 literacy development. Finally, Nagy et al. (1993) and Hancin-Bhatt and Nagy (1994) have found that Spanish L1 ELLs are better able to make use of spelling than morphological similarities to recognize cognates, although use of morphological similarities increased with grade level. Thus, instruction in specific morphological similarities between cognates might contribute to the L2 literacy development of ELLs by enhancing their knowledge of these otherwise underused cognate relationships.

In sum, findings from research on specific components of reading and writing support the conclusion that L2 literacy development can be influenced by both common or metalinguistic abilities as well as by features of language specific to the L1 or L2. Research focusing on phonological awareness provides clear evidence that such awareness appears to emanate from a common underlying ability that can be developed either through the L1 or the L2 and is manifested in both L1 and L2 literacy development in virtually the same way. However, more crosslinguistic studies of metaphonological awareness are needed to ascertain to what extent and in what ways this is true. Research also indicates that such metalinguistic abilities can be developed autonomously in the L2, even when learners have limited proficiency in the L2.

Research concerned with ELLs' orthographic development found evidence for influences from the L1 as well as from the L2, in the latter case leading to developmental patterns that are similar to those of native speakers of the L2. Research that has investigated cognate relationships between vocabularies in the L1 and the L2 provides a clear example of how ELLs can draw on knowledge that is specific to the L1 in developing vocabulary in the L2.

Research focusing on orthographic patterns and cognate relationships between languages both suggest that ELLs can benefit from direct instruction about systematic functional and structural differences and similarities between languages and such instruction enhances crosslinguistic facilitation. Arguably, the use of L1 language-specific knowledge or abilities during L2 literacy tasks may serve to fill gaps in the learners' competence when they have not yet acquired target-appropriate knowledge of the L2. Learning patterns that echo those of native-speaking readers and writers seem to emerge as L2 learners advance in their L2 literacy development, as is to be expected. Clearly, transfer of orthographic and cognate vocabulary knowledge is more likely in languages that are typologically similar (Spanish and English) than for typologically different languages (e.g., English and Chinese). Much more research is needed to explore cross-language relationships in languages that are not alphabetic and that are otherwise typologically different from English.

Further research in these areas, especially with different language pairs, is needed to further our knowledge of the precise nature of putative common underlying abilities, as well as to determine how systematic relationships between the L1 and the L2 can be exploited by ELLs in their L2 literacy development.

L1 LITERACY AND L2 LITERACY DEVELOPMENT

Research on the effects of L1 literacy on L2 literacy development is the final issue in our survey of crosslinguistic/crossmodal relationships. Although the "time on task" view of L2 development might oppose promotion of L1 literacy on the grounds that it reduces the time ELLs have to devote to L2 literacy development and others argue that it is a source of interference or confusion, research such as that by Nguyen and Shin (2001) supports the view that competence in L1 literacy does not retard L2 literacy development. Much of the evidence concerning the effects of L1 literacy development on L2 literacy development comes from research on program comparisons, initial language of instruction, and various instructional strategies – all of which is reviewed in other chapters. These studies, reviewed elsewhere in this volume, examined this issue in relatively general terms by comparing students' general levels of reading and writing achievement in both languages.

What remains to be discussed in this section are more specific developmental relationships between the two literacies; that is, the specific ways in which L2 literacy develops in bilingual contexts. This has been examined by examining specific aspects of literacy and specific types of learners (e.g., successful and unsuccessful ELL readers/writers). In this section, the concept of a common underlying proficiency (as proposed by Cummins) is reconceptualized as a common underlying reservoir of literacy abilities. The concept of a reservoir suggests that ELLs develop various literacy abilities that are then available to them when reading or writing in either language. Furthermore, ELLs who remain proficient in their L1 also develop abilities specific to their bilingual state (e.g., use of cognates); thus, the concept of a reservoir becomes a bilingual reservoir. As the following section sugggests, differences in literacy performance may be due to different ways in which ELLs develop and draw on this common underlying reservoir of literacy abilities. A summary of the research included in this section of our synthesis is provided in Table A.3.4.

Effects of L1 Literacy on L2 Literacy Development

A number of studies mentioned previously with regard to the relationship between oral proficiency and L2 literacy also explored the effect of L1 literacy on the development of L2 literacy (e.g., Royer and Carlo, 1991; Langer et al., 1990; Reese et al., 2000). These studies found that the relationship between literacy in the L1 and the L2 is at least as significant as, if not more significant than, that between L2 oral development and L2 literacy. These findings, in turn, argue that developing literacy in the L1 does not detract from literacy development in the L2 but rather supports it. To be more specific, Reese et al. (2000), discussed previously, found that ELLs who were identified as the best L1 readers were deemed able to transition to English reading instruction earlier than other students and that early L1 reading abilities were a significant predictor of English reading abilities assessed eight years later. Additional evidence in support of the additive effects of L1 literacy development comes from Collier (1987) who, in a cross-sectional study, examined the link between length-of-residence and age-of-arrival on ELLs' English reading achievement. She found that late elementary grade ELLs with at least two years of L1 reading instruction reached grade-level equivalence in English reading more rapidly than those with little or no schooling in the L1. However, older ELLs (who arguably face relatively cognitively demanding L2 academic tasks) did not achieve grade-level equivalence as quickly as younger ELL students despite the fact that the former had had more years of L1 literacy development, suggesting that the issue is complicated by the nature and level of the reading tasks required of the learner. Royer and Carlo (1991) found that the L1 reading abilities of ELLs in Grade 5 were the best predictor of their L2 reading achievement in Grade 6, thereby providing corroborative evidence for the supportive effect of the L1. These findings suggest that L1 literacy needs to develop to a certain level if it is to benefit L2 literacy development.

A number of studies that have looked at the acquisition and use of specific literacy abilities across languages corroborate this general relationship. Buriel and Cardoza (1998), Lanauze and Snow (1989), Langer et al. (1990), Jimenez et al. (1996), and Jimenez (2000) have all found evidence for specific parallel abilities across languages. For example, in a study of L2 writing among Grades 4 and 5 Hispanic ELLs, Lanauze and Snow (1989) found that ELLs exhibited similar profiles with respect to the complexity, sophistication, and semantic content of their writing in both their L1 and L2; this was evident even for students who were not orally proficient in their L2. These findings suggest that ELLs are able to apply abilities developed in their L1 to L2 literacy tasks. This pattern is further illustrated when the literacy profiles of successful and less successful readers are compared. Langer et al. (1990), Jimenez et al. (1996), and Jimenez (2000) found that ELLs who were successful readers were successful in both languages, and ELLs who were unsuccessful readers were unsuccessful in both languages. These studies all uphold the notion that successful literacy development in both languages appears to be supported by a common underlying reservoir of literacy abilities and that L1 literacy can contribute to the development of this reservoir of abilities.

L1 and L2 Literacy Strategies

Research that has examined the strategies used by ELLs during L2 literacy tasks provides further insight into the nature of the additive relationship between L1 and L2 literacy. Research in this corpus has examined this issue in two ways: by comparing the strategies used by ELLs during both L1 and L2 literacy tasks; and by comparing the strategies used by ELLs during L2 English reading tasks with those used by native English speakers.

Research that has compared the strategies used by ELLs during L1 and L2 literacy tasks has found that successful and "unsuccessful" ELL readers/writers employ different strategies (Calero-Breckheimer and Goetz, 1993; Jimenez, 2000; Jimenez et al., 1996; Langer et al., 1990, Miramontes, 1987). More specifically, but perhaps not surprising, success-ful ELL readers/writers employ a number of effective strategies, such as using context and inferencing, monitoring comprehension, and invoking prior knowledge, whereas unsuccessful ELL readers employ a variety of ineffective or less sophisticated strategies (Padron and Waxman, 1988). They fail to draw or adjust inferences; they often invoke irrelevant prior knowledge; and they view completion as more important than compre-hension (Jimenez et al., 1996). Of perhaps more interest, this research also found that successful readers/writers demonstrate use of the same strate-gies during both L1 and L2 literacy tasks, and they view reading in the L1 and L2 as similar activities or processes with language-specific differences. Jimenez et al. (1996) reported that successful ELL readers/writers were able to deploy a variety of effective "bilingual" strategies, such as searching for cognates, judicious translation, or use of prior knowledge developed in the L1. In contrast, the less successful ELLs viewed reading in the L1 and the L2 as separate abilities and saw the L1 as a source of confusion. That the unsuccessful ELL readers/writers viewed L1 and L2 reading in these ways suggests that they had not developed an understanding of the common-alities in L1 and L2 literacy and, as a result, were unable to draw on sim-ilarities and connections between their two languages in the service of L2 reading and writing. Jimenez (2000) suggests that unsuccessful ELL read-ers may need opportunities to learn about similarities between the writing systems of their two languages and to become more aware of bilingual strategies that would encourage them to draw on knowledge resources in the L1 to enhance their literacy abilities in the L2 (see also Langer et al., 1990).

At the same time, research that has compared L2 (i.e., ELL) with L1 English readers/writers has found that their strategies differ. More specif-ically, L1 English readers have been shown to use significantly more and different strategies in general than ELL readers (Padron, Knight, and Wax-man, 1986; Knight, Padron, and Waxman, 1985). Bean, Levine, and Graham (1982) and Miramontes (1987, 1990) found that ELLs pay closer attention to textual features than L1 English readers. For example, Miramontes (1987, 1990) found that good Spanish readers paid significantly more attention to graphic representation and grammatical structure in both L1 and L2 reading than good English readers. Although these researchers report no apparent loss in comprehension by ELLs, they suggest that the strategies used by ELLs in their English reading are inappropriate because they are not the same as those employed by successful L1 English readers. However, the reading performance of the ELLs as reported in this study does not back up this claim. Rather, the pattern of strategies employed by successful ELL readers and writers may be more appropriately construed as an equally effective but different path to literacy development in comparison to that exhibited by L1 readers and writers.

An explanation of the differences between successful ELL and L1 readers can be offered in terms of the former's having access to a bilingual reservoir of literacy abilities and strategies in contrast to the latter's monolingual pool of resources. Langer et al. (1990) and Jimenez et al. (1996) add support to this possibility by providing evidence that successful ELL readers maximize what they know by using their L1 to translate, elaborate, and hypothesize when making sense of English text. Edelsky and Jilbert (1985) have made a similar claim: "children's bilingualism increases their options for making meaning" (p. 69). Such a notion sees reading in an L2 as part of a larger, *bilingual* process. Such a process is also supported by the research discussed earlier with respect to L1 spelling patterns and cognate vocabulary (see also Nagy, McClure, and Mir, 1997, for evidence concerning L1 syntactic influences on determining unfamiliar word meanings in L2 reading). It follows that attempts to get ELLs to adopt strategies that are similar to those of monolingual English readers may be misguided because they fail to acknowledge and draw on the full capacities of bilingual learners, which necessarily encompass contributions and knowledge from two languages.

Other Issues: Text Types and Genre

We finish this chapter with a final issue that deserves consideration but has received scant empirical attention; namely, ELLs' need to develop proficiency in different types and genres of literacy if they are to achieve their full literacy potential. Jimenez et al. (1996) and Langer et al. (1990) note that some ELLs have difficulty with academic or cognitively demanding types of texts (e.g., they find reports more difficult to read and understand than stories). Jimenez et al. (1996) also note, in comparing successful L1 English readers with successful ELL readers in English, that the two groups differed qualitatively in terms of their concern for detail and the types and level of sophistication of the connections they made during literacy tasks. Bermudez and Prater (1994) suggest the need to provide opportunities for ELLs to develop more sophisticated expertise in the use of persuasive discourse, while Langer et al. (1990) observe that ELLs who are transitioning to English literacy have difficulty interpreting decontextualized reading comprehension questions, a finding also reported by Field (1996) in a descriptive study of ELLs who were transitioning to English literacy. Two studies that differ significantly in their focus, and due to the case-study nature need to be interpreted with caution, also support the notion that ELL readers/writers can develop social and critical aspects of L2 literacy in ways similar to that of English L1 readers/writers (Samway, 1993; Urzua, 1987). Bringing these broader literacy issues back to a consideration of the construct of common underlying proficiencies, as Jimenez (2000) and Galindo (1993) suggest, ELLs need literacy-development experiences that are connected to their bilingual abilities and bicultural status.

In summary, research that has sought to define the relationship between L1 literacy and L2 literacy has found that L1 literacy does not detract from L2 literacy development but rather contributes to and supports its development. In effect, ELLs with successful L1 literacy experience progress more quickly and successfully in their L2 literacy development than ELLs with no prior L1 literacy. Research also provides evidence for parallel abilities across languages, thereby supporting the construct of a common underlying reservoir of literacy abilities. In brief, the evidence reviewed in this section indicates that there can be additive developmental effects of L1 literacy development on L2 literacy development. This does not mean that L2 development is unimportant because, as Reese et al. found, ELLs with pre-school literacy experiences in either the L2 or the L1 are advantaged with respect to later reading acquisition. This issue is discussed further in Chapter 4.

Research that has examined the strategies employed by ELLs in L1 and L2 literacy tasks provides further insight into the processes of L2 reading and writing. Studies show that successful ELL readers and writers use similar strategies in both languages, whereas less successful ELL readers and writers do not, apparently not capitalizing on the commonalities of literacy across languages. Furthermore, successful ELLs also make use of effective strategies not available to successful monolinguals; strategies that draw on knowledge of and relationships between the L1 and the L2.

Finally, studies that have focused on the context and content of literacy activities suggest that more attention needs to be given to developing ELLs' abilities with respect to deeper and more cognitively demanding aspects of literacy. Research has shown that certain text types, such as factual reports as opposed to narratives, pose more difficulty for ELLs, as do more decontextualized literacy tasks. Researchers suggest that development and success in these more demanding literacy tasks can be facilitated by drawing on ELLs' sociocultural knowledge, including their L1 as well as L2 experiences.

CONCLUSIONS

The various L1 and L2 as well as oral and written proficiencies discussed in this chapter contribute in different yet complementary ways to L2 literacy development. These abilities appear to contribute to the development of a common bilingual reservoir that serves both L1 and L2 literacy and create an awareness of systematic relationships between languages, allowing ELLs to draw on existing L1 knowledge in the service of L2 literacy. Furthermore, it appears L2 literacy is, in a sense, more than the sum of its parts, as ELLs appear to have unique abilities that result from their bilingual status.

Research that has focused on the relationship between L2 literacy and oral language proficiency in the L1 and L2 reveals a relationship between oral and written language in ELLs that is specific and complex. In particular, research that has examined the influence of L1 oral proficiency on L2 literacy found that not only does it not detract from L2 literacy development, but also that specific aspects of L1 oral language proficiency, such as L1 emergent literacy, are more influential in L2 literacy development than general aspects of L2 oral proficiency. It also appears that ELLs make use of L1 oral proficiency to draw on prior knowledge and experience, either in the absence of or in addition to similar levels of L2 oral proficiency, in the service of L2 literacy tasks. Findings from research concerned with the relationship between L2 oral proficiency and L2 literacy development suggest that a certain level of L2 oral proficiency needs to be attained for a significant relationship to be evident. Furthermore, as with L1 oral language proficiency, specific literacy-related aspects of L2 oral proficiency, such as diversity of vocabulary and in-depth text understanding, appear to be more highly related to L2 literacy abilities than do more general or surface-level L2 oral abilities. Moreover, it appears that L2 literacy development can proceed to some extent even with limited L2 oral proficiency, provided that consideration is given to linguistic and prior experiential knowledge that ELLs have already acquired through the medium of their L1. If future research supports this conclusion, it would follow that instructional consideration of aspects of both L1 and L2 oral language could optimize L2 literacy development, arguably beyond what can be achieved through the L2 alone. In sum, L1 and L2 oral abilities can contribute to L2 literacy development in a complementary fashion.

Results from research that has examined specific components of reading and writing further define L2 literacy development to include a complex set of influences, including common underlying proficiencies, influences from the L1, the learners' knowledge of relationships between their languages, and typical developmental processes linked to the L2. Research on phonological awareness suggests that such awareness is a common underlying ability that, once acquired, is manifest in both L1 and L2 literacy development. The findings reviewed here suggest that phonological awareness can be developed through the L1 and applied to the L2 or developed through the L2, even if ELLs have limited L2 proficiency. The influence of the L1 is evident from research that has looked at the development of L2 spelling. Studies using word lists that contrast spelling patterns between the L1 and the L2 show L1 influence or "negative transfer in ELLs" spelling errors. On the other hand, studies that examined spelling errors spontaneously produced by ELLs found that other types of errors correspond to developmental patterns specific to the L2, similar to those made by native speakers. Research that has looked at the effect of cognate relationships between the L1 and L2 on L2 literacy development provides specific evidence of how ELLs can utilize knowledge of the L1 in acquiring vocabulary in the L2. However, this same research indicates that knowledge of specific orthographic and morphological correspondences can be enhanced, suggesting that there is a potential for crosslinguistic facilitation that is underutilized in L2 literacy development.

Perhaps the most direct crosslinguistic relationship discovered in this review is that between L1 literacy and L2 literacy. Research on this relationship finds that L1 literacy supports L2 literacy development. ELLs with initial L1 literacy experiences, such as emergent and family literacy, as well as those with well-developed L1 literacy experiences, progress more quickly and successfully in L2 literacy development. Research findings reviewed here also provide evidence for parallel abilities across languages, supporting the common underlying proficiency, or reservoir of abilities, construct. These parallel abilities are evidenced quite consistently in studies that focus on the strategies used by ELLs in L1 and L2 literacy tasks, where ELLs who are successful in L2 literacy tasks use similar strategies in both their L1 and their L2, viewing literacy in either language as a similar event. Less successful ELL readers and writers use different and less effective strategies and see L1 and L2 literacy tasks as different. Furthermore, ELLs appear to utilize different yet effective strategies in L2 literacy tasks in comparison to monolinguals, strategies that appear to stem from their bilingualism. The research reviewed in this section supports an additive effect of L1 literacy on L2 literacy development and support the construct of a common bilingual reservoir. It also provides the basis and impetus for future research to investigate ELLs' literacy abilities in both languages in terms of shared and effective strategies, as well as their unique bilingual strategies.

The final set of studies reviewed in this chapter calls attention to an additional set of issues related to the content and types of literacy tasks that ELLs confront in school. This research suggests that ELLs need more exposure to and instruction relevant to complex genres of literacy.

When considered together, the crosslinguistic and crossmodal influences on L2 literacy development that have been reviewed in this chapter form a complex yet coherent picture. At the same time, it is important to note that the picture is at best preliminary and considerably more research in most domains is required to draw stable and definitive conclusions.

References

Adams, M. 1990. *Beginning to read.* Cambridge: MIT Press.
Bean, T., Levine, M. G., & Graham, R. C. 1982. Beginning ESL readers' attention to the graphemic features of print. *Reading Improvement 18*(4), 346–9.
Bermudez, A. B., and Prater, D. L. 1994. Examining the effects of gender and second language proficiency on Hispanic writers' persuasive discourse. *Bilingual Research Journal 18*(3–4), 47–62.
Buriel, R., and Cardoza, D. 1998. Sociocultural correlates of achievement among three generations of Mexican-American high school seniors. *American Educational Research Journal 25*(2), 177–92.
Calero-Breckheimer, A., and Goetz, E. 1993. Reading strategies of biliterate children for English and Spanish texts. *Reading Psychology: An International Quarterly 14*, 177–204.
Carlisle, J., Beeman, M., Davis, L., and Sparim, G. 1999. Relationship of metalinguistic capabilities and reading achievement for children who are becoming bilingual. *Applied Psycholinguistics 20*(4), 459–78.
Collier, V. 1987. Age and rate of acquisition of second language for academic purposes. *TESOL Quarterly 21*(4), 617–41.
Cronnell, B. 1985. Language influences in the English writing of third- and sixth-grade Mexican-American students. *Journal of Educational Research 78*, 168–73.
Cummins, J. 1979. Linguistic interdependence and the educational development of bilingual children. *Review of Educational Research 49*, 222–51.
　1981. The role of primary language development in promoting educational success for language minority students. In *Schooling and Language Minority Students: A Theoretical Framework* (pp. 3–49). Los Angeles: National Dissemination and Assessment Center.
　1991. Interdependence of first- and second-language proficiency in bilingual children. In E. Bialystok (ed.), *Language Processing in Bilingual Children* (pp. 70–89). Cambridge, UK: Cambridge University Press.
　1992. Empowerment through biliteracy. In J. V. Tinajero and A. F. Ada (eds.), *The power of two languages: Literacy and biliteracy for Spanish-speaking students.* New York: McGraw-Hill.
　1997. Cultural and linguistic diversity in education: A mainstream issue? *Educational Review 49*, 99–107.
　2000. *Language, power and pedagogy: Bilingual children in the crossfire.* Clevedon, UK: Multilingual Matters.
Durgunoglu, A., Nagy, W., and Hancin-Bhatt, B. 1993. Cross-language transfer of phonological awareness. *Journal of Educational Psychology 85*(3), 453–65.
Edelsky, C., and Jilbert, K. 1985. Bilingual children and writing: Lessons for all of us. *Volta Review 87*(5), 57–72.
Ellis, R. 1986. *Understanding second language acquisition.* Oxford: Oxford University Press.

Fashola, O., Drum, P., Mayer, R., and Kang, S. 1996. A cognitive theory of ortho-graphic transitioning: Predictable errors in how Spanish speaking children spell English words. *American Educational Research Journal 33*(4), 825–43.

Fernandez, R. M., and Nielsen, F. 1986. Bilingualism and Hispanic scholastic achievement: Some baseline results. *Social Science Research 15*(1), 43–70.

Field, M. 1996. Pragmatic issues related to reading comprehension questions: A case study from a Latino bilingual classroom. *Issues in Applied Linguistics 7*(2), 209–24.

Galindo, R. 1993. The influence of peer culture on Mexican-origin bilingual chil-dren's interpretations of a literacy event. *The Bilingual Research Journal 17*(3–4), 71–99.

Goldstein, B., Harris, K., and Klein, M. 1993. Assessment of oral storytelling abil-ities of Latino junior high school students with learning handicaps. *Journal of Learning Disabilities 26*(2), 138–43.

Hancin-Bhatt, B., and Nagy, W. 1994. Lexical transfer and second language mor-phological development. *Applied Psycholinguistics 15*(3), 289–310.

Heath, S. 1983. *Ways with words.* Cambridge, UK: Cambridge University Press.

Hsia, S. 1992. Developmental knowledge of inter- and intraword boundaries: Evidence from American and Mandarin Chinese speaking beginning readers. *Applied Psycholinguistics 13*(3), 341–72.

Hudelson, S. 1994. Literacy development of second language children. In F. Genesee (ed.), *Educating second language children: The whole child, the whole curriculum, the whole community* (pp. 129–58). Cambridge, UK: Cambridge University Press.

Jimenez, R. T. 2000. Literacy and the identity development of Latina/o students. *American Educational Research Journal 37*(4), 971–1000.

Jimenez, R., Garcia, G. E., and Pearson, P. D. 1996. The reading strategies of bilin-gual Latina/o students who are successful English readers: Opportunities and obstacles. *Reading Research Quarterly 31*(1), 90–112.

Kennedy, E., and Park, H. 1994. Home language as a predictor of academic achievement: A comparative study of Mexican- and Asian-American youth. *The Journal of Research and Development in Education 27*(3), 188–94.

Knight, S., Padron, Y., and Waxman, H. 1985. The cognitive reading strategies of ESL students. *TESOL Quarterly 19*(4), 789–91.

Lado, R. 1957. *Linguistics across cultures.* Ann Arbor, MI: University of Michigan Press.

Lanauze, M., and Snow, C. 1989. The relation between first- and second-language writing skills: Evidence from Puerto Rican elementary school children in bilin-gual programs. *Linguistics and Education 1*(4), 323–39.

Langer, J. A., Barolome, L., and Vasquez, O. 1990. Meaning construction in school literacy tasks: A study of bilingual students. *American Educational Research Journal 27*(3), 427–71.

Lindholm, K., and Aclan, Z. 1991. Bilingual proficiency as a bridge to academic achievement: Results from bilingual/immersion programs. *Journal of Education 173*(2), 99–113.

MacSwan, J., and Rolstad, K. 2003. Linguistic diversity, schooling, and social class: Rethinking our conception of language proficiency in language minority education. In C. B. Paulston and G. R. Tucker (eds.), *Sociolinguistics: The essential readings* (pp. 329–40). Malden, MA: Blackwell.

Maguire, M. H., and Graves, B. 2001. Speaking personalities in primary school children's writing. *TESOL Quarterly 35*, 561–93.

Miramontes, O. 1987. Oral reading miscues of Hispanic students: Implications for assessment of learning disabilities. *Journal of Learning Disabilities 20*(10), 627–32.

1990. A comparative study of English oral reading skills in differently schooled groups of Hispanic students. *Journal of Reading Behavior 22*(4), 373–94.

Nagy, W., Garcia, G., Durgunoglu, A., and Hancin-Bhatt, B. 1993. Spanish-English bilingual students' use of cognates in English reading. *Journal of Reading Behavior 25*(3), 241–59.

Nagy, W. E., McClure, E. F., and Mir, M. 1997. Linguistic transfer and the use of context by Spanish-English bilinguals. *Applied Psycholinguistics 18*(4), 431–52.

Nguyen, A., and Shin, F. 2001. Development of the first language is not a barrier to second language acquisition: Evidence from Vietnamese immigrants to the United States. *International Journal of Bilingual Education and Bilingualism 4*(3), 159–64.

Nielsen, F., and Lerner, S. 1986. Language skills and school achievement of bilingual Hispanics. *Social Science Research 15*, 209–40.

Padron, Y., Knight, S., and Waxman, H. 1986) Analyzing bilingual and monolingual students' perceptions of their reading strategies. *The Reading Teacher 39*(5), 430–3.

Padron, Y., and Waxman, H. 1988. The effect of ESL students' perceptions of their cognitive strategies on reading achievement. *TESOL Quarterly 22*(1), 146–50.

Peregoy, S. 1989. Relationship between second language oral proficiency and reading comprehension of bilingual fifth grade students. *NABE Journal 13*(3), 217–34.

Peregoy, S., and Boyle, O. 1991. Second language oral proficiency characteristics of low, intermediate and high second language readers. *Hispanic Journal of Behavioral Sciences 13*(1), 35–47.

Perez, E. 1981. Oral language competence improves reading skills of Mexican American third graders. *The Reading Teacher, 35*(1), 24–7.

Porter, R. 1990. *Forked tongue: The politics of bilingual education.* New York: Basic Books.

Reese, L., Garnier, H., Gallimore, R., and Goldenberg, C. 2000. Longitudinal analysis of the antecedents of emergent Spanish literacy and middle-school English reading achievement of Spanish-speaking students. *American Educational Research Journal 37*(3), 633–62.

Roberts, T., and Corbett, C. 1997. *Efficacy of explicit English instruction in phonemic awareness and the alphabetic principle for English learners and English proficient kindergarten children in relationship to oral language proficiency, primary language and verbal memory.* (ERIC Document Reproduction Service No. ED 417 403.)

Rossell, C. H., and Baker, K. 1996. The educational effectiveness of bilingual education. *Research in the Teaching of English 30*(1), 7–74.

Royer, J., and Carlo, M. 1991. Transfer of comprehension skills from native to second language. *Journal of Reading 34*(6), 450–5.

Samway, K. D. 1993. This is hard, isn't it?: Children evaluating writing. *TESOL Quarterly 27*(2), 233–57.

Saville-Troike, M. 1984. What really matters in second language learning for academic achievement? *TESOL Quarterly 18*(2), 199–219.

Snow, C. E., Burns, M. S., and Griffin, P. 1998. *Preventing reading difficulties in young children*. Washington, DC: National Academy of Sciences.

Sulzby, E., and Teale, W. 1991. Emergent literacy. In R. Barr, M. Kamil, P. Mosenthal, and P. Pearson (eds.), *Handbook of reading research* (Vol. 11, pp. 727–58). New York: Longman.

Terrasi, S. 2000. *Phonemic awareness skills in kindergarten students from English and non-English speaking homes* (ERIC Document Reproduction Service No. ED 441 220).

Tompkins, G. E., Abramson, S., and Pritchard, R. H. 1999. A multilingual perspective on spelling development in third and fourth grades. *Multicultural Education 6*(3), 12–18.

Torgesen, J. K., Alexander, A. W., Wagner, R. K., Rashotte, C. A., Voeller, K. S., and Conway, T. 2001. Intensive remedial instruction for children with severe reading disabilities: Immediate and long-term outcomes from two instructional approaches. *Journal of Learning Disabilities 34*, 35–58.

Toukomaa, P., and Skutnabb-Kangas, T. 1977. *The intensive teaching of the mother tongue to migrant children of pre-school age and children in the lower level of comprehensive school*. Helsinki: The Finnish National Commission for UNESCO.

Urzua, C. 1987. You stopped too soon: Second language children composing and revising. *TESOL Quarterly 21*(2), 279–303.

Wagner, R. K., and Torgesen, J. K. 1987. The nature of phonological processing and its causal role in the acquisition of reading skills. *Psychological Bulletin 101*, 192–212.

Zutell, J., and Allen, V. 1988. The English spelling strategies of Spanish-speaking bilingual children. *TESOL Quarterly 22*(2), 333–40.

APPENDIX TO CHAPTER 3

TABLE A.3.1. *Summary of Studies on L1 Oral Proficiency and L2 Literacy*

Authors	Sample Characteristics	Grades	Research Design	Outcome Measures (partial listing)	Results
Buriel and Cardoza (1998)	1st, 2nd, 3rd generation Hispanic, various programs, southwestern USA	10, 12	Within gp and btwn gp comparisons, convenience samples – n = approx. 11,300 – Stats, ANOVA; correlations; multiple regression analysis	– Survey/questionnaire: educational aspirations; Span language background (4 pt scale for oral and written Span proficiency, home language and mother tongue) – SES variables – Standardized reading test scores	1st and 2nd generation: – Greater L1 oral proficiency and literacy skills than 3rd generation – No relationship btwn language background and reading scores 3rd generation: – Those with greater L1 oral proficiency had lower reading scores
Fernandez and Nielsen (1986)	– Eng monolingual and bilingual Hispanics – Eng monolingual and bilingual whites – In various programs	High school: (grades unspecified)	Within and btwn gp comparisons, convenience samples – n = 16,046 – Stats; regression analysis	– Reading and vocabulary test scores – Self-assessed Eng proficiency in reading and writing – Self-assessed Span or other language proficiency in reading and writing – Use of other language	– Proficiency in Eng and other language positively related to achievement

| Kennedy and Park (1994) | Hispanic- and Asian-Americans, nationwide sample, various programs | 8 | – Within gp and btwn gp comparisons, convenience samples
– Hispanic-Americans (n = 1,952)
– Asian-Americans (n = 1,131)
– Stats: descriptive multiple regression analysis, correlations | – Survey/questionnaire: home language background; social psychological variables; student effort
– Self-reported Eng grades
– Standardized reading test scores | – Speaking language other than Eng at home irrelevant to grades and standardized reading scores for Hispanics
– Negative relationship btwn speaking language other than Eng at home and standardized test scores in reading for Asians |
| Lanauze and Snow (1989) | Span L1 Hispanics, in bilingual programs, New Haven, CT | 4, 5 | – Btwn gp comparisons of lang proficiency level, convenience samples
– n = 38
– Stats, correlations | – Span and Eng teacher-assessed language proficiency level (oral, aural and reading skills combined, but based primarily on oral skills; 2 point [good or poor] scale)
– Picture description writing task scored for complexity, sophistication, and semantic content | – Children good in Span but poor in Eng gp and children good in both languages used more complex and sophisticated language than children poor in both languages
– Children good in both languages had independent writing skills
– Children good in Span but poor in Eng transferred skills from Span to Eng
– Children poor in both languages were not transferring skills |

(continued)

TABLE A.3.1 (*continued*)

Authors	Sample Characteristics	Grades	Research Design	Outcome Measures (partial listing)	Results
Langer, Barolome, and Vasquez (1990)	Hispanics from bilingual homes, bilingual program in northern CA	5	Within gp comparisons, convenience samples – Detailed ethnographic study – Case studies – n = 12 – Stats: descriptive, qualitative measures	– Student interviews and school records: L1 and L2 proficiencies – Classroom observation – Passage reading sessions: 2 different genre/text type passages (story and report) comparisons; during reading "envisionment" questions; post-reading "probing" questions; oral and written passage recall – Oral L2 proficiency ratings	– Students relied on knowledge of Span to support understanding of Eng text, increasingly so with more difficult texts – Competence in Span enriched reading in L1 and L2
Nielsen and Lerner (1986)	Bilingual Hispanics, nationwide, various programs	12	Within gp comparisons, convenience sample – n = approx. 1,000 – Stats, factor analysis	– Survey: Eng reading and writing proficiency; Span reading and writing proficiency; SES, LOR – Reading and vocabulary tests scores	– Language proficiency and reading ability not highly related, other factors more significant – No negative effect of bilingualism on school achievement
Reese et al. (2000)	Span L1 ELLs, Los Angeles, CA area	K-7	Within gp comparisons – Longitudinal – Random sample – n = 66	– In-depth home interviews: family literacy practices (parents use of Eng or Span literacy at work, reading aloud to child)	– Family literacy practices predicted emergent Span literacy and Eng proficiency, which in turn predicted Grade 7 reading achievement

Study	Grade	Participants	Analysis	Measures	Findings
			– Stats: path analysis, correlational as analysis	– Span early literacy assessment (e.g., identify letters and corresponding sounds, oral comprehension on story read aloud, knowledge of print conventions) – Standardized reading tests in language of instruction (EABE, CTBS) – School records – Standardized tests of Eng reading performance in Grade 7 – Eng language proficiency: Bilingual Syntax Measure or Idea Proficiency Test – Span proficiency assumed	
Saville-Troike (1984)	2–6	ELLs from diverse L1 backgrounds, L1 literate, from well-educated families, mainstream Eng program with ESL and L1 instruction (30 min/day)	Within gp comparisons, convenience sample – n = 19 – Descriptive stats, retrospective analysis	– Informal parent and teacher interviews: home language; personality factors – Interviews with students in Eng: language use; grammatical and content info – ESL classroom observations: language use; verbal interaction – Northwest Syntax Screening Test (Eng) – Functional Language Survey (Eng) – Bilingual Syntax Measure (Eng) – Reading subtest scores of the CTBS	– 3 out of 5 top achievers used native language to figure out Eng reading

91

TABLE A.3.2. *Summary of Studies on L2 Oral Proficiency and L2 Literacy*

Authors	Sample Characteristics	Grade	Research Design	Outcome Measures (partial listing)	Results
Goldstein, Harris, and Klein (1993)	Hispanic ELLs from 2 schools in 2 districts of southern California, in programs for learning handicapped, received bilingual education in earlier grades	7, 8, 9	Within gp comparisons, convenience sample – n = 31 – Stats, correlational analysis	– Reading comprehension subtest of Peabody Individual Achievement Test – Oral production subscale of Language Assessment Scale (standardized story retell task), 2 scoring methods: standard scoring procedure (surface – sentence structure and vocabulary use in development of coherent storyline); story structure analysis (deeper – types of story structures)	– Significant positive correlation btwn adapted story structure analysis and reading comprehension – Greater relationship btwn storytelling ability and reading comprehension scores than surface structure analysis and reading comprehension scores
Lindholm and Aclan (1991)	Hispanic and English L1, northern California, two-way Span/Eng immersion (initial reading instruction in Span)	1, 2, 3, 4	Within and btwn gp comparisons, convenience samples: – Span L1 (n = 159) – Eng L1 (n = 90) divided by grade: – Grade 1 (n = 87) – Grade 2 (n = 71) – Grade 3 (n = 75) – Grade 4 (n = 16) and bilingual proficiency gp: – High (L2H, L1H) – Medium (L2M, L1M) – Low (L2L, L1H/M) – Stats, ANOVA	– bilingual proficiency, Eng and Sp scores on Student Oral Language Observation Matrix – CTBS (reading) scores	Grade 3: – High gp significantly outscored Medium and Low gp on reading scores – Eng reading instruction only started in Grade 3 Grade 4: – High gp performing at grade level average in Eng reading

Study		Sample / Design	Measures	Findings
Peregoy (1989)	5	Span L1 ELLs, transitional bilingual program	Multiple-case study, comparison of Eng reading proficiency level gps, convenience samples: – High (n = 2) – Intermediate (n = 2) – Low (n = 2) – Stats: Descriptive	– Placement in Eng reading instruction levels by teacher, based in part on oral proficiency test scores – Eng oral language production measure: storytelling from 4-frame picture sequence scored for fluency, semantic content, grammatical complexity, and grammatical correctness – Eng reading comprehension measures of 4 reading passages: 1st read orally; 2nd and 3rd read silently, followed by multiple-choice comprehension questions; 4th read one line at a time, required to make interpretations and predictions after each line	– General correspondence btwn L2 oral proficiency and L2 reading comprehension – Limited vocabulary and syntactic knowledge impeded reading comprehension; however, assistance provided facilitated reading comprehension for low gp
Peregoy and Boyle (1991)	3	Hispanic ELLs, 38 urban and semirural schools in northern CA, bilingual education and mainstream Eng programs	Within and btwn gp comparisons of reading gp levels, convenience samples: – High (n = 20) – Intermediate (n = 18) – Low (n = 19) (assigned according to performance on auditory vocabulary and word reading subtest of Stanford Diagnostic Reading Test)	– Oral and silent reading of appropriate L2 passages followed by multiple-choice questions, and explanations for choice – L2 oral proficiency assessed through individual administration of simulated science lesson: transcribed and coded for surface structure (grammatical complexity and well-formedness) and deep structure (informativeness and comprehension) aspects of L2 oral proficiency	L2 reading – Low group demonstrated extreme difficulty in decoding and comprehending – Intermediate gp able to decode and comprehend with difficulty – High gp able to decode and comprehend with relative ease (on par with native Eng peers)

(continued)

TABLE A.3.2 (continued)

Authors	Sample Characteristics	Grade	Research Design	Outcome Measures (partial listing)	Results
			– Total n = 57 (38 in bilingual education program, 19 in mainstream Eng program; 25 began reading instruction in Eng, 32 began in Span) – Stats: not defined		L2 oral proficiency – Significant difference on all measures btwn low and high reading gps – Significant differences on well-formedness and informativeness btwn intermediate and high gp
Perez (1981)	Hispanic, majority Span L1, Texas public school, program unspecified	3	Within and btwn gp with unspecified assignment to – TR: Instructional Intervention (n = 75) – CO: regular instruction (n = 75) – Pre- and post-tests – Unspecified stats	– Prescriptive Reading Inventory pre- and post-test – Instructional Intervention: teacher led, oral language activities related to concepts in readers	– TR (not defined) gp showed significant improvement on post-test Inventory compared to controls
Reese et al. (2000)	Span L1 ELLs, Los Angeles, CA, area	K-7	Within gp comparisons – Longitudinal – Random sample – n = 66 – Path analysis, correlations	– In-depth home interviews: family literacy practices (parents use of Eng or Span literacy at work, reading aloud to child) – Span early literacy assessment (e.g., identify letters and corresponding sounds, oral comprehension on story read aloud, knowledge of print conventions) – Standardized reading tests in language of instruction (EABE, CTBS)	Grade 7: – Family literacy practices predicted emergent Span literacy and Eng proficiency, which in turn predicted reading achievement – Greater oral Eng proficiency highly predictive of reading performance

Study	Population	Grade	Design	Measures	Findings
Royer and Carlo (1991)	Span L1 ELLs	5–6	– Within gp comparisons, convenience sample – n = 49 – Longitudinal – Stats: correlational and regression analyses	– School records – Standardized tests of Eng reading performance in Grade 7 – Eng language proficiency: Bilingual Syntax Measure or IDEA Proficiency test – Span proficiency assumed – L1 and L2 listening comprehension scores – L1 and L2 reading comprehension scores	– Span reading comprehension at Grade 5 best predictor of Eng reading comprehension at Grade 6 – Eng listening skills second best predictor of Eng reading
Saville-Troike (1984)	ELLs from diverse L1 backgrounds, L1 literate, from well-educated families, mainstream Eng program with ESL and L1 instruction (30 min/day)	2–6	– Within gp comparisons, convenience sample – n = 19 – Descriptive stats, retrospective analysis	– Informal parent and teacher interviews: home language; personality factors – Interviews with students in Eng; language use; grammatical and content info – ESL classroom observations: language use; verbal interaction – Northwest Syntax Screening Test (Eng) – Functional Language Survey (Eng) – Bilingual Syntax Measure (Eng) – Reading subtest scores of the CTBS	– Language test scores did not predict achievement on reading subtest – Number of different vocabulary items used in oral Eng production (interview data) significantly correlated with reading achievement, verbosity did not

TABLE A.3.3. *Summary of Studies on Component Skills of L2 Literacy Development*

Authors	Sample Characteristics	Grade	Research Design	Outcome Measures (partial listing)	Results
Carlisle et al. (1999)	Span L1 ELLs, Chicago, maintenance bilingual program	1, 2, 3	Within gp comparisons, convenience sample – Fall and Spring testings – n = 57 – Stats, regression analysis	– Span and Eng receptive vocabulary tests (PPVT-R/TVIP) – Test of Auditory Analysis Skills (TAAS) in Eng – Listening comprehension and letter-word identification tests in Eng – Eng phonological awareness – Eng and Span vocabulary definition task (formal and informal definitions) – Eng reading comprehension (subtest of CAT)	– Significant portion of variance in reading comprehension explained by extensiveness of vocabulary in L1 and L2 and phonological awareness – Phonological awareness significantly correlated with Eng vocabulary
Cronnell (1985)	Span L1 ELLs, some bilingual classes, Los Angeles, CA	3, 6	Within and btwn gp comparisons, convenience sample – Grade 3 (n = 78) – Grade 6 (n = 92) – Stats: descriptive	– Eng spelling errors in writing samples classified by type: Span spelling, pronunciation, grammar, vocabulary	– Significant portion of errors can be attributed to Span, interlanguage or Chicano Eng

Study	Population	Grade	Design	Measures	Findings
Durgunoglu, Nagy, and Hancin-Bhatt (1993)	Span L1 ELLs, transitional bilingual program	1	Within gp comparisons, convenience sample – n = 27 – Stats: correlational analysis, multiple regression analysis	– Letter naming ability test – Span phonological awareness test – Span and Eng oral proficiency tests (pre-LAS) – Span and Eng word recognition tests – Transfer tests: Span to Eng word recognition	– Span phonological awareness a significant predictor of both Span and Eng word recognition – Span and Eng oral proficiency did not correlate with word recognition or phonological awareness
Fashola et al. (1996)	Span L1 ELLs and Eng L1, southern CA, program unspecified	2, 3, 5, 6	Within and btwn gp comparisons, convenience samples – L1 Span (n = 38) – L1 Eng (n = 34) – Stats	– 40 common Eng words selected for Eng/Span contrastive spellings – Eng spelling test	– Significant difference btwn Span and Eng, and younger and older students on predicted (Span to Eng contrastive analysis) errors
Hancin-Bhatt and Nagy (1994)	Span L1 ELLs, 3 urban schools in predominantly Spanish-speaking areas of large Midwest city, 10 bilingual classrooms	4, 6, 8	Within and btwn gp comparisons, convenience samples: – Grade 4 (n = 96) – Grade 6 (n = 41) – Grade 8 (n = 59) – Stats: ANOVA, multiple regression analysis	– Background questionnaire – Language use questionnaire – Eng to Span cognate and non-cognate translation task – Span yes/no vocabulary test: recognition – Eng-Span systematic suffix relationship matching task	– Developmental trend in recognition of cognates compared to non-cognates – Limited knowledge of Span – Eng systematic relationships btwn suffixes – Knowledge of Span cognates accounted for significant amount of variance in translation task; relationship btwn cognate translation ability and language background/use factors

(continued)

TABLE A.3.3 (continued)

Authors	Sample Characteristics	Grade	Research Design	Outcome Measures (partial listing)	Results
Hsia (1992)	Eng L1 Kindergarten and Mandarin L1 K to Grade 1, greater Boston area, from middle-, upper-middle class homes – Mandarin L1s attended Chinese language weekend school and attended/had attended American preschool and K	K, 1	Within and btwn gp comparisons, convenience samples – L1 Eng K (n = 15) – L1 Mandarin K (n = 15) – L1 Mandarin Grade 1 (n = 15) – 2 testing sessions, 6 months apart – Stats, ANOVA	– Reading readiness test – Children's invented spellings – Mandarin phoneme segmentation task – Eng sentence segmentation task	– No significant main effects – Native-like constraints acquired over time
Jimenez, Garcia, and Pearson (1996)	Hispanic ELLs (orally bilingual and biliterate) and Eng L1, 3 schools in 2 school districts, some bilingual schooling	6, 7	Within and btwn gp comparisons, convenience samples – Hispanic successful readers in Eng (n = 8) – Hispanic marginally successful readers in Eng (n = 3) – Monolingual Eng successful readers in Eng (n = 3) – Descriptive stats, qualitative analysis	– Prior knowledge assessment background questionnaire – Teacher and standardized test categorization into successful and unsuccessful readers – Prompted/ unprompted think aloud strategy assessment – Text retellings – Student interviews	– Cognate searching strategy and translating used by all 8 Hispanic successful readers

Study	Grade	Sample	Design/Analysis	Findings
Nagy et al. (1993)	4, 5, 6	Span L1 ELLs, 2 urban elementary schools, bilingual education and Eng-only programs	Within gp comparisons, convenience sample – n = 74 – Stats, MANOVA, multiple regression analysis	– Multiple-choice test of target cognates – Span and Eng yes/no vocabulary tests of target/non-target cognates and non-cognates – Eng reading comprehension – Significant difference in cognate over non-cognate recognition – Transfer of Span lexical knowledge to Eng, dependent on metalinguistic awareness of recognizing words as cognates; could be enhanced with morphological training
Roberts and Corbett (1997)	K	ELLs and Eng L1s, suburban northern CA, program unspecified	Within and btwn gp comparisons with convenience assignment – TR: Specific phonological instruction in Eng (n = 16 L1 Hmong ELLs; 13 L1 Eng) – CO: Regular instruction (n = 17 L1 Hmong, 1 L1 Laos ELLs, 11 L1 Eng) – 2 additional comparison classes (n = similar to CO) – Pre- and post-testing of all groups – Stats, multivariate analysis	– Classroom observation, interviews, family literacy interviews – Eng phonological awareness tasks – For ELLs – Pre-LAS Eng proficiency test – ELLs in TR gp scored significantly higher on some measures of phonological awareness than ELLs in CO gp – ELLs not significantly different than L1 Eng in TR or CO gps – Significant improvement in Hmong rhyming, segmenting and blending for Hmong L1s in TR gp
Terrasi (2000)	K	Primarily Hispanic and Eng L1 students, urban schools south of Boston, program unspecified	Within and btwn gp comparisons, convenience samples – Primarily Hispanic ELLs (n = 40) – L1 Eng (n = 227)	– 6 Eng phonological awareness subtests – Significant gains for both gps – Larger gains for ELLs

(continued)

Authors	Sample Characteristics	Grade	Research Design	Outcome Measures (partial listing)	Results
			– Pre- and post-tested – Intervention: specific phonological instruction in Eng – Stats: descriptive		
Tompkins, Abramson, and Pritchard (1999)	ELLs with diverse L1s and Eng L1s, 2 schools, 1 low income and 1 affluent, programs unspecified, central CA	3, 4	Within and btwn gp comparisons (language background, grade and school), random selection: Low-income school – n = 5 (Grade 3), n = 5 (Grade 4), from each lg gp (Sp, Hmong, Lao, Khmer) (subtotal n = 40) – n = 5 (Grade 3), n = 5 (Grade 4) L1 Eng (subtotal n = 10) Affluent school – Grades 3 and 4, L1 Eng (n = 10) – Stats, ANOVA, qualitative analyses	– Eng spelling errors in journal writings	– Similar spelling patterns regardless of language gp – Significant differences btwn schools – Qualitative analysis showed errors to be largely interlanguage developmental
Zutell and Allen (1988)	Span L1 ELLs, large urban mideastern schools, bilingual programs	2, 3, 4	Within gp comparisons, convenience sample – n = 108 – Stats: descriptive	– 5 word categories selected for Span-Eng contrasting sound-letter name relationships – Eng spelling test	– No differences when grouped by grade – When grouped according to test success – less successful students produced more predicted Span-influenced spellings

TABLE A.3.4. *Summary of Studies on L1 Literacy and L2 Literacy*

Authors	Sample Characteristics	Grade	Research Design	Outcome Measures (partial listing)	Results
Bean, Levine, and Graham (1982)	Gifted and remedial Eng L1s; intermediate and beginner ELLs in ESL program, Los Angeles, CA	11	Btwn gp comparisons, convenience samples – L1 Eng gifted (n = 16) – L1 Eng Remedial (n = 14) – Intermediate ESL (n = 18) – Beginner ESL (n = 12) – Stats: ANOVA	– Graphemic identification task	– Beginning ESL students paid significantly more attention to graphemic level of reading
Bermudez and Prater (1994)	Span L1 ELLs, 2 inner-city schools in Southwest USA, ESL and mainstream programs	4	Btwn gp analyses, convenience samples – In ESL (n = 18) – Already mainstreamed into Eng (n = 19) – Stats, ANOVA	– Essay samples, written in response to standard prompt: persuasive writing coded for persuasive discourse markers	– No significant difference btwn gps, suggesting that mainstreamed ELLs do not have a higher level of persuasive discourse needed to develop as writers
Buriel and Cardoza (1998)	1st, 2nd, 3rd generation Hispanic, Southwest USA, various programs	10, 12	Within gp and btwn gp comparisons, convenience samples – n = approx. 11,300 – Stats: ANOVA; correlations; multiple regression analysis	– Survey questionnaire: educational aspirations; Span-language background (4-pt scale for oral and written Span proficiency, home language, and mother tongue) – SES variables – Standardized reading test scores	– 3rd-generation students with greater Span literacy skills scored higher on reading test

(continued)

Authors	Sample Characteristics	Grade	Research Design	Outcome Measures (partial listing)	Results
Calero-Breckheimer and Goetz (1993)	Span L1 ELLs, major Texan city, bilingual education program	3, 4	Within gp comparisons, convenience sample – n = 26 – Stats, ANOVA and correlational analysis	– Line by line reading of Eng and Span texts on computer (reading time and lookbacks recorded) – Multiple-choice comprehension questions – After reading free reporting of strategy use – Strategy use checklist	– Students used same number of strategies regardless of language, strategy types highly correlated – More strategies in Eng positively correlated with higher scores on comprehension questions – More strategies in Span, positively correlated with more gist recall
Collier (1987)	ELLs from 75 different language backgrounds, large public school system on East Coast, ESL program	4, 6, 8, 11	Cross-sectional data from 1977–86, age of arrival, length of residence, and grade-level comparisons – n = 1,548 – Stats: descriptive	– Eng proficiency upon arrival – Literacy skills upon arrival – Number of years of schooling in Eng – SRA test scores in reading	– Minimum of 2 years of schooling in L1 for most rapid progress in academic development of L2 <u>Age 8–11:</u> – Achieved grade-level norms most rapidly <u>Age 12–15:</u> – Experienced greatest difficulty with academic aspects of L2; probably due to more complex subject matter
Field (1996)	Span L1 ELLs, transitional bilingual classroom, Santa Barbara, CA	4	Within gp, convenience sample – n = 10 – Qualitative analysis	– Written answers to reading comprehension questions – Video-taped/audio-taped gp discussion in Eng and Span	– Students had difficulty inferencing, and correctly interpreting pragmatics of comprehension questions

Study		Sample / Design	Methods	Findings
Galindo (1993)	1	Span L1 ELLs, urban setting in Southwest USA, previously attended bilingual K	Within gp, convenience sample - n = 4 - Qualitative analysis	- Observation, audio recordings of classroom literacy events - Dialogue journals btwn writing partners	- Students interpreted literacy events in terms of their own interests and in a manner to meet teacher's requirements
Jimenez (2000)	4, 5, 6	- Span L1 ELLs, transitioned to mainstream Eng - Eng L1 Hispanic, mainstream Eng - midwestern city	- Classroom and focal students, convenience samples from two Grade 4 and one Grade 5 regular bilingual classes and one Grade 4–6 bilingual special education class: - Span L1 ELLs (n = 84) - Eng L1 Hispanic (n = 1) - Focal students from each class (n = 4 – 6) - Teachers (n = 4) Instructional intervention: - Bilingual strategic reading instruction - Qualitative analysis	- Classroom observations - Teacher interviews - Think-alouds during reading and interviews with focal students	- Emergent findings showed increased awareness of literacy and basic cognitive operations related to test processing - Support for linguistically sensitive, culturally relevant, and cognitively challenging instruction, which helps students view dual-language background as a strength
Jimenez, Garcia, and Pearson (1996)	6, 7	Hispanic ELLs (orally bilingual and biliterate) and Eng L1s, at 3 schools in 2 school districts, some bilingual schooling	Within and btwn gp comparisons, convenience samples - Hispanic successful readers in Eng (n = 8) - Hispanic marginally successful readers in Eng (n = 3) - Monolingual Eng successful readers in Eng (n = 3) - Descriptive stats, qualitative analysis	- Prior knowledge assessment background questionnaire - Teacher and standardized test categorization into successful and unsuccessful readers - Prompted/unprompted think-aloud strategy assessment - Text retellings - Student interviews	- Cognate searching strategy and translating used by all 8 Hispanic successful readers

(continued)

TABLE A.3.4 (continued)

Authors	Sample Characteristics	Grade	Research Design	Outcome Measures (partial listing)	Results
Lanauze and Snow (1989)	Span L1 Hispanics, had been in bilingual program for 1–4 years, New Haven, CT	4, 5	– Btwn gp comparison of language proficiency level, convenience samples – Good in Span and Eng (n = 17) – Poor in Eng but good in Span (n = 12) – Poor in Span and Eng (n = 9) – Stats, ANOVA, correlations	– Span and Eng teacher-assessed language proficiency: oral, aural, and reading skills combined (based primarily on oral skills; 2-point scale, good or poor) – Picture description writing task: complexity, sophistication, and semantic content	– Children good in Span but poor in Eng gp and children good in both languages used more complex and sophisticated language than children poor in both languages – Children good in both languages had independent writing skills – Children good in Span but poor in Eng transferred skills from Span to Eng – Children poor in both languages were not transferring skills
Langer, Barolome, and Vasquez (1990)	Hispanics from bilingual homes, northern California, bilingual program	5	– Within gp comparisons, convenience samples – Detailed ethnographic study – Case studies – n = 12 – Stats, ANOVA, descriptive stats, qualitative measures	– Student interviews and school records to assess L1 and L2 proficiencies – Classroom observation – Passage reading sessions: 2 different genre/text type passages (story and report) comparisons; during reading "envisionment" questions; post-reading "probing" questions; oral and written passage recall – Oral L2 proficiency ratings	– Significant main effects for genre (better understanding of stories over reports) and language (Span over Eng); and type of question – Better readers provided more abstract and decontextualized responses; poorer readers examples and explanations – Those students with good meaning-making strategies used these strategies in both languages

Study	Context	Grades	Methods	Sample	Findings
Miramontes (1987)	Hispanic, 4 schools in large urban school district in CA, Span/Eng bilingual program	4, 5, 6	– Miscue reading inventory – Graded reading selections – Miscue analysis and retellings	Within and btwn gp comparisons, convenience sample – Good readers in Eng (n = 10) – Good readers in Span (n = 10) – Reading disabled in Eng (n = 10) – Reading disabled in Span (n = 9) – Stats, ANOVA, Scheffé and factor analysis	– Good strategies rather than Eng proficiency differentiated good and poor readers – Competence in Span enriched reading in L1 and L2 – Both gps of Span readers adhered significantly more closely to the text – Good Span readers consistently used decoding strategies that adhered more closely to text in both languages – Learning disabled in Span reading gp did not retain meaning of text in Eng, suggesting general lack of Eng proficiency – not reading disability
Miramontes (1990)	Hispanics, 2 large urban school districts in the Southwest, Span-Eng full bilingual program	4, 5, 6	– Oral reading sessions – Miscue analysis – Retelling	Within and btwn gp comparison, convenience assignment – Good Eng readers: Eng at home, initial literacy in Eng (n = 10) – Good Span readers: initial literacy Span (n = 10) – Mixed-dominance: L1 Span at home, Eng at school (n = 20)	– Good Span readers significantly paid more attention to form of text in both languages – Good Span readers successfully used Span reading strategies and different strategies in Eng reading from good Eng and Mixed Dominance gps, but equally effective in comprehension

(continued)

Authors	Sample Characteristics	Grade	Research Design	Outcome Measures (partial listing)	Results
			– Stats, ANOVA, Scheffé, correlational and factor analyses		– Good Span readers had significantly lower scores in retelling, but may be result of more limited oral Eng proficiency
Nagy, McClure, and Mir (1997)	Span L1 Hispanic ELLs and Eng L1s, urban school district, bilingual and mainstream program	7, 8	Within and btwn gp comparisons, convenience samples – Span L1 ELLs in bilingual program (n = 41) – Span L1 in Eng mainstream program (n = 45) – Eng L1 (n = 15) – Stats, ANOVA and correlational analyses	– Language background questionnaire – Eng reading proficiency, TABE – Span reading proficiency (bilingual program only) – Multiple choice, meaning of nonsense words in Eng context	– Bilinguals influenced by L1 syntactic knowledge when guessing meaning of unfamiliar words in Eng reading context
Nguyen and Shin (2001)	Vietnamese ELLs, program unspecified	5–8	Within gp comparisons, convenience sample – n = 170 – Stats, rank order correlation	– Self-report questionnaire (Likert scale, 16 Qs) of L1 and L2 competence, preference, attitudes – SAT (reading and language combined) scores	– Near zero correlation of SAT scores and self-report competence in L1 literacy – No evidence that competence in L1 holds back Eng L2 literacy development
Padron, Knight, and Waxman (1986) Knight, Padron, and Waxman (1985)	Span L1 ELLs, Eng L1s, program unspecified, Houston, TX	3, 5	Within and btwn gp comparisons, convenience sample	– San Diego quick assessment graded word list	– Monolinguals used significantly more strategies than bilinguals

Study	Population/Setting	Grades	Design & Statistics	Measures	Findings
			– Span L1 bilinguals (n = 23) – Eng L1 monolinguals (n = 15) – Stats, t-tests	– Think aloud while reading passages from Ekwall reading inventory	– Gps used different strategies – Monolinguals used concentrating, searching for details, and self-generating questions significantly more – Teacher expectations most often cited by bilinguals
Padron and Waxman (1988)	Span L1 ELLs, small industrial town near major southwestern city, ESL program	3, 4, 5	– Within gp comparison, convenience sample – Pre- and post-testing of reading test and strategy questionnaire – n = 82 – Stats, multiple regression analysis	– Stanford diagnostic reading test – 14-item reading strategy questionnaire	– 2 negative strategies negatively associated with reading gains – Less successful students used less sophisticated and inappropriate strategies
Reese et al. (2000)	Span L1 ELLs, Los Angeles, CA, area	K–7	– Within gp comparisons – Longitudinal – Random sample – n = 66 – Stats: path analysis, correlational analysis	– In-depth home interviews: family literacy practices (parents use of Eng or Span literacy at work, reading aloud to child) – Span early literacy assessment (e.g., identify letters and corresponding sounds, oral comprehension on story read aloud, knowledge of print conventions) – Standardized reading tests in language of instruction (EABE, CTBS)	– Family literacy practices predicted emergent Span literacy and Eng proficiency, which in turn predicted Grade 7 reading achievement – Best Span readers earliest to transition to Eng reading instruction

(continued)

Authors	Sample Characteristics	Grade	Research Design	Outcome Measures (partial listing)	Results
				– School records – Standardized tests of Eng reading performance in Grade 7 – Eng language proficiency: Bilingual Syntax Measure or Idea Proficiency Test – Span proficiency assumed	– Span reading comprehension at Grade 5 best predictor of Eng reading comprehension at Grade 6 – Eng listening skills second best predictor of Eng reading
Royer and Carlo (1991)	Span L1 ELLs, transitional bilingual program, Holyoke, MA	5–6	Within gp comparison, convenience samples – n = 49 – Stats, correlational and regression analyses	– L1 and L2 listening comprehension scores – L1 and L2 reading comprehension scores	
Samway (1993)	ELLs, large school district in upstate New York, pull-out ESL classes	2, 3, 4, 6	Within and btwn gp comparisons, convenience samples – Grade 2 (n = 4) – Grade 3 (n = 1) – Grade 4 (n = 2) – Grade 6 (n = 2) – Qualitative analysis	– Classroom observation – Audio-taped writing conferences – Informal interviews – Children's evaluation of peer and own stories	– Qualitative analysis showed students had awareness of many facets of writing evidenced through their evaluations of writing
Urzua (1987)	Southeast Asian ELLs, transitioned to mainstream	4, 6	Observational study – n = 2	– Audio-taped process; writing sessions, feedback, etc. – dialogue journal writing	– ELLs develop skills areas of a sense of audience, voice and power of language similar to native Eng-speaking children

4

Literacy

Instructional Issues

Fred Genesee and Caroline Riches

INTRODUCTION

Literacy instruction is undoubtedly one of the critical focal points in the education of all children – native English speakers as well as English language learners (ELLs). Literacy is both an end in itself and a means to other ends since, without formal education, most children would not learn to read and write and, without reading and writing skills, children would not be able to learn and function effectively in school and beyond. Clearly, there are challenges in teaching reading and writing to ELLs that exceed those that educators face when teaching native English speakers. The focus of this chapter is on research that has examined the instructional, family and community, and assessment issues related to reading and writing by ELLs. For purposes of this review, *reading and writing include the production or comprehension of written language and behaviors related to the production and comprehension of written language – for example, strategies for comprehending unknown written words or engagement in reading and writing activities.* This encompasses a broad range of outcome measures, as will become evident in the following review. The studies were categorized into four broad topics:

1. Instructional Approaches
2. Language of Instruction
3. Family and Community
4. Assessment

INSTRUCTIONAL APPROACHES

Research reviewed in this section has examined a wide variety of different methods, techniques, and strategies for promoting the reading and writing skills of ELLs. Each study was classified according to one of three major approaches to instruction: (1) direct, (2) interactive, and (3) process-based (see Hillocks, 1984, for a similar taxonomy). Briefly, direct instruction emphasizes the explicit and direct instruction of specific reading/writing skills or strategies. Interactive instruction emphasizes learning that is mediated through interaction with other learners or more competent readers and writers (e.g., the teacher). The goals of interactive approaches include specific literacy skills and strategies, and they also include literacy-related outcomes including, for example, engagement in reading/writing and interest in literacy. Finally, process-based instruction emphasizes engagement in authentic use of written language for communication or self-expression. Process-based approaches deemphasize teaching the component skills and strategies of reading and writing in favor of learning through induction.

These approaches are not mutually exclusive. A given classroom intervention can entail features of more than one approach. For example, to some extent, all instruction involves the teaching of specific skills and a social context in which teaching and learning take place; and, all instruction entails some kind of interaction, at the very least with the teacher. In fact, many of the studies classified as direct instruction involve interactive methods. For example, Padron (1992) taught specific comprehension strategies using reciprocal training methods, and Klingner and Vaughn (1996) used cooperative learning and cross-age tutoring methods. We view the studies as falling along a continuum of approaches from direct instruction to interactive to process-based approaches. Some studies had a relatively distinct constellation of features with a central focus that fitted into one of these three classifications. Such studies are treated in that category. Some studies, like Padron (1992) and Klingner and Vaughn (1996), were composed of different approaches with equal emphases. These are discussed in conjunction with each appropriate approach. Thus, Padron (1992) is included in the Direct and the Interactive Instructional sections because it examines classrooms in which a combination of direct instruction and reciprocal teaching were employed. A handful of studies did not fit into any of these categories (e.g., a study on suggestopedia, a method that emphasizes relaxation and the use of music to prepare students to learn a new language). Such studies were excluded on the grounds that single studies of unique techniques lack sufficient generalizability to be useful. The majority of studies examined reading as opposed to writing and students in elementary school as opposed to middle or high school. In other words, most of this research focused on various aspects of the reading development of ELLs in elementary school.

In the sections that follow, we describe each generic approach in greater detail, and we review evidence for the effectiveness of each. All relevant studies are summarized in Tables A.4.1, A.4.2, and A.4.3. Details about students, specific instructional methods, research designs, outcome measures, and results are included. Space limitations do not permit discussion of all studies, and the reader is referred to the tables for details of studies that are not reviewed in the text.

Direct Instruction

The studies in this category highlight direct instruction of specific skills that are considered essential for all students learning to read and write. Direct approaches to instruction are based on the twin assumptions that reading and writing consist of interrelated but discrete subskills and that these skills are best taught explicitly. For example, students are taught new vocabulary items explicitly or given practice discriminating among sounds and matching sounds to letters. Another characteristic of direct instruction is its orientation to evaluation. The effectiveness of direct instruction is assessed directly and with respect to discrete skills, for example, by testing students' vocabulary knowledge or their spelling skills explicitly. Direct instruction is thought to be particularly appropriate and desirable for minority language students on the grounds that they are at risk for reading and writing development and, thus, they require explicit and focused instruction in the requisite skills that comprise reading and writing.

A summary of the studies that are reviewed in this section is presented in Table A.4.1. Despite arguments in favor of direct instruction (e.g., Snow, Burns, and Griffin, 1998), our search identified few studies that met our inclusion criteria – only ten. Research on direct instruction has focused on reading and paid little attention to writing (except see Bermudez and Prater, 1990; Echevarria, Short, and Powers, 2003). Within the domain of reading, text-level skills enjoyed the greatest attention (Bermudez and Prater, 1990; Hernandez, 1991; Kucer, 1992 [also included in Interactive Instruction section]; McLaughlin et al., 2000; Padron, 1992; Rousseau and Tam, 1993), while three studies examined vocabulary skills (Avila and Sadoski, 1996; McLaughlin et al., 2000; Ulanoff and Pucci, 1999). With the exception of the Kramer, Schell, and Rubison study, which examined Hispanic ELLs in Grades 1–3, research has focused on learners in Grades 3 to 7/8. Consequently, there is little empirical evidence concerning the effects of direct instruction on writing at any grade level or on reading and writing among early primary school (K-2) or high school ELLs. Moreover, none of the studies examined ELLs whose L1 was not Spanish and, in particular, ELLs whose native language is typologically distinct from English, such as Chinese.

All three studies that examined vocabulary report significant improvements in performance (Avila and Sadoski, 1996; McLaughlin et al., 2000; Ulanoff and Pucci, 1999). More specifically, McLaughlin et al. evaluated the effectiveness of a vocabulary-enriched curriculum that included "direct instruction in vocabulary to deepen word knowledge of high-frequency, grade-appropriate words; instruction in strategies such as how to infer meaning from text, using cognates and recognize root words; and activities outside the classroom to extend and deepen students' understanding of word meanings" (McLaughlin et al., 2000; p. 134). The participants were Grades 4 and 5 ELLs of Hispanic background and English-only students. Half of each language group was assigned to the treatment group while half were assigned to the control group; assignment was based on convenience. The control and treatment group students were drawn from the same schools, but no description is provided of the former's instructional experiences. After two years of exposure to the treatment, ELLs performed significantly better than control students on measures of knowledge of target vocabulary, polysemy, morphology, and semantic associations; there was no significant difference between the groups on the PPVT. Moreover, the gap between the ELLs and English L1 students was attenuated by 40 percent after two years of exposure to the treatment condition. However, the ELLs continued to score significantly lower than the English L1 students.

In the Avila and Sadoski (1996) study, Grade 5 ELLs of Hispanic background were taught new English vocabulary using a Spanish keyword method. Students in the control condition were taught new English words using a translation method. Students exposed to the keyword method demonstrated significantly superior word-knowledge skills in English in comparison to the control group. The advantages of the treatment were evident immediately following intervention and after a delay of one week. These findings also attest to the effectiveness of cross-language skills training, an issue we return to later. Finally, Ulanoff and Pucci (1999) found that Grade 3 ELLs exposed to a preview-review method of vocabulary development had greater post-treatment scores (m = 14.87) than did ELLs who had been exposed to a concurrent translation treatment (m = 7.33) and control ELL students (m = 10.44). In fact, the concurrent-translation group scored significantly lower than the control students. There were no significant differences between groups at pre-test.

We identified only three studies that analyzed the effects of direct instruction on English text-level reading skills that used statistical procedures (Bermudez and Prater, 1990; McLaughlin et al., 2000; and Padron, 1992); among these, two reported significant advantages (McLaughlin, 2000; Padron, 1992) and one reported nonsignificant advantages (Bermudez and Prater, 1990) for students who received direct instruction. Three additional studies in this group provide narrative descriptions of the effects of direct instruction on reading performance (Hernandez, 1991; Kucer, 1992; Rousseau and Tam, 1993) and, thus, must be interpreted with reservation.

Padron (1992) examined the effects of direct instruction on Grades 3 to 5 Hispanic students' use of specific comprehension strategies: (1) question generating, (2) summarizing, (3) predicting, and (4) clarifying. There were two treatment groups, each of which entailed twice-weekly, 30-minute sessions for one month; one treatment group was given reciprocal training and the other question-answer–relations training. In the reciprocal-training group, teachers discussed why some students experience difficulties understanding text. This was followed by sessions during which the teacher modeled the four targeted comprehension strategies, following which students were given opportunities to use the strategies. In the question-answer group, the targeted strategies were taught by having students classify comprehension questions according to what strategies they could use to arrive at an answer. Students' use of the strategies was assessed by the Reading Strategy Questionnaire (RSQ), a self-report measure. Students in Control Group 1 were introduced to the same story as that read by the students in the treatment groups, and then read it silently, with none of the special training. Students in Control Group 2 took the RSQ but had no special intervention; they then remained in the class and received instruction in a subject other than reading. Control 2 assessed the effects of prior exposure to the questionnaire on post-test performance. In response to the RSQ, students in the reciprocal-teaching group indicated that they used more "strong" reading strategies (i.e., "summarizing" and "self-generated questions") than the control students, while students in both treatment groups reported using fewer "weak" strategies (e.g., "thinking about something else" and "writing down every word in the story") than the control students. There were no differences between the treatment and control groups on the remaining ten strategies surveyed in the questionnaire. The design of this study is exemplary in its inclusion of alternative treatment and control groups. However, the question remains whether their self-reported increase in the use of certain strong strategies was actually associated with greater use and whether it resulted in greater comprehension; this was not examined by Padron. This is a more general issue of relevance to studies of strategy use; namely, whether increased use of specific strategies that are the object of direct instruction actually improves reading comprehension (see also Kucer, 1992).

Rousseau and Tam (1993) examined the decoding and comprehension skills of eleven- to twelve-year-old Hispanic students with speech/language impairment following direct instruction using a keyword method alone, a listening preview method alone, or a combined keyword plus listening preview method. Student performance was scored numerically, but there were no statistical analyses of their results and, thus, these findings must be qualified accordingly. Although the lack of statistical analyses limits the significance of these results, this small sample study (n = 5) is noteworthy for its research design. Each student was observed initially during a baseline condition, followed, in order, by keyword alone, listening preview alone, and combined keyword plus listening preview treatments. This design allowed the researchers to examine the relative effects of these two types of intervention, alone and in combination, holding individual student differences constant. This study is also noteworthy for its attention to ELLs with speech and language impairment, a group that is not well represented in current research. The keyword method alone produced better performance than listening preview alone but not as high as the combined treatment condition.

Bermudez and Prater (1990) examined the effects of direct instruction on both reading comprehension and writing in Grades 3 and 4 ELLs of Hispanic, low SES backgrounds. Writing performance was assessed using measures of fluency, elaboration of ideas, and organization of ideas. Students' comprehension was assessed post-treatment by a series of questions that tapped their literal and inferential understanding of three selections from their basal reader. Students in the treatment condition first read three selections from their basal reader; they then engaged in brainstorming and clustering of ideas about the topic of the stories, with the assistance of the teacher; and, finally, they wrote a paragraph about the topic. The intervention was brief, lasting only two days. Students in the control condition also read the stories from the basal reader and wrote a paragraph about them. They too were engaged in a teacher-led discussion of the stories prior to writing about them; but, in contrast to the treatment condition, their discussion was based on questions from the basal reader. Students in the treatment group received significantly higher scores than the control group on elaboration of ideas in their writing; but there were no differences between the groups on written fluency and organization. Moreover, there was no significant difference between the treatment and control group on the comprehension measure.

McLaughlin et al. (2000), as reported previously, found that Grade 5 ELLs who had been taught using a vocabulary-enriched curriculum for two years scored significantly higher on a cloze/comprehension test than ELLs who had not had this instruction. Moreover, the gap in reading comprehension between the ELLs and English L1 students was reduced from 1.06 standard deviations after year one of the project to 0.50 standard deviations at the end of year two, a reduction of approximately 45 percent.

A number of additional studies have examined reading comprehension but provide only narrative descriptions of student performance (Hernández, 1991; Kucer, 1992, 1995; Rousseau and Tam, 1993). We have included these studies in our review despite this limitation because of the paucity of studies on direct instruction and in order to give a comprehensive overview of extant work with this focus. All three of these studies report post-treatment improvements in ELLs' reading performance, but these findings must be interpreted with caution. Hernández (1991) found that instruction in reading-comprehension strategies delivered in Spanish to Hispanic students in the summer prior to Grade 7 resulted in statistically significant gains in their reading comprehension in Spanish and, most important also resulted in use of these strategies during English reading. Because Hernández's analysis of the transfer data is only descriptive and the data were based on only seven students, the results must be interpreted cautiously. These results, along with those from Avila and Sadoski, are nevertheless theoretically and practically significant because they address the issue of crosslanguage transfer of reading comprehension strategies. More research is clearly called for to examine this possibility further.

Kucer (1992) used modified cloze reading lessons to teach Mexican-American ELLs how to use context clues when they encounter words they do not know how to read. The intervention took place over the course of the Grade 3 school year. Kucer observed that 93 percent of the students' responses to unknown words in the cloze passages were contextually appropriate. However, interviews with the students indicated that, despite their good performance on the cloze passages, they often misunderstood the teachers' intent in using them. Kucer cautions that it is not sufficient to directly teach reading and writing strategies. Students also need explicit explanations of how and why they are useful, and they must be motivated to use them.

The effects of direct-skills training have also been examined on auditory discrimination (Kramer, Schell, and Rubison, 1983) and writing (Bermudez and Prater, 1990; Echevarria, Short, and Powers, 2003). The Kramer et al. study is included on the premise that auditory discrimination is a precursor to acquiring sound-letter knowledge and early decoding skills. Kramer et al. (1983) examined the effectiveness of a four-week auditory discrimination training program in English for Grades 1 to 3 Spanish-speaking ELLs. The premise of the intervention was that poor discrimination skills may hamper Spanish-speaking students' initial decoding skills in English. The sound pairs in English that were taught during the training sessions were selected because they are difficult for native speakers of Spanish. Post-treatment testing included contrasts that were taught as well as some that were not taught. Control students received none of the discrimination training. The treatment students discriminated significantly better than the control students on all sound pairs that were taught and, as well, on additional pairs that were not taught.

Echevarria et al. (2003) compared the writing skills of Grades 6, 7, and 8 ELLs with diverse L1s following one year of instruction by trained teachers using the Sheltered Instruction (SIOP) method developed by Echevarria, Vogt, and Short (2000). The end-of-year writing scores of the SIOP students were compared to those of a similar group of ELLs. Analysis of covariance with beginning-of-year scores as the covariate were conducted to compare the students' results at the end of the school year. There were statistically significant differences in favor of the SIOP students on total writing score, language production, organization, and mechanics; there were no between-group differences on the focus and elaborations scores. As noted previously, Bermudez and Prater (1990) report advantages for ELLs following direct-writing instruction using brainstorming and clustering on elaboration but not on fluency or organization.

Interactive Instruction

A recurrent issue in literacy education concerns the nature of the broader social context in which students learn to read and write. A number of theoreticians emphasize the importance of interactive learning environments to promote reading and writing proficiency (e.g., Cummins, 1984; Slavin, 1995; Tharp, 1997). In interactive learning environments, learners engage in literacy activities with one or more other learners or with more mature readers and writers (like teachers, parents, or older students). In this way, students learn from others, initially by observation and subsequently by internalizing more mature literate behaviors exhibited by others. In contrast to learning in direct instruction, learning in interactive instructional environments is indirect or mediated by such social interaction. Interactive approaches are favored by some on the grounds that teachers and parents who are competent readers and writers can provide learners with individualized guided instruction that corresponds to their zone of proximal development, in line with Vygotsky's theory of development and learning.

Some researchers have argued that interactive learning environments are especially relevant to ELLs because of the diverse sociocultural backgrounds of these students. More specifically, interactive approaches support individualized teaching and learning in line with the heterogeneous learning needs and styles of ELLs. Interactive learning environments are also thought to reinforce participant structures that some ELLs are used to in their homes but which differ from mainstream American culture. These participant structures emphasize group versus individualized participation, collaborative versus competitive demonstrations of competence, and learning by observing versus learning by talking. Interactive learning environments entail multiple participants engaged in collaborative work and, consequently, extended opportunities to learn through observation. Learning from models is also thought to be advantageous for students from minority-language backgrounds who have not had extensive extracurricular experiences with adult models of literacy; the same could be said of majority-language students from low-literacy backgrounds. A further argument in favor of interactive approaches comes from the notion that reading and writing are more than mere cognitive activities. They are linked to a culture of literacy (Hudelson, 1994). Interactive strategies recognize and promote the acquisition of this culture in addition to the specific language/cognitive skills that comprise reading and writing as cognitive activities. Descriptions of the learning environments

TABLE 4.1. *Sample Descriptions of Interactive Learning Environments*

---

e.g. 1: from Calderon et al. (1998, p. 157) "teachers assign students to four–member, heterogeneous learning teams of students, who work together to help each other learn..." "... the interaction and practice with peers helped students develop fluency and comfort with English."

e.g. 2: from Fayden (1997, p. 25): "The teacher was the model for reading. As she and the children reread the book many times over a period of several days, the teacher gradually withdrew herself as the children assumed more and more responsibility for reaching the book."

e.g. 3: from Klingner & Vaughn (1996, p. 276): "At first, the teacher models use of these strategies by 'thinking aloud' as she reads through a text. The teacher then leads students in a text–related discussion, assisting them in strategy use and gradually withdrawing support as it is no longer necessary. As students become more proficient... they take turns being the 'teacher' and leading discussions about text content."

e.g. 4: from Klingner & Vaughn (2000, p. 70): "... it is based on the theory that cognitive development occurs when concepts first learned through social interaction become internalized and made one's own."

---

of a number of the studies reviewed in this section are presented in Table 4.1.

In keeping with the broad range of goals of interactive approaches to literacy instruction, a wide variety of specific interactive teaching/learning environments has been implemented and examined in the literature (see Table A.4.2). The diversity of interactive techniques for literacy instruction exhibited in this body of research is, in turn, reflected in a diversity of reading, writing, and literacy-related outcome measures. Table A.4.2 provides a description of the outcomes examined in each study that were relevant to our review. A number of the studies used norm-referenced measures of general reading; others used discrete-point tests of specific reading skills related to vocabulary, letter identification, and the lexical and propositional content of written text, to give but a few examples. Still others examined students' use of reading strategies and reading-related behaviors, such as helping, engagement in reading, perceptions of control of reading, and interests and attitudes. The latter are termed "reading-related" in this review since they assess reading indirectly. Some teachers and literacy specialists argue that such behaviors, while ancillary to reading per se, are important components of a developmentally appropriate program of reading instruction. They argue further that these ancillary skills are particularly important in instruction for ELLs who have no or limited exposure to literacy outside of schooling and, thus, require instruction that attends to the broader context of reading; the same could be said of native English speakers with limited literacy experiences before coming to school.

The majority of studies examined text-level reading comprehension skills (Calderon, Hertz-Lazarowitz, and Slavin, 1998; Cohen and Rodriquez, 1980; Doherty et al., 2003; Echevarria, 1996; Goldenberg, 1992/93; Klingner and Vaughn, 1996; Saunders and Goldenberg, 1999; and Syvanen, 1997), including the use of strategies related to reading comprehension (Fayden, 1997; Klingner Vaughn, 1996; Padron, 1992). Three studies examined vocabulary comprehension skills (Doherty et al., 2003; Klingner and Vaughn, 2000; Kucer, 1992), and only two examined writing (Calderón et al., 1998; Goldenberg, 1992/93). A number of studies examined other reading-related behaviors, including reading fluency and accuracy (Blum et al., 1995; Li and Nes, 2001), engagement in reading (Blum et al., 1995; Klingner and Vaughn, 2000; Martinez-Roldan and Lopez-Robertson, 2000, also included in Process Approaches), and use of academic discourse (Echevarria, 1996). With the exception of Echevarria, all other studies that examined reading-related behaviors provide narrative descriptions of their results and, thus, must be interpreted with caution. With the exception of Echevarria (1996) and Klingner and Vaughn (1996), both of whom examined middle-school students, all other studies examined students in elementary school. There were no studies of pre-school or high school students.

A number of general trends emerge from these studies. First, it appears that interactive instructional strategies can be effective with ELLs, as argued by its advocates. Virtually every study in this corpus reported that ELLs in interactive learning environments demonstrated improvements in reading and writing or behaviors related to reading and writing as a consequence of participation in an interactive learning environment. This was shown in studies that used between-group designs (Calderón et al., 1998; Padron, 1992), within-group (pre-post) designs (Fayden, 1997; Klingner and Vaughn, 1996, 2000), and regression designs (Doherty et al., 2003). It was also shown in studies that provide only narrative descriptions with no numeric or statistical data (Blum et al., 1995; Kucer, 1992; Li and Nes, 2001; Martinez-Roldan and Lopez-Robertson, 2000). A number of these narrative reports also suffer from small sample sizes – five or less in some studies (Blum et al., 1995, Kucer, 1992; and Li and Nes, 2001).

The exceptions to the overall pattern of improvement following interactive lessons were Syvanen (1997), Goldenberg (1992/93), and Cohen and Rodriquez (1980). More specifically, Syvanen (1997) found no significant difference in improvement from pre- to post-test among Grades 4 and 5 ELLs who had participated in a cross-age tutoring treatment on a district reading achievement test in comparison to a sample of seventy students in regular classes elsewhere in the district. Without proper control measures, however, it is difficult to know if the comparison group was comparable in other respects to the ELLs who were the subjects of this study. Goldenberg (1992/93) reports no significant differences in literal comprehension between students who had participated in instructional conversation (IC) lessons in comparison to students who had had basal reading (BR) lessons, although he reported that the IC group demonstrated more complex and sophisticated conceptualizations of the theme of the reading lesson in their written essays.

As well, Cohen and Rodriquez (1980) report no advantage for Grade 1 Hispanic ELLs who participated in interactive group-oriented classrooms. The latter study warrants some discussion since it compared the reading achievement of students exposed to two contrasting modes of instruction – high intensity (direct) skills instruction (HIL) and group-oriented interactive instruction. This is a powerful design since it serves to evaluate the impact of different approaches rather than simply show that a specific approach can result in improvement. Cohen and Rodriquez (1980) found that ELLs in HIL classrooms demonstrated higher reading comprehension scores on the CTBS than did students in the interactive classrooms.

Notwithstanding these exceptions, this corpus of studies indicates that interactive instruction can enhance reading comprehension skills related to both vocabulary and text-level material, writing skills (although the evidence here is scant), and other reading-related behaviors, as described previously. Again, however, it is important to keep in mind that the research on these other behaviors must be interpreted cautiously owing to its narrative reporting procedures.

The Saunders and Goldenberg (1999) study warrants some discussion here because it exemplifies a "component building" approach to instructional development and evaluation that could serve as a model for others. Specifically, they examined the effects of two instructional components – IC and literature logs (LL), on the performance of Grades 4 and 5 ELLs of Hispanic background. Students were randomly assigned to one of four groups: LL only, IC only, IC+LL, or control. Students' were tested for their factual and interpretive comprehension and for their understanding of the themes of a story about "giving." In the LL lessons, teachers met the assigned group of students briefly, gave them prompts, and asked them to write about personal experiences that were related to the story. Students then wrote learning logs independently, and the teacher subsequently engaged them in a discussion about the similarities and differences in their experiences and those of the characters in the stories. In the IC lessons, "teachers attempted through discussion to clarify the factual content of the story and develop students' understandings of the more sophisticated concept of giving…" (Saunders and Goldenberg, 1999, p. 287). Students in the control group did not participate in small group discussions with the teacher. Instead, they worked alone or with a teaching assistant on reading and writing activities related to social studies. Students in the LL + IC group scored significantly higher than the control group on story comprehension, and students in all three treatment groups were more likely to demonstrate an understanding of the story themes than students in the control group.

There was an interesting and important interaction effect for the "understanding of story theme" measure that involved the ELLs and English-only students. In particular, English-only students benefited from all three treatments, whereas only ELLs in the combined LL+IC group benefited significantly (statistically); in other words, there were no significant differences between ELLs in the IC-only and LL-only groups in comparison to the control group. With respect to factual and interpretive comprehension, all students showed enhanced performance in the combined condition in comparison to all other conditions. Overall, the effects of IC were somewhat stronger than those of LL, arguing that given a choice, teachers are advised to choose the former. Implementation of the combined approach is recommended otherwise since it clearly benefits ELLs the most (see also Rousseau and Tam, 1993).

A second trend to emerge from this group of studies is the effectiveness of interactive approaches with ELLs from a variety of backgrounds, more specifically, with ELLs from low socioeconomic status (SES) families (Doherty et al., 2003; Fayden, 1997; Padron, 1992; Goldenberg, 1992/93; Saunders and Goldenberg, 1991, 1999), ELLs with learning disabilities (Echevarria, 1996; Klingner and Vaughn, 1996), and ELLs with emergent literacy skills (Blum et al., 1995). The findings from Blum et al. must be interpreted with caution owing to the descriptive nature of their data. There is also evidence that interactive learning environments benefit ELLs from diverse ethnolinguistic backgrounds: Native American (Fayden, 1997), Chinese American (Li and Nes, 2001), and Hispanic American students (e.g., Calderón et al., 1998; Doherty et al., 2003; Echevarria, 1996; Goldenberg, 1992/93; Klingner and Vaughn, 1996, 2000; Kucer, 1992; Padron, 1992; Saunders and Goldenberg, 1999). Li and Nes's results on Chinese Americans are based on narrative descriptions only and, thus, must be interpreted with caution. Overall, students of Hispanic background were the focus of attention in most studies. In light of the apparent language socialization differences among families from different cultural backgrounds (Ochs and Schieffelin, 1984), more carefully designed, in-depth research is warranted on the effectiveness of interactive approaches with learners of other backgrounds.

Third, interactive approaches also appear to be effective with ELLs in middle school (Echevarria, 1996; Klingner and Vaughn, 1996) as well as in elementary school (see Table A.4.2 for those studies). However, as noted previously, studies on ELLs in high school are lacking. This gap is of particular concern given the critical role that reading and writing play in the mastery of academic subjects, such as mathematics and science, in the higher grades.

Finally, interactive approaches appear to be effective in promoting reading-related behaviors; that is, engagement in reading and writing and an understanding and appreciation of literacy in its broader sense, as well as text- and word-level comprehension skills. As noted previously, however, all of the studies that examined reading-related outcomes provide only narrative descriptions, arguably owing to the general and complex nature of these outcomes.

Process Approaches

Process approaches emphasize student engagement in authentic literacy activities with significant communicative goals. Typically, students are given extended opportunities to engage in free reading or writing and in reading and writing activities in which communication is emphasized, such as dialogue journals, literature logs, or free reading/writing. Engagement in reading and writing activities may be individual or interactive – dialogue journals or free writing, for example, are usually individual activities, whereas shared literature can entail group activity. Children's literature is a common vehicle for implementing process approaches since literature exposes learners to authentic written text, is engaging, and allows learners to relate to written language via their own experiences, if materials are well chosen. As Roser, Hoffman, and Farest (1990) indicate, literature-based literacy programs provide a number of advantages to ELLs: they "(1) offer exposure to a variety of children's books, (2) contribute to a rich literary environment, (3) motivate responsive reading, (4) encourage voluntary reading, (5) expand the learners' reading interests, (6) help learners grow in language, reading, writing, and thinking, and (7) help learners discover their own connections with literature."

Process approaches are distinguished by the view that language is holistic – reading, writing, speaking, and listening (as well as their component subskills) co-occur under authentic conditions and they, therefore, should be taught and learned together. See Table 4.2 for some sample descriptors of process-based instruction in studies reviewed in this section. Proponents of the process approach view the distinctions between the subcomponents of reading and writing that are emphasized in direct skills-based approaches and even some interactive approaches as artificial. Moreover, they argue that focusing instruction on subskills is less likely to succeed because it focuses students' attention unduly on the component elements of literacy while distracting them from the ultimate goal – reading and writing for authentic communication and self-expression. This is not to say that process approaches are indifferent to the mastery of spelling, grammar skills, and so forth rather, they view the acquisition of these subskills as a natural by-product of engagement in communicatively oriented reading

TABLE 4.2. *Sample Descriptions of Process Approaches*

- **e.g. 1**: from Gomez et al. (1996, p. 218): "Students in the Free Writing group ... selected their own topics, and could write for as long as they wanted. Students' writing was not subjected to error corrections ... teachers responded to each student's writing through written comments. Students were then invited to respond ..., thus creating a written dialogue. In the Structured Writing group ... topics were assigned by the teacher, and the students wrote intensively, in nine minutes of concentrated writing time. Students were instructed to work alone and quietly ... Writing samples were subjected to error correction by the teacher. ... Students were directed to focus on avoiding those errors on their next writing sample."
- **e.g. 2**: from Kuball Peck (1997, p. 217): "The classroom was a print-rich environment in which skills were learned in context as part of a whole. For instance, the teachers modeled reading and writing on a daily basis. Recipes, songs, stories, and daily news were charted in front of the students. Child-dictated stories were transcribed by the morning teacher ... thus, skills were presented in context. Fragmented instruction, in which skills are taught in isolation, was not offered."

and writing. In fact, most evaluations of process approaches included in our review use direct assessments of reading and writing skills (see, for example, Roser et al., 1990; Schon, Hopkins, and Davis, 1982; and Schon, Hopkins, and Vojir, 1984). The question is, how effective are they at promoting acquisition of specific reading and writing skills in the absence of focused or direct instruction in such skills?

Whole language can be viewed as a special case of the process approach since it shares these tenets of other process approaches. Indeed, a defining characteristic of whole language is its emphasis on the integrity of reading, writing, speaking, and listening (and their respective subskills). Whole-language philosophy asserts that the acquisition of literacy skills occurs naturally, like the acquisition of oral and aural language, through involvement in authentic, meaningful uses of written language. There is wide variation among whole-language programs with respect to the instruction of the component skills of reading and writing.

As was the case for the other approaches discussed in this chapter, there are a number of ways in which process approaches are conceptualized, operationalized, and evaluated (de la Luz Reyes, 1991). Table A.4.3 summarizes the variety of instructional techniques and foci that were investigated and the outcome measures used to evaluate them in the studies included in this review. The description of the outcome measures in Table A.4.3 is not intended to be complete. Rather, it illustrates the wide range of outcome measures that have been used in this research, in keeping with each program's particular conceptualization of the approach. To be more specific, a number of socioaffective variables (e.g., attitudes toward reading;

self-concept as a reader/writer; engagement in reading) figured in a number of these studies along with more conventional outcomes measures, such as spelling, grammar, and standardized test scores. Proponents of process approaches regard it as the preferred method of instruction for ELLs on the assumption that they are particularly responsive to the special language learning needs of ELLs.

Like research on the other approaches, the research in this corpus focused on word level (Schon et al., 1982) and text-level reading skills or reading-related behavior (Carger, 1993; Kucer and Silva, 1999; Kucer,1995; Martinez-Roldan and Lopez-Robertson, 2000; Roser et al., 1990; Schon et al., 1982; Schon et al., 1984). In contrast, there was also a focus on the development of writing (Carger, 1993; de la Luz Reyes, 1991; Gomez, Parker, and Lara-Alecio, 1996; Kuball and Peck, 1997; Kucer and Silva, 1999). All of the studies examined students in elementary grades, except Schon et al. (1984), who examined students in high school (Grades 9–12). ELLs of Hispanic backgrounds were the only student group to be investigated.

Overall, evidence of the effectiveness of process approaches is mixed. Six studies report advantages for students exposed to process instruction (Carger, 1993; Gomez et al., 1996; Kuball, and Peck, 1997; Kucer and Silva, 1999; Martinez-Roldán and Lopez-Robertson, 2000; Roser et al., 1990), but with the exception of Kucer and Silva, all other studies provide only narrative descriptions with no statistical analyses of their results; and two report results only for reading-related behaviors (Carger (1993): expression of emotion during pretend reading in one child; Martinez-Roldán and Lopez-Robertson (2000): engagement in reading. Two studies report no statistically significant advantages on standardized tests of reading (i.e., Inter-America Reading Test, MAT) for ELLs who experienced process-based literacy activities in comparison to control students (Schon et al., 1982; Schon et al., 1984). Schon et al. (1982) examined Hispanic ELLs from low SES families who were in Grades 2–4, while Schon et al. (1984) examined Hispanic ELLs from low SES families in Grades 9–12. Yet others report less favorable outcomes for students in process-based literacy classrooms (de la Luz Reyes, 1991; Gomez et al., 1996). Of particular note, Gomez et al. (1996) report that Hispanic ELL students who received "structure-based lessons" in the summer prior to entering Grade 6 outperformed students who received extended opportunities for free writing, an activity that is often associated with process instruction.

Evidence for the effectiveness of process approaches to literacy instruction is even more tentative when careful consideration is given to methodological factors. While these studies vary with respect to the detail and thoroughness of the descriptions they provided of the instructional approaches under investigation, overall, many suffer from inadequate descriptions of the actual literacy activities. This is especially true of those that examined whole-language classrooms, but it is not only these studies that suffer such problems. For example, Schon et al. (1984) note that "Teachers in the experimental group were instructed to provide at least sixty minutes a week of free reading time and *to do everything they could to help their students develop positive attitudes towards reading.*" (emphasis added) (p. 14).

A number of researchers, even those who argue for a process approach, called for a balanced approach that incorporates some direct instruction of specific skills, as needed, embedded in process-based activities. For example, Kucer and Silva (1999), noted earlier, comment that "...it is overly simplistic to assert that students will improve their literacy abilities by being immersed in a garden of print; that is, students will improve in their reading and writing due to the maturation process, regardless of instruction...." (p. 365). A similar conclusion is drawn by de la Luz Reyes (1991) following a study of the writing abilities of Grade 6 Hispanic ELLs in classrooms where dialogue journals and literature logs were used to promote development: "Overall, mere exposure to standardized writing conventions did not improve the students' use of them" (p. 291). In response to this situation, Kucer and Silva recommend that "...when it is determined that a child is encountering repeated difficulty with a particular dimension of written language, focused instructional events would be developed that explicitly teach over time the matter in which the child is experiencing difficulty. In these lessons, not only is the child shown what to do, but also how it is to be accomplished" (p. 366).

Clearly, considerably more research is necessary to come to firm conclusions about process approaches. In particular, more research is called for that identifies the critical features of this approach as well as the necessary conditions for successful implementation of such approaches. In the meantime, current evidence suggests that process approaches alone are not particularly effective at promoting the acquisition of reading- and writing-specific skills unless provision is made for such a focus.

Methodological Considerations

Methodological concerns that are particularly relevant to specific approaches have been discussed in the preceding sections. Here we address methodological issues that emerge from a consideration of all three bodies of research. There is clearly variation in the methodological strength of individual studies. In their favor, many studies are noteworthy for the detail and care that was taken to provide descriptions of the actual implementation of specific instructional strategies. Doherty et al. (2003) and Echevarria (1996), moreover, assessed the fidelity of implementation of the IC approach that was the focus of their investigations. While highly recommended, this is not a common practice in this entire body of research.

Future research on the effectiveness of alternative instructional approaches would benefit from a number of methodological improvements. Systematic use of objective measures of learner outcomes and appropriate statistical analyses of these outcomes is critical to determine the magnitude and reliability of instructional effects; a number of studies noted in summary Tables A.4.1, A.4.2, and A.4.3 provided only narrative descriptions. As well, some studies used small sample sizes, making generalizability difficult. Small sample sizes can be justified in ethnographic studies that entail in-depth descriptions of student involvement in reading and in studies of special populations that are difficult to identify (e.g., ELLs with learning/language disabilities [see Echevarria, 1996, for an example]). At the same time, follow-up studies with larger samples are called for to confirm trends noted in such studies. None of the small-n studies reported such follow-up research. Long-term as well as short-term assessment of the impact of instruction is also highly desirable, for obvious reasons. In the majority of studies reviewed here, students from Hispanic/Latino backgrounds were examined, leaving open to question the generalizability of findings to other groups. Clearly, there is a need to investigate ELLs from a variety of minority ethnolinguistic groups.

A number of studies examined the effectiveness of specific instructional approaches for students with special challenges. In most cases, these students were identified as learning disabled or impaired on the basis of their standing relative to district norms. It is possible that students identified in this way face a heterogeneous group of challenges, including language impairment, dyslexia, and learning disability. While these impairments converge the longer students are in school, there are good theoretical and practical reasons to believe that they are initially different forms of impairment that, arguably, call for different forms of remediation (e.g., Bishop and Snowling, 2004). For example, specific language impairment is not the same as a general learning disability (see Leonard, 2000, for a review), and appropriate intervention for the former is different from appropriate intervention for the latter. Future researchers are encouraged to differentiate special learning needs of ELLs and to identify learners with different needs using appropriate selection criteria. Without more differentiation of students with special challenges, our understanding of how to meet their particular needs will remain sketchy.

When examined as a whole, this body of research suffers from the "one-off" syndrome – that is, single studies by a researcher or team of researchers on a specific pedagogical issue or approach in a specific school and district. This style of research may reflect the pressures on university-based researchers to "publish or perish" and/or the need to provide answers quickly. Whatever the precise explanation, such an approach leaves many unanswered questions about the reliability and generalizability of reported results. Future research that entails long-term, sustained efforts and multiple samples in different communities would contribute significantly to our understanding of how and when these approaches work. Also relevant to the issue of generalizability is the diversity of ways in which variations of an approach, such as process-based approaches, are operationalized. On the one hand, flexibility in the way an approach is or can be operationalized is realistic and desirable so that the particular needs and resources within particular classrooms can be addressed. On the other hand, the lack of uniformity or coherence in the way approaches are implemented compromises generalizability and replicability substantially. It is incumbent on researchers to provide not only sufficient detail about the implementation of the approach they are investigating to ensure that they are studying what they say they are studying but also to provide information about the reliability of their descriptions, which, as noted earlier, is lacking in many cases.

LANGUAGE OF INSTRUCTION

An ongoing issue among theoreticians, researchers, and professional educators has been the benefits, or disadvantages, of providing instruction through the medium of ELLs' L1 (for more discussion of this issue, see Chapter 5, this volume). A number of arguments for this (Cummins, 2000; Thomas and Collier, 1997) and against it (Porter, 1990; Rossell and Baker, 1996) have been made. These will not be reviewed in detail here because of space limitations. However, in short, proponents of L1 support argue that L2 reading acquisition is facilitated if instruction is provided in a language that students already know so that skills acquired in the L1 can transfer to the acquisition of reading and writing in the L2. Opponents of L1 support argue that it detracts from acquisition of the L2 because it gives the learner less instructional time relevant to the L2 – the time-on-task argument.

A lot of research has assessed the impact of instruction through the L1 versus instruction through English alone. The primary way in which this issue has been addressed is by comparing the performance of ELLs who have received instruction in the primary grades through the medium of only English to that of ELLs who have received instruction in their L1 along with English instruction. Studies using these methods comprise the majority of studies that were uncovered. Another way in which this issue has been addressed is by examining the performance of ELLs in bilingual education to that of native English speakers to ascertain if ELLs in bilingual programs are more or less likely to achieve parity with native English speakers (see Burnham-Massey and Piña, 1990). The corpus of studies reviewed here is summarized in Table A.4.4. Chapter 5 provides an extended review and critique of this and related research from the perspective of academic achievement.

Before proceeding with a discussion of the results of this research, it is useful to provide a methodological overview of them. The focus of this work has been on elementary-level students since the case for bilingual instruction or initial instruction through the students' L1 applies primarily to students who are receiving initial reading and writing instruction. The choice of language of instruction to optimize educational outcomes is also an issue for ELLs at the middle and high school levels, but we did not identify any research on these age groups. A number of studies have examined the *short-term* impact of bilingual instruction on students' literacy development in Grades 1, 2, and 3 (Calderón et al., 1998; Carlisle and Beeman, 2000; Fulton-Scott and Calvin, 1983; Lindholm and Aclan, 1991; Saldate, Mishra, and Medina, 1985); other studies have examined the *medium-term* impact of bilingual instruction on students in the senior elementary Grades 4, 5, and 6 (Burnham-Massey and Piña, 1990; Friedenberg, 1990; Fulton-Scott and Calvin, 1983; Gersten and Woodward, 1995; Howard, Christian, and Genesee, 2004; Lindholm and Aclan, 1991; Mortensen, 1984; Ramirez, 1992); and some have examined the *long-term* impact on students in Grades 7 and 8 (Bacon, Kidd, and Seaberg, 1982; Burnham-Massey and Piña, 1990; Gersten and Woodward, 1995) and in one case in Grade 11 (Burnham-Massey and Piña, 1990). Examination of impact of bilingual forms of education on student achievement in the early as well as later elementary and middle grades is important because it highlights the importance of sustained, coherent instruction through the L1; we return to this point later.

The majority of studies have employed standardized tests, including the California Test of Basic Skills, Stanford Achievement Test, Iowa Test of Basic Skills, Woodcock-Johnson, Metropolitan Achievement, SRA, and Texas Assessment of Academic Skills. The use of standardized tests is an important feature of these studies since it makes it possible to evaluate practices related to language of instruction in the same way as in English-only programs. Moreover, the population of students who contribute to the norming of standardized tests is carefully selected to represent target levels of achievement in school and, thus, use of such assessment instruments ensures objectivity and generalizability that could be compromised if only local instruments were used. Other outcome measures have also been employed in single studies: GPAs (Fulton-Scott and Calvin, 1983) and locally devised rubrics for scoring writing or oral language skills (Ferris and Politzer, 1981; Howard, Christian, and Genesee, 2004; Kuball and Peck, 1997).

Overall, the studies within this corpus report similar results; namely, that, in the long term, ELLs who receive some reading instruction in the L1 in the primary grades demonstrate the same or better performance in L2 reading as ELLs of similar linguistic and cultural background who have received initial literacy and academic instruction in English only (Bacon,

Kidd, and Seaberg, 1982; Calderón, Hertz-Lazarowitz, and Slavin, 1998; Carlisle and Beeman, 2000; Friedenberg, 1990; Fulton-Scott and Calvin, 1983; Gersten and Woodward, 1995; Lindholm and Aclan, 1991; Mortensen, 1984).

ELLs who receive initial instruction through the L1 do not always demonstrate parity with comparison groups or test norms in the early grades when L1 instruction is predominant. A number of studies have found that it takes several years before parity is achieved. Gersten and Woodward (1995) report advantages for ELLs in an English immersion program in Grades 4 to 6 compared to ELLs in a transitional bilingual program but no differences in Grade 7. Fulton-Scott and Calvin (1983) report that there were few differences between ELLs in bilingual-multicultural programs and ESL programs in the primary grades, but that the performance of bilingually instructed students was superior to that of the comparison group by Grade 6. Calderón et al. (1998), Mortensen (1984), and Saldate et al. (1985) also report that ELLs who received bilingual instruction demonstrated superior reading performance relative to comparison groups, but again after participating in the program for some years.

Evidence of equal (or superior) reading achievement in English among ELLs who received reading instruction in the L1 has also been reported for ELLs with learning disabilities (Maldonado, 1994) and for ELLs of Cherokee background (Bacon, Kidd, and Seaberg, 1982), two groups of learners who are at added risk in school – risk due to their minority language status and their learning handicap in the case of Maldonado's learners and risk due to their minority indigenous cultural status in the case of students in the Bacon et al. study. The Maldonado study is particularly noteworthy because it entailed random assignment of ELLs with disabilities to bilingual and English-only classrooms. More specifically, twenty students with learning disabilities from one school were randomly assigned to either an experimental group that received integrated bilingual special education or a control group that received traditional special education in English. The two groups were taught for three years in otherwise similar classrooms by similar teachers. The experimental group received instruction in Spanish for all but 45 minutes per day during the first year and received balanced language instruction (50 percent English; 50 percent Spanish) the second year. English was the only language of instruction during the final year. Instruction for the control group was conducted only in English. Performance on the CTBS (pre- and post-test) showed that students in the bilingual special education class were superior to students in the English-only group at post-test. The students in the bilingual special education program actually scored lower than the control group at pre-test, indicating that they had made even greater gains than the control group than their post-test results alone would indicate. Replication of the Maldonado study is warranted to address methodological weaknesses, in particular, to ensure that the only or primary instructional difference between the learning disabled group who received instruction through the L1 and those who did not was the language of instruction.

The cumulative effects of participation in alternative educational programs for ELLs has been examined in a large-scale, longitudinal study by Thomas and Collier (2002). Since that study is discussed in detail in Chapter 5, it is not reviewed in detail here. Suffice to say that they report that ELLs who were in mainstream English-only programs and had received no special services scored lower by the end of high school than ELLs who had participated in some form of bilingual education (i.e., early- or late-exit bilingual or two-way immersion).

In a longitudinal study of the performance of Hispanic ELLs and English L1 students in two-way immersion programs in Grades 3 to 5, Howard et al. (2004) found that both ELL and English L1 students showed significant improvements in English reading and writing from Grades 3 to 5, but that the ELLs performed significantly lower than the English L1 students on both measures at all grade levels. ELLs in TWI programs received initial literacy instruction in Spanish. The difference between the ELL and English L1 groups could be due to a number of factors. First, the ELL students were significantly more likely than the English L1 students to come from lower socioeconomic backgrounds, as measured by parental occupation or free/reduced lunch. Second, the ELL students may not have been in the two-way immersion program long enough to reach parity with their English-speaking peers. In support of this possibility, Collier (1987) has reported that it can take from five to seven years for ELLs to achieve grade-appropriate scores on standardized reading and language tests in English (see also Cummins, 2000). ELLs have the triple challenge of acquiring the societal language for both social and academic purposes, acquiring new academic skills and knowledge, and adapting culturally to their new environments, all at the same time. This calls for developmentally coherent curricula that span several grades and for adaptations to assessment programs that take into account ELLs' long-term developmental trajectories. Longitudinal studies are critical if we are to ascertain and understand the long-term results of particular instructional strategies or approaches, a point we return to in Chapter 6.

Finally, Burnham-Massey and Piña (1990) compared the CTBS reading and language subtest scores of ELLs who began instruction in Spanish with those of English-only students longitudinally from Grades 1 to 12. The ELLs' percentile scores increased from Grades 1 to 5, at which time they had reached the 46th percentile in reading and the 50th percentile in language. Later comparisons in Grades 7 and 8 showed that the ELLs scored at the same level as the English-only students; both scored around the 50th percentile on language, but only at the 35th–41st percentile levels on reading. The results were not compared statistically, and no explanation is given for the drop in reading scores from Grade 5 to 7. The students were subsequently compared in Grades 9 to 12 using GPAs and scores on the High School Proficiency Test. The ELLs performed as well as the English-only students at all grade levels on reading and writing, but again no statistical analyses were carried out. Although these results must be interpreted with caution for reasons that have been discussed, overall, they suggest that the long-term language and reading development of ELLs who begin elementary education in Spanish can be equivalent to that of English-only students.

Taken together, the results of these studies provide little support for the time-on-task argument against bilingual forms of education for ELLs. Further evidence against this argument comes from a longitudinal investigation by Ramirez (1992) of three program alternatives for ELLs: structured immersion, early-exit bilingual, and late-exit bilingual. A subset of Ramirez's analyses compared the performance of ELLs in three versions of late-exit bilingual education that varied with respect to the amount and consistency of L1 instruction. Ramirez reports that ELLs "who were provided with a substantial and consistent primary language development program learned ... English language and English reading skills as fast or faster than the norming population in the study" (Ramirez, 1992, p. 39). In other words, more exposure to the L1 in school did not result in slower L2 development, as would be predicted by the time-on-task argument. Ramirez took considerable care to document the instructional practices of the target programs in his investigation.

Additional evidence that questions the time-on-task hypothesis comes from Ferris and Politzer (1981), who compared the writing skills of native Mexican-born and U.S.-born ELLs. The former group had received their first three years of education in Spanish in Mexico and their subsequent education, until Grade 8, in English in the United States. The second group was born in the United States and had received all their education in English. Although the writing skills of the U.S.-born and educated group were superior with respect to verb inflection, verb tense, and pronoun agreement, there were no significant differences on many other measures of writing: number of details, clarity, coherence, completeness; on frequency counts of fused sentences, incorrect punctuation, article agreement, use of possessives; or on T-unit analyses (average number of words per T-units, average number of clauses per T-unit, average clause length).

Before leaving this section, a comment on random assignment might be useful. Previous critiques of evaluations of bilingual education have discounted this research on the grounds that most studies do not include random assignment (Rossell and Baker, 1996). One of the primary arguments for the use of random assignment is linked to the issue of generalizability. Random assignment of subjects to experimental conditions permits researchers to rule out potentially confounding extraneous factors that might account for significant or nonsignificant effects. However, random assignment is not always possible or appropriate when it comes to real schools. First, it is difficult, for ethical and political reasons, for a school district or ethics review board to enforce random assignment, without parental permission, to such different educational options as English-only and bilingual. Second, there is no realistic or legal way to ensure that participants in bilingual programs would remain in programs following initial random assignment; as a result, long-term participants in such programs could no longer be said to be randomly assigned. In addition, since choice is the hallmark of education in the United States and in current implementations of bilingual education, a randomly assigned group of students would not be a valid reflection of the kinds of students and families who typically select such programs. However, convergent findings from studies that have employed different assessment instruments and analytic techniques, as well as different groups of students in different regions of the country, is a realistic way of providing evidence for the generalizability of the effectiveness of bilingual or any other form of instruction for ELLs (see NRC Principle 5: Replicate and Generalize Across Studies, 2002). The research reviewed here, arguably, provides this kind of evidence (see also Chapter 5, this volume).

FAMILY AND COMMUNITY

The studies reviewed in this section examine literacy development in relation to home-related factors, such as SES, language use at home, number of books and literacy practices at home, parents' values and aspirations, and home-based factors, such as the impact of school-initiated interventions in the home (e.g., the impact of using audio-books at home on students' reading performance; Blum et al., 1995). Factors related to oral language development in the home and its impact on phonological awareness, or other reading-related skills, are discussed in more detail in Chapter 3. In principle, one might also expect community-related factors to play a role in the development of reading and writing skills in ELLs (e.g., the extent to which written forms of language are evident and useful in the community). In fact, we uncovered no studies of this nature.

Investigations of family and community factors are important because it is often argued that ELLs are at-risk for reading failure or difficulty because of their lack of exposure to or engagement in literacy outside school. This assumption is itself subject to empirical verification. A thorough understanding of the language experiences of ELLs in the home and community would be useful for developing school-based literacy activities that build on these students' total language experiences, especially those language experiences that support literacy development. Moreover, evidence that home- and community-based literacy activities can enhance ELLs' literacy development would be welcomed news because it could provide additional resources for promoting literacy development in school by drawing on the assistance of parents and communities.

Two predominant variables in this research are socioeconomic status and home-related literacy practices and resources. These two variables are highly interrelated. SES was assessed in terms of eligibility for free lunch. Eligibility for free lunch is linked to parental income which, in turn, may be linked to parental occupation and education and, ultimately, to a variety of literacy practices and resources in the home (e.g., literacy skills of parents, their engagement in reading and writing on their own behalf and with their children, and availability and use of books). It is important to recognize that there may be a discrepancy between the current SES of parents of ELLs and their education because immigrant parents may be relegated to low-level jobs in their new communities despite high levels of education and occupation in their communities of origin. We review these two issues separately but recognize that they are likely concerned with the same proximal family influences.

SES and Literacy Development

With respect to SES, Kennedy and Park (1994) and Reese et al. (2000) both report significant correlations between SES and the standardized reading test scores of middle-school ELLs. Kennedy and Park examined Grade 8 Asian and Mexican American ELLs while Reese et al. examined Grade 7 Latino students. Tompkins, Abramson, and Pritchard (1999) report that ELLs with diverse L1 backgrounds attending relatively high SES schools were more likely to use conventional English spelling patterns than ELLs in less affluent schools. In contrast, Buriel and Cardoza (1988) report that SES was unrelated to the standardized English reading and vocabulary scores of Grade 9 first- and second-generation Mexican American ELLs living in the Southwest. Personal aspirations were the most significant predictors of these first- and second-generation students' test results. SES made a modest contribution to the vocabulary scores of third-generation students, explaining an additional 3 percent of variance; SES did not account for additional variance in the third-generation students' reading scores. Ima and Rumbaut failed to find a significant difference in SES between limited-English proficient (LEP) and English proficient ELLs of Southeast Asian background in regression analyses that examined the influence of a variety of factors on school achievement. In line with the Ima and Rumbaut results, Thomas and Collier (2002) also report that SES accounted for a relatively small proportion of variance in the reading scores of ELLs in different program options.

The discrepancy in these findings may relate to mitigating factors. SES is itself not a causal variable but represents a number of other proximal variables that are causal in nature, such as reading practices and the availability of reading material at home. Thus, studies that include a constellation of such proximal variables may yield different results with respect to the influence of SES depending on which specific predictor variables are included in the analyses and the validity and reliability of these other variables. In other words, some multivariate studies may have eliminated the statistical influence of SES on reading and/or writing scores, thereby giving the impression that SES is unrelated to literacy development. In fact, from developmental and pedagogical perspectives, the family, individual, and sociocultural variables associated with SES are of more significance than SES per se because they carry with them practical implications of some import. In contrast, SES alone implies little of actionable consequence. This is evident as we turn to the next set of studies, those that look at family-related literacy practices and their relationship to literacy.

Family Literacy Practices

Studies of proficient and precocious ELL readers provide one source of evidence for an association between home-related factors and literacy development (Jackson and Wen-Hui, 1992; Pucci and Ulanoff, 1998). Pucci and Ulanoff (1998) found that proficient ELL readers from minority-language backgrounds had more books at home, enjoyed reading more, and felt they were more proficient than less proficient ELL readers. The students in this study were in Grade 4 and were Hispanic. In an interesting related study of precocious ELL and precocious English L1 readers (in Kindergarten and Grade 1), Jackson and Wen-Hui (1992) found that the two groups were similar with respect to home-literacy experiences. More specifically, the parents of both groups reported that their children read at home at least two or three times a week; both groups were read to at home; both groups had someone help them identify letter names, spell words, and understand word meanings; and, in addition, both had attended some kind of pre-school. However, the samples of these studies were quite small (twelve in both cases), making generalizability difficult. More important, it is not clear what the causal factors are in these studies – were these ELLs proficient readers because of parental involvement in their children's reading or did these children's precocity/proficiency in reading prompt parental involvement, or both?

In a variation of these studies that have examined naturally occurring home-based literacy practices, Blum et al. (1995) examined the effectiveness of a school-initiated intervention that was conducted in the homes of ELLs of diverse L1 backgrounds with no L1 reading ability. In the intervention, audio recordings of stories were sent home with students to support their reading at home in the absence of other sources of support. Blum et al.

report that the reading performance of these Grade 1 students benefited from this initiative. However, their results are based on observation only and their sample was small – only five students. This type of intervention warrants more attention, with methodological enhancements, because of its potential educational importance. The Blum et al. (1995) results along with the Pucci and Ulanoff (1998) and Jackson and Wen-Hui (1992) results have important implications for extending opportunities for literacy development to include parents and home literacy training.

At the other end of the literacy spectrum, Hughes, Schumm, and Vaughn (1999) examined the homes and parental literacy practices of ELLs with learning disabilities (LD). More specifically, Hughes et al. compared the homes of Grade 3 and Grade 4 Hispanic students with LD to those of similar students with typical patterns of development with respect to types of reading and writing activities, the desirability and feasibility of reading activities, and facilitators and barriers to parents helping their children to read. They found few differences between the homes of these two groups of students – the most common activities in the homes of both groups were reading to the children or having the children read to the parents; both groups of parents valued home reading, but the parents of children with LD found it more difficult to help their children read than did parents with average or above-average readers; and both groups of parents reported that the most common barriers to supporting their children's reading development at home were lack of communication with the school and lack of knowledge of English. Evidence from this research on home-related factors suggests that while parental and home-related factors may be associated with learning/reading proficiency, they are less important in explaining learning (i.e., reading) disability. Arguably, the latter is due to endogenous limitations in children's general cognitive or language-specific capacity and, thus, may be relatively insensitive to variations in family influences.

L1 Use at Home

A major issue concerning home/community factors and English literacy development is the extent to which use of and/or proficiency in the L1 affects ELLs' proficiency in English literacy. This question has been examined in a number of studies in which multiple independent variables have been used to predict L2 literacy outcomes including, for example parental levels of education and SES (as noted previously); educational aspirations, expectations, and values; homework patterns; use of the L1 and L2 at home; and immigration and medical background (Buriel and Cardoza, 1988; Duran and Weffer, 1992; Hansen, 1989; Ima and Rumbaut, 1989; Kennedy and Park, 1994; Reese et al., 2000). Taken together, the results from these studies suggest a complex multivariate relationship between

L1/L2 use outside school and L2 literacy development in school. Implicated in this complex relationship are generational status (e.g., whether students are first-, second-, or third-generation immigrants; see Buriel and Cardoza, 1988), the cultural backgrounds of students (e.g., whether students are Mexican American or Asian American; see Kennedy and Park, 1994), type of outcome measure (e.g., auditory vocabulary versus text comprehension; see Hansen, 1989; and standardized test scores versus course grades; see Kennedy and Park, 1994), and type of predictor measure (e.g., oral language use versus literacy; see Reese et al., 2000).

Hansen (1989), also reviewed in Chapter 2, investigated the relationship between gains in English reading (and auditory vocabulary) scores on the one hand, and language use in the classroom, at home, and with peers on the other hand, among Grade 2 and Grade 5 students from Spanish-dominant homes in the San Francisco Bay area. They report that, after prior levels of reading comprehension were accounted for, students' use of English at home and in the classroom accounted for significant portions of variance in reading scores (18 and 9 percent, respectively). In other words, ELLs who used more English at home and in the classroom scored higher on tests of English reading than did ELLs who used English less often in these settings.

Research by Kennedy and Park (1994) suggests that the significance of L1/L2 use in the home depends on both students' cultural background and type of outcome measure. To be specific, they found that in the case of Mexican American ELLs, English use in the home was not a significant predictor of English course grades ($r = 0.012$) or of standardized English test scores ($r = -0.002$). In the case of Asian American ELLs, English use in the home was not related to course grades ($r = 0.05$) but was moderately related to standardized test scores ($r = 0.08^*$). Kennedy and Park note that the explanatory power of their final regression models, which included other predictor variables, was quite small in all cases, accounting for between 8 and 23 percent of the total variance in outcome measures, depending on the measure and the background of the students. Home language use was a much stronger correlate of standardized test results than of course grades.

Buriel and Cardoza (1988) report that the influence of L1 use in the home on L2 literacy development may also depend on the immigration history of the student. The students in their study were first-, second-, or third-generation Grade 9 students of Mexican descent living in the U.S. Southwest. Regression analyses indicated that home language use was not a significant predictor of English reading outcomes (as measured by self-reported course grades and standardized reading tests) in first- and second-generation students. In contrast, among third-generation students, greater English dominance (based on self-reports of the extent to which English was the first language, the current language of use in the home, and usual individual language, among others) was associated with higher scores on standardized English reading tests and vice versa for students with less English dominance. Conversely, high Spanish-dominant third-generation ELLs scored less well on English reading tests than low Spanish-dominant students. In short, for these third-generation ELLs, there was a positive correlation between extent of English use outside school and level of English reading ability. At the same time, third-generation students with greater literacy skills in Spanish scored higher on the English reading test than did students with lower Spanish literacy skills. Home language use did not predict English vocabulary scores among third-generation students to any significant extent. In brief, high levels of both English language use at home and Spanish literacy were correlated positively with level of English literacy.

The dual significance of both oral English language use/proficiency and Spanish literacy development is echoed in a study by Reese et al. (2000) in which they monitored the English reading development of Spanish-speaking students longitudinally from Kindergarten to Grade 7. Using path analyses with multiple predictor variables and Grade 7 reading test scores as the outcome variable, they report that the average number of years that ELLs' parents lived in the United States predicted students' level of oral proficiency in English ($r = 0.32^{***}$), which in turn predicted their English reading scores in Grade 7 ($r = 0.43^{***}$). In other words, greater oral English proficiency enhanced English literacy development. Duran and Weffer (1992) and Ima and Rumbaut (1989) have similarly found that number of years in the United States has a significant positive correlation with English reading scores of Grade 10 Mexican American and Grades 7 to 12 Southeast Asian ELLs, respectively. Returning to Reese et al., they also found that family literacy practices predicted early Spanish literacy ($r = 0.22^{*}$), which in turn predicted Grade 7 English reading scores ($r = 0.30^{**}$). Interestingly, their index of "family literacy practices" did not distinguish between English and Spanish literacy and, thus, can be interpreted as an index of literacy in either language. Thus, students who entered school with some prior oral proficiency in English were advantaged in the long run for the acquisition of English reading, as were ELLs who entered Kindergarten with literacy skills in Spanish.

ASSESSMENT

Assessment is undoubtedly one of the most critical aspects of education for English language learners. It is implicated in virtually every aspect of their education – from screening or admission, to identification of special and individual needs that figure in instructional planning, to promotion or retention. While there exists an extensive body of research on assessment for native English speakers, this research is of dubious generalizability to ELLs for a variety of reasons. Most obviously, standardized or norm-referenced tests are only valid for students on whom the test has been normed, and use of such tests with other types of students can lead to egregiously faulty results and decisions. For example, a standardized test of mathematics or science administered in English to ELLs is just as much about the student's language proficiency as it is about his/her knowledge of mathematics or science. Standardized tests that have been developed for mainstream English-speaking students may contain cultural biases that can result in underestimations of the competence of students from different cultural and/or linguistic backgrounds (Cabello, 1984).

To be effective, education must be based on an accurate assessment of students' knowledge and skills; otherwise, students will be provided instruction that is too advanced or not advanced enough, redundant, or simply irrelevant. Despite its singular importance, research on assessment of ELLs is dramatically lacking. Of the entire body of research reviewed for this volume, only ten empirical studies related to assessment issues were uncovered and retained. While these studies address issues of some importance, their significance is weakened by conceptual fragmentation; that is, each study looks at a different assessment issue. Thus, the findings reported by these studies lack utility because we cannot ascertain their reliability and generalizability.

The diversity of this research can best be illustrated by providing a brief overview. McEvoy and Johnson (1989) examined the utility of using a test of general intelligence (WPPSI) as a predictor of early reading scores among Mexican American students. They found that, indeed, the WPPSI predicted a significant amount of variance in reading scores when predicting from age 5 to Grades 1 to 4. Jansky et al. (1989) failed to find good predictive validity for a five-test screening battery for ELLs of Hispanic background when initial screening occurred at Kindergarten or Grade 1 with follow-up for five to six years. Accordingly, they argue for careful selection of screening tests that are fine-tuned to the specific needs and characteristics of the students being tested. In contrast, Frontera and Horowizt (1995) report that teachers can be a valuable and valid source of information concerning students who are at risk for reading failure based on questionnaire responses.

Miramontes (1987) examined the miscues of good and disabled readers whose first language was Spanish versus those whose first language was English. She found that the miscues of students whose first language was Spanish (whether they were good or disabled readers) adhered more consistently to the expected graphic and sound cues represented in the text than did those of students whose first language of reading was English. She emphasizes the importance of assessing ELLs' reading abilities in both languages and also of examining reading processes, not just levels. In another study, Miramontes (1990) makes the same claims as a result of research on the miscues of Hispanic students with mixed language

dominance/proficiency. Umbel et al. (1992) also argue for assessment of
ELLs' skills in both languages in order to arrive at valid assessments of
vocabulary skills. Cabello (1984) documents alternative forms of cultural
bias in tests used to assess ELLs – bias linked to lexico-syntactic, content
and concepts, social, and cognitive aspects of assessment. She recommends
the use of test items that are relatively free of bias when assessing students
with different linguistic and cultural backgrounds. Similarly, Garcia (1991)
found that the performance of Hispanic students on an English language
reading test was seriously underestimated because of their limited prior
knowledge of certain test topics and concludes that simply diversifying
the topics in a test is inadequate to overcome this bias. In a large survey of
5,472 students of Southeast Asian background, Ima and Rumbaut (1989)
argue that educators must consider the diversity of learners within this
group of ELLs if their educational efforts, including assessment activities,
are to be appropriate and effective.

Collectively, these studies address a number of important general issues.
However, it is difficult to provide recommendations from this corpus
because the research is so fragmented. Some observations that can be
derived from this corpus relate to importance of:

1. Assessment in both languages in order to arrive at complete and
   valid assessments of ELLs' abilities and difficulties (Miramontes,
   1987; Umbel et al., 1992).
2. Multiple sources of information when assessing the learning needs
   of ELLs (Frontera and Horowitz, 1995; McEvoy and Johnson, 1989).
3. Different kinds of information about ELLs and tests that are dynamic
   and tailored to specific needs and characteristic of ELLs; in particular,
   assessments should be free of cultural bias, sensitive to students'
   relative proficiency in each language, and sensitive to developmental
   patterns and to first-language reading (Miramontes, 1987).
4. Distinctive patterns of reading and language development among
   ELL subgroups that can serve as valid points of reference for diag-
   nosis – in other words, one should not assume that there are singular
   or simple profiles that validly characterize the reading difficulties of
   all ELLs who are below grade level (Goldstein, Harris, and Klein,
   1993; Ima and Rumbaut, 1989; Merino, 1983; Miramontes, 1990).

There is clearly a need for much more research in this field if we are
to address these issues with empirical evidence. Additional key questions
deserve attention:

1. How can we best identify the strengths and weaknesses in ELLs'
   L2 (and L1) reading skills and, in particular, those who are below
   grade level in reading performance? In a related vein, do ELLs from

different L1 backgrounds demonstrate the same patterns of difficulty and strength?

2. Can the L2 reading skills of ELLs be calibrated in some way that would permit appropriate placement of students in English reading programs?
3. How can we distinguish ELLs who are suspected of impaired reading from those who simply have incomplete mastery of the L2?
4. Can standardized English and content-area tests that are mandated by state regulations be adapted for use with ELLs to make valid inferences about their reading and academic progress relative to mainstream students?
5. Is it possible to develop tests of English reading and language that are not biased against ELLs in inappropriate ways?

CONCLUSIONS

Studies of alternative approaches to reading and writing instruction indicate that interactive approaches have much to recommend them. Most evaluative studies on interactive approaches attest to their effectiveness. Moreover, they are effective for students with typical as well as those with impaired capacities for learning, although the evidence is limited and definitions of impairment are often overly general and lacking in precision. We previously cautioned that the distinctions used to categorize studies of instruction are not mutually exclusive. In fact, a number of studies consist of combinations of approaches. Direct and interactive instruction was frequently combined – a number of studies of classrooms that were categorized as direct instruction included interactive components (e.g., Padron, 1992), and many interactive learning environments included direct-skills instruction (Doherty et al., 2003; Goldenberg, 1992; Saunders and Goldenberg, 1999). The evidence suggests that different forms of direct instruction can be effective for teaching word-level and text-level language skills and that it can be effective crosslinguistically. Our present understanding of the effectiveness of direct instruction is limited by the relative paucity of research on this approach.

The importance of direct instruction as a component of an overall plan of instruction is indicated by the results of process-based approaches. The effectiveness of process approaches is mixed at best, with some studies reporting advantages for students who were in process-oriented literacy classrooms, but many reported null advantages and even disadvantages. Researchers who examined process approaches pointed out that simply exposing students to literacy-rich learning environments is not sufficient to promote acquisition of the specific skills that comprise reading and writing. They argued that focused and explicit instruction in particular skills and subskills is called for if ELLs are to become efficient and effective readers and writers. Thus, the fundamental tenet of process-based approaches that direct-skills instruction be avoided is the source of its weakness. Unless process-based instruction is able to provide additional evidence to the contrary, the results to date do not recommend this approach.

The best recommendation to emerge from our review favors instruction that combines interactive and direct approaches. Classrooms that combine interactive with direct instruction provide instruction in specific reading and writing skills within carefully designed interactive contexts, such as Instructional Conversations. Interaction between learners and teachers, be they adults or more competent students, is a mechanism through which adaptation and accommodation of individual differences and preferences can be accomplished. Carefully planned interactions in the classroom are also both the medium for delivering appropriate instruction about literacy and academic material and the message, insofar as the very language that is used during interactive instruction embodies many key features of language for literacy and broader academic purposes. Direct instruction of specific skills ensures student mastery of literacy-related skills that are often embedded in complex literacy or academic tasks. Presenting direct instruction in interactive learning environments ensures that it is meaningful, contextualized, and individualized. The choice of methods will depend in large part on the objectives of instruction and learner characteristics. Certain methods, such as the keyword method, will be appropriate for vocabulary development, while others, such as brainstorming, will be appropriate for text comprehension and writing. At the same time, it is important to point out that the emphasis on authentic, meaningful, and individualized literacy activities that is the hallmark of process approaches is probably a critical element of all literacy programs. It is a matter of balance and focus – extant evidence suggests that an exclusive focus of the sort emphasized by process approaches is probably not optimal.

A comprehensive and coherent plan for instruction calls for more than specific techniques or methods, be they interactive or direct in nature. Educators need comprehensive frameworks for planning and delivering a whole curriculum. The Five Standards for Effective Pedagogy (Tharp et al., 2000) provides such an overarching framework. "The Five Standards articulate both philosophical and pragmatic guidelines for effective education.... they do not endorse a specific curriculum but, rather, establish principles for best teaching practices ... for both majority and minority students" (see CREDE, 2002, for more details). The standards emphasize teaching and learning through interaction but also accommodate direct instruction as appropriate. In light of the evident need to focus on specific components of oral language and reading and writing for academic purposes, the SIOP framework developed by Echevarria, Vogt, and Short (2000) deserves consideration at the same time. SIOP is of particular relevance to the present discussion because it focuses on how language can be adapted to make academic content comprehensible and, vice versa, how academic instruction can promote acquisition of language for academic purposes. It incorporates both interactive and direct instructional approaches.

While direct and interactive instruction are generally effective, we do not have a full understanding of the scope of their effectiveness. More evidence with respect to the specific language-skills domains over which each approach can be said to be effective is needed. There is considerable evidence with respect to text-level reading skills but limited evidence concerning vocabulary, spelling, phonological awareness and decoding, and writing skills. By strategically focusing on different learner outcomes, researchers could expand our understanding of the scope of effectiveness of these approaches.

Research concerning the effectiveness of direct and interactive forms of instruction alone or in combination at different grade/age levels would provide valuable information about how to adapt these approaches to learners as they progress developmentally. One might imagine that direct instruction is particularly effective for acquisition of certain skills at certain stages of development and less effective at other times for other kinds of skills. Similarly, interactive instruction and particular forms of interactive instruction alone or in combination with direct instruction might be particularly effective for teaching certain skills at particular stages of development. The studies by Saunders and Goldenberg (1999) and Doherty et al. (2003) provide research models for better understanding the effectiveness of combined approaches to instruction and the components that they comprise. More research that examines the relative merits of alternative approaches to instruction would provide educators with valuable comparative data with which to decide among alternatives, as well.

Research with respect to language of instruction has focused on whether use of ELLs' L1 for initial schooling (and especially literacy instruction) enhances, impedes, or has no effect on the development of reading and writing skills in English. Collectively, this body of research indicates that use of the L1 during the primary grades of schooling does not retard L2 literacy development. To the contrary, in some cases, ELLs who participate in primary school programs that provide L1 support generally achieve the same or superior levels of reading and writing skills as ELLs in English-only programs by the end of elementary school or middle school. Thus, contrary to the time-on-task hypothesis, ELLs can accommodate instruction in two languages without costs to their English-language development. At the same time, ELLs who receive initial instruction in their L1 can achieve parity in English literacy with native English speakers and, when they do, it usually takes several years of schooling. Participation in a bilingual program does not lead to parity with native English speakers in all cases, indicating that it is not sufficient to simply provide instruction in

ELLs' L1 and English to achieve parity with native English speakers. Attention must also focus on type and quality of instruction. It is for this reason that research on alternative instructional approaches for ELLs is so critical. Unfortunately, there is insufficient research concerning additional instructional factors in bilingual classrooms to draw conclusions regarding the joint effectiveness of language of instruction and instructional approach. Moreover, the precise impact of use of the L1 for initial literacy instruction is not entirely clear since the sole independent variable in most of this research is language of instruction with little control in most cases for other possible mitigating factors.

Research on the role of family and community factors on L2 literacy development reveals an interesting but complex picture. On the one hand, ELLs who begin school with advanced levels of oral English language proficiency tend to achieve higher levels of English literacy than students who lack proficiency in English and, conversely, ELLs who are Spanish dominant upon school entry tend to achieve lower levels of proficiency in L2 literacy. On the other hand, ELLs with enriched literacy experiences during the pre-school years in the home, whether in the L1 or the L2, and ELLs with literacy skills in Spanish prior to school entry are likely to achieve higher levels of proficiency in English L2 literacy than ELLs with less enriched literacy experiences and less developed L1 literacy skills. The influence of English language use/proficiency outside school on English literacy development in school may also depend on the cultural background of students as well as their parents' length of residence in the United States. English language proficiency upon entry to school appears to play a more important role in English literacy development in school the longer the family history of residence in the United States. Other factors, such as personal aspirations, appear to be more important than L2 proficiency among first- and second-generation immigrants. Oral English proficiency also appears to be more important among Asian American than among Mexican American ELLs, although these results are statistically modest and are based on a single study and, thus, deserve replication before substantive conclusions can be drawn about the role of cultural background.

Taken in conjunction with the language-of-instruction findings, we see that the acquisition of the home language and ESL is not a zero-sum game. Proficiency in the home language does not have to result in reduced English language skills and, conversely, the development of English language skills does not have to entail loss of the home language. However, careful consideration has to be given to what aspects of L1 and L2 development are promoted in the pre-school years. The evidence reviewed in this chapter and in Chapter 3 indicates that it is not sufficient to simply promote bilingual proficiency in day-to-day oral language skills for ELLs to succeed fully in English-language school environments. ELLs are more likely to succeed at English-language literacy if they have had enriched literacy skills, either in the L1 or the L2, prior to school entry. Results reported in Chapter 3 indicate further that L1 oral language skills that are implicated in literacy development are also likely to benefit L2 literacy development.

Parents and schools must play a greater role in promoting literacy in the home, especially during the pre-school years so that ELLs are better prepared for literacy instruction when they begin school. The same is probably true for native English speakers who are at risk for literacy development. Much more research is needed to examine family-based language interventions so that we have a better understanding of what works, with what kinds of learners, and under what conditions. At present, our understanding of the effect of home-based language interventions on English-language literacy development in school is restricted. To date, ELLs of Hispanic background have been the primary focus of research attention, and studies of non-Hispanic children have not disaggregated their results by language and cultural background. There are good reasons to expect that specific types of home-based interventions will be differentially effective for different learner groups (Steinberg, Dornbusch, and Brown, 1992). Future research on these issues would fill these gaps in our knowledge.

Finally, with respect to assessment, it is difficult to draw precise or broad-based conclusions because there is extremely little empirical research on assessment issues related to ELLs, and the extant research is conceptually fragmented. A number of critical questions about assessment of ELLs remains to be answered.

References

Avila, E., and Sadoski, M. 1996. Exploring new applications of the keyword method to acquire English vocabulary. *Language Learning 46*(3), 379–95.

Bacon, H., Kidd, G., and Seaberg, J. 1982. The effectiveness of bilingual instruction with Cherokee Indian students. *Journal of American Indian Education 21*(2), 34–43.

Bermudez, A., and Prater, D. 1990. Using brainstorming and clustering with LEP writers to develop elaboration skills. *TESOL Quarterly, 24*, 523–8.

Bishop, D. V. M., and Snowling, M. J. 2004. Developmental dyslexia and specific language impairment: Same or different? *Psychological Bulletin 130*, 858–86.

Blum, I. H., Koskinen, P. S., Tennant, N., Parker, M. E., Straub, M., and Curry, C. 1995. Using audiotaped books to extend classroom literacy instruction into the homes of second-language learners. *Journal of Reading Behavior 27*(4), 535–63.

Buriel, R., and Cardoza, D. 1998. Sociocultural correlates of achievement among three generations of Mexican-American high school seniors. *American Educational Research Journal 25*(2), 177–92.

Burnham-Massey, L., and Piña, M. 1990. Effects of bilingual instruction on English academic achievement of LEP students. *Reading Improvement 27*(2), 129–32.

Cabello, B. 1984. Cultural interference in reading comprehension: An alternative explanation. *Bilingual Review 11*(1), 12–20.

Calderón, M., Hertz-Lazarowitz, R., and Slavin, R. 1998. Effects of bilingual cooperative integrated reading and composition on students making the transition from Spanish to English reading. *The Elementary School Journal* 99(2), 153–65.

Carger, C. L. 1993. Louie comes to life: Pretend reading with second language emergent readers. *Language Arts* 70(7), 542–7.

Carlisle, J. F., and Beeman, M. M. 2000. The effects of language of instruction on the reading and writing achievement of first-grade Hispanic children. *Scientific Studies of Reading* 4(4), 331–53.

Center for Research on Education, Diversity, & Excellence (CREDE) 2002. *The Five Standards for Effective Pedagogy.* http://crede.ucsc.edu/standards/standards.html.

Cohen, A. S., and Rodriquez, S. 1980. Experimental results that question the Ramirez–Castaneda model for teaching reading to first-grade Mexican-Americans. *Reading Teacher* 34(1), 12–18.

Collier, V. 1987. Age and rate of acquisition of second language for academic purposes. *TESOL Quarterly* 21(4), 617–41.

Cummins, J. 1984. *Bilingualism and special education: Issues in assessment and pedagogy.* San Diego: College Hill Press.

————— 2000. *Language, power, and pedagogy.* Clevedon, UK: Multilingual Matters.

de la Luz Reyes, M. 1991. A process approach to literacy using dialogue journals and literature logs with second language learners. *Research in the Teaching of English* 25(3), 291–313.

Doherty, R. W., Hilberg, R. S., Pinal, A., and Tharp, R. 2003. Five standards and student achievement. *NABE Journal of Research and Practice Winter*, 1–24.

Duran, B., and Weffer, R. 1992. Immigrants' aspirations, high school process, and academic outcomes. *American Educational Research Journal* 29(1), 163–81.

Echevarria, J. 1996. The effects of instructional conversations on the language and concept development of Latino students with learning disabilities. *The Bilingual Research Journal* 20(2), 339–63.

Echevarria, J., Short, D., and Powers, K. 2003. *School reform and standards-based education: How do teachers help English language learners?* Technical Report. Santa Cruz: Center for Research on Education, Diversity, & Excellence.

Echevarria, J., Vogt, M. E., and Short, D. J. 2000. *Making content comprehensible for English language learners: The SIOP Model.* Needham Heights, MA: Allyn & Bacon.

Fayden, T. 1997. What is the effect of shared reading on rural Native American and Hispanic kindergarten children. *Reading Improvement* 34(1), 22–30.

Ferris, M., and Politzer, R. 1981. Effects of early and delayed second language acquisition: English composition skills of Spanish speaking junior high school students. *TESOL Quarterly* 15(3), 263–74.

Friedenberg, J. 1990. The effects of simultaneous bilingual reading instruction on the development of English reading skills. *Acta Paedologica* 1(2), 117–24.

Frontera, L., and Horowitz, R. 1995. Reading study behaviors of fourth grade Hispanics: Can teachers assess risk? *Hispanic Journal of Behavioral Sciences* 17(1), 100–20.

Fulton-Scott, M., and Calvin, A. 1983. Bilingual multi-cultural education vs. integrated and non-integrated ESL instruction. *NABE: The Journal for the National Association for Bilingual Education* 7(3), 12.

Garcia, G. E. 1991. Factors influencing the English reading test performance of Spanish-speaking Hispanic students. *International Reading Association 26*, 371–92.

Gersten, R., and Woodward, J. 1995. A longitudinal study of transitional and immersion bilingual education programs in one district. *The Elementary School Journal 95*(3), 223–39.

Goldenberg, C. 1992/93. Instructional conversations: Promoting comprehension through discussion. *The Reading Teacher 46*, 316–326.

Goldstein, B., Harris, K., and Klein, M. 1993. Assessment of oral storytelling abilities of Latino junior high school students with learning handicaps. *Journal of Learning Disabilities 26*(2), 138–43.

Gomez, R., Parker, R., and Lara-Alecio, R. 1996. Process versus product writing with limited English proficient students. *The Bilingual Research Journal 20*(2), 209–33.

Greene, J. P. 1998. *A meta-analysis of the effectiveness of bilingual education research.* Claremont, CA: The Tomas Rivera Policy Institute.

Hansen, D. 1989. Locating learning: Second language gains and language use in family, peer and classroom contexts. *NABE: The Journal for the National Association for Bilingual Education 13*(2), 161–80.

Hernandez, J. S. 1991. Assisted performance in reading comprehension strategies with non-English proficient students. *The Journal of Educational Issues of Language Minority Students 8*, 91–112.

Hillocks, G., Jr. 1984. What works in teaching composition: A meta-analysis of experimental treatment studies. *American Journal of Education 93*(1), 133–70.

Howard, E. R., Christian, D., and Genesee, F. 2004. The development of bilingualism and biliteracy from grades 3 to 5: A summary of findings from the CAL/CREDE study of two-way immersion education. CREDE Research Report. Washington, DC, and Santa Cruz, CA: Center for Applied Linguistics and Center for Research on Education, Diversity, & Excellence.

Hudelson, S. 1994. Literacy development of second language children. In F. Genesee (ed.), *Educating second language children* (pp. 129–58). New York: Cambridge University Press.

Hughes, M. T., Schumm, J. S., and Vaughn, S. 1999. Home literacy activities: Perceptions and practices of Hispanic parents of children with learning disabilities. *Learning Disability Quarterly 22*(3), 224–35.

Ima, K., and Rumbaut, R. G. 1989. Southeast Asian refugees in American schools: A comparison of fluent-English-proficient and limited-English-proficient students. *Topics in Language Disorders 9*(3), 54–75.

Jackson, N. E., and Wen-Hui, L. 1992. Bilingual precocious readers of English. *Roeper Review 14*(3), 115–19.

Jansky, J., Hoffman, M., Layton, J., and Sugar, F. 1989. Prediction: A six-year follow-up. *Annals of Dyslexia, 39*, 227–46.

Jimenez, R. 1997. The strategic reading abilities and potential of five low-literacy Latina/o readers in middle school. *Reading Research Quarterly 32*(3), 224–43.

Kennedy, E., and Park, H. S. 1994. Home language as a predictor of academic achievement: A comparative study of Mexican- and Asian-American youth. *The Journal of Research and Development in Education 27*(3), 188–94.

Klingner, J., and Vaughn, S. 1996. Reciprocal teaching of reading comprehension strategies for students with learning disabilities who use English as a second language. *The Elementary School Journal 96*(3), 275–93.

2000. The helping behaviors of fifth graders while using collaborative strategic reading during ESL content classes. *TESOL Quarterly 31*(1), 69–98.

Kramer, V. R., Schell, L. M., and Rubison, R. M. 1983. Auditory discrimination training in English of Spanish-speaking children. *Reading Improvement 20*(3), 162–8.

Kuball, Y. E., and Peck, S. 1997. The effect of whole language instruction on the writing development of Spanish-speaking and English-speaking kindergartners. *Bilingual Research Journal 21*(2–3), 213–31.

Kucer, S. 1992. Six bilingual Mexican-American students and their teacher's interpretations of cloze literacy lessons. *The Elementary School Journal 92*(5), 557–72.

1995. Guiding bilingual students "through" the literacy process. *Language Arts 72*(1), 20–9.

Kucer, S. B., and Silva, C. 1999. The English literacy development of bilingual students within a transition whole-language curriculum. *Bilingual Research Journal 23*(4), 345–71.

Leonard, L. B. 2000. *Children with specific language impairment*. Cambridge, MA: MIT Press.

Li, D., and Nes, S. 2001. Using paired reading to help ESL students become fluent and accurate readers. *Reading Improvement 38*(2), 50–61.

Lindholm, K., and Aclan, Z. 1991. Bilingual proficiency as a bridge to academic achievement: Results from bilingual/immersion programs. *Journal of Education 173*(2), 99–113.

Maldonado, J. A. 1994. Bilingual special education: Specific learning disabilities in language and reading. *Journal of Educational Issues of Language Minority Students 14*, 127–47.

Martinez-Roldan, C., and Lopez-Robertson, J. 2000. Initiating literature circles in a first grade bilingual classroom. *The Reading Teacher 53*(4), 270–81.

McEvoy, R., and Johnson, D. 1989. Comparison of an intelligence test and a screening battery as predictors of reading ability in low income, Mexican-American children. *Hispanic Journal of Behavioral Sciences 11*(3), 274–82.

McLaughlin, B., August, D., Snow, C. E., Carlo, M., Dressler, C., White, C., Lively, T., and Lippman, D. 2000. *Vocabulary improvement and reading in English language learners: An intervention study*. Proceedings of a Research Symposium on High Standards in Reading for Students from Diverse Language Groups. Washington, DC: U.S. Department of Education.

Merino, B. J. 1983. Language development in normal and language handicapped Spanish-speaking children. *Hispanic Journal of Behavioral Sciences, 5*(4), 379–400.

Miramontes, O. 1987. Oral reading miscues of Hispanic students: Implications for assessment of learning disabilities. *Journal of Learning Disabilities 20*(10), 627–32.

1990. A comparative study of English oral reading skills in differently schooled groups of Hispanic students. *Journal of Reading Behavior 22*(4), 373–94.

Mortensen, E. 1984. Reading achievement of native Spanish-speaking elementary students in bilingual vs. monolingual programs. *Bilingual Review 11*(3), 31–36.

Ochs, E., and Schieffelin, B. B. 1984. Language acquisition and socialization: Three developmental stories and their implications. In R. A. Schweder and R. A. LeVine (eds.), *Culture theory: Essays on mind, self, and emotion*. New York: Harper and Row.

Padron, Y. N. 1992. The effect of strategy instruction on bilingual students' cognitive strategy use in reading. *Bilingual Research Journal* 16(3–4), 35–51.

Porter, R. P. 1990. *Forked tongue*. New York: Basic Books.

Pucci, S., and Ulanoff, S. 1998. What predicts second language reading success? A study of home and school variables. *Review of Applied Linguistics* 121–22, 1–18.

Ramirez, D. 1992. Executive summary. *Bilingual Research Journal* 16, 1–62.

Ramirez, S. Z. 1986. The effects of Suggestopedia in teaching English vocabulary to Spanish-dominant Chicano third graders. *The Elementary School Journal* 86(3), 325–33.

Reese, L., Garnier, H., Gallimore, R., and Goldenberg, C. 2000. Longitudinal analysis of the antecedents of emergent Spanish literacy and middle-school English reading achievement of Spanish-speaking students. *American Educational Research Journal* 37(3), 633–62.

Roser, N., Hoffman, J., and Farest, C. 1990. Language, literature, and at-risk children. *The Reading Teacher* 43(8), 554–59.

Rossell, C. H., and Baker, K. 1996. The educational effectiveness of bilingual education. *Research in the Teaching of English* 30, 7–74.

Rousseau, M. K., and Tam, B. K. Y. 1993. Increasing reading proficiency of language-minority students with speech and language impairments. *Education and Treatment of Children* 16(3), 254–71.

Saldate, M., IV, Mishra, S. P., and Medina, M., Jr. 1985. Bilingual instruction and academic achievement: A longitudinal study. *Journal of Instructional Psychology* 12(1), 24–30.

Saunders, W., and Goldenberg, C. 1999. The effects of instructional conversations and literature logs on the story comprehension and thematic understanding of English proficient and limited English proficient students. *The Elementary School Journal* 99(4), 277–301.

Schon, I., Hopkins, K. D., and Davis, W. A. 1982. The effects of books in Spanish and free reading time on Hispanic students' reading abilities and attitudes. *NABE: The Journal for the National Association for Bilingual Education* 7(1), 13–20.

Schon, I., Hopkins, K. D., and Vojir, C. 1984. The effects of Spanish reading emphasis on the English and Spanish reading abilities of Hispanic high school students. *The Bilingual Review,* 11(1), 33–9.

Slavin, R. 1995. *Cooperative learning: Theory, research and practice* (2nd Ed.). Boston: Allyn & Bacon.

Slavin, R. E., and Madden, N. A. 1999. Effects of bilingual and English as a second language adaptations of Success for All on the reading achievement of students acquiring English. *Journal of Education for Students Placed at Risk* 4, 393–416.

2001. *One million children: Success for All*. Thousand Oaks, CA: Corwin.

Snow, C. E., Burns, M. S., and Griffin, P. 1998. *Preventing reading difficulties in young children*. Washington: National Academy of Sciences.

Steinberg, L., Dornbusch, S. M., and Brown, B. B. 1992. Ethnic differences in adolescent achievement: An ecological perspective. *American Psychologist* 47, 723–9.

Syvanen, C. 1997. English as a second language students as cross-age tutors. *ORTESOL Journal 18*, 33–41.

Tharp, R. 1997. *From at-risk to excellence: Research, theory and principles of practice.* Research Report 1. Santa Cruz, CA: Center for Research on Education, Diversity, & Excellence.

Tharp, R. G., Estrada, P., Dalton, S. S., and Yamauchi, L. 2000. *Teaching transformed: Achieving excellence, fairness, inclusion and harmony.* Boulder, CO: Westview Press.

Thomas, W. P., and Collier, V. P. 2002. *A national study of school effectiveness for language minority students' long-term academic achievement.* Santa Cruz, CA: Center for Research on Education, Diversity & Excellence.

Thomas, W., Collier., V. P. 1997. *School effectiveness for language minority students.* Washington: National Clearinghouse for Bilingual Education. (www.ncbe. gwu.edu).

2002. *A national study of school effectiveness for language minority students' long term academic achievement.* Santa Cruz, CA: CREDE.

Tompkins, G. E., Abramson, S., and Pritchard, R. H. 1999. A multilingual perspective on spelling development in third and fourth grades. *Multicultural Education 6*(3), 12–18.

Ulanoff, S. H., and Pucci, S. L. 1999. Learning words from books: The effects of Read Aloud on second language vocabulary acquisition. *Bilingual Research Journal 23*(4), 409–22.

Umbel, V., Pearson, B., Fernandez, M., and Oller, D. 1992. Measuring bilingual children's receptive vocabulary. *Child Development 63*(4), 1012–20.

Vygotsky, L. 1962. *Thought and language.* Cambridge, MA: MIT Press.

Willig, A. C. 1985. A meta-analysis of selected studies of the effectiveness of bilingual education. *Review of Educational Research 55*, 269–317.

TABLE A.4.1. *Summary of Studies on Direct Instruction*

Authors	Sample Characteristics	Grade	Instructional Method(s)	Research Design	Outcome Measures (partial listing)	Results
Avila and Sadoski (1996)	Hispanic, low achieving	5	Keyword method in Spanish to enhance acquisition of new English vocabulary	Random assignment to: – TR: keyword method – CO: translation – n = 63 – Immediate and delayed recall (1 wk)	– Cued recall of new vocabulary – Sentence completion using new vocabulary – Immediate and delayed recall of new vocabulary	– TR > CO immediate and delayed recall of Eng words
Bermudez and Prater (1990)	Hispanic, urban, low income	3, 4	Brainstorming and clustering to enhance rdg comp and wtg skills: Fluency, elaboration, and organization of ideas – 45 minutes/ day for 6 days	Random assignment to: – TR: Brainstorming + clustering – CO: Discussion of questions from basal reader – n = 16 each	– Comprehension of stories – Retention of story information – Writing: Fluency, elaboration, and organization measures	– TR > CO elaboration – No sign differences on fluency, organization, comp, or retention

(continued)

TABLE A.4.1 (*continued*)

Authors	Sample Characteristics	Grade	Instructional Method(s)	Research Design	Outcome Measures (partial listing)	Results
Echevarria, Short, and Powers (2003)	ELLs in 1 East Coast (large, urban district) & 2 West Coast (large urban) districts of the United States, Hispanic, Asian/Pacific, European background, diverse L1s	6, 7, 8	Sheltered Instruction (SI)	Convenience assignment to: – TR: SI (n = 346) – CO: Regular instruction (n = 94) – Pre – post-testing of both groups	– Expository writing: Lang production, focus, support/ elaboration, organization, and mechanics (6-pt scale for each)	– TR > CO at post-test on total score, lang production, organization, mechanics – TR = CO at post-test on focus and elaboration
Hernandez (1991)	Hispanic, LEP	Summer Pre – Grade 7	Modeling, monitoring checklist, and direct instruction to promote use of reading comp strategies: Question-generating, summarizing, predicting	Within group design with pre – post-testing – Stats analysis of gains in Span read comp – Narrative description of use of strategies in Eng – n = 7	– Comp of Span stories – Use of strategies while reading Eng stories	– Stat. sign post-test improvement in Span reading comp – All students exhibited use of strategies during Eng reading – Evidence of transfer of skills training from Span to Eng

| Kramer, Schell, and Rubison (1983) | Hispanic, urban Kansas | 1, 2, 3 | Auditory discrimination training of 4 contrasting sounds in English | Random assign to:
– TR = Discrimination training (n = 15)
– CO: No training (n = 15) | – Discrimination of target and non-target sounds | TR > CO: Pre- to post-test gains on trained and untrained contrasts |
| Kucer (1992) | Hispanic, bilingual, working class, metropolitan school | 3 | – Cloze texts to teach strategies for comprehending unknown words in text | Single subject design
– n = 6
– Narrative description of post-intervention performance | – Videotapes and field notes of lessons: Teacher's understanding of lessons
– Literacy artifacts: Students' use of strategies
– Interviews: Students' and teachers' retrospective understanding of lessons | – 93% of students' responses during cloze were contextually appropriate
– Students used cloze-based strategies as taught but did not always explicitly understand purpose of instruction in the same way as the teacher intended |

(*continued*)

151

TABLE A.4.1 (*continued*)

Authors	Sample Characteristics	Grade	Instructional Method(s)	Research Design	Outcome Measures (partial listing)	Results
McLaughlin et al. (2000)	Hispanic ELL and Eng L1; schools in Massachusetts, California, and Virginia	4, 5	– Vocab-enriched lessons aimed at improving vocabulary and reading comp (12-week intervention)	Convenience assignment to: – TR: Vocab-enriched lessons – CO: No intervention – n = 150 in Grade 4 – n = 150 in Grade 5 – Pre-post-testing	– Test of knowledge of target words – PPVT – Test of polysemy production – Test of morphology – Test of breadth of knowledge of vocab – Cloze test (comprehension)	Vocabulary: – After 1 yr: TR > CO (ELL) on knowledge of target vocab; no sign diff on PPVT or polysemy – After 2 yrs: TR > CO (ELL) on vocab, polysemy, morphology, and semantic associations for both ELL & Eng L1 gps; no sign diff on PPVT – 2 yr participants = 1 yr participants – Gap btwn Gr 5 ELL and Eng L1 reduced by 40% following treatment – ELL < Eng L1 on all outcome measures in yr 1

| Padron (1992) | Hispanic, bilingual, low income, suburban Southwest | 3, 4, 5 | Direct instruction plus reciprocal teaching or Question-Answer method to promote use of: Question-generating, summarizing, predicting, and clarifying strategies | Random assignment to:
– TR1: Reciprocal teaching of comp strategies (n = 25)
– TR2: Classify comp questions according to how they can be answered (n = 24)
– CO1: Silent reading + answer questions (n = 21)
– CO2: Took RSQ + lesson in social studies (n = 19)
– Pre- post-test | – Reading Strategy Questionnaire (RSQ) – Likert-type scale of 14 strategies: 7 scales negatively related to reading achievement and 7 positively related to reading achievement

Reading Comprehension (cloze):
– After 1 yr: TR = CO (ELL)
– After 2 yrs: TR > CO; 1 yr gp = 2 yr gp
– Gap btwn Grade 5 ELL and Eng L1 students reduced by 45%
– Overall shift from use of weak to use of strong reading strategies from Grade 3 to 4
– TR gps used strong strategies (i.e., summarizing, generating questions) more than CO and used weak strategies (thinking about something else while reading, writing down every word in the story) less than CO gp
– No gp differences on other 10 strategies |

(continued)

TABLE A.4.1 (*continued*)

Authors	Sample Characteristics	Grade	Instructional Method(s)	Research Design	Outcome Measures (partial listing)	Results
Rousseau and Tam (1993)	Hispanic, with speech & language impairment, inner-city metropolitan school	11–12 yrs old	– Keyword and listening previewing methods to enhance reading: Oral decoding and reading comp	– Single subject design with alternating treatments and reversal design (n = 5) – Numeric results but no stat analyses	– Words read correctly – Correct answers to comprehension questions	– Keyword was more effective than preview method – Combined approach was more effective than single approach
Ulanoff and Pucci (1999)	Hispanic, transitional bilingual program	3	– Concurrent Translation and Preview – Review techniques to promote vocabulary acquisition	Random assignment to: – TR_1; Conc. Translation (n = 21) – TR2 = Preview-Review (n = 23) – CO = no treatment (n = 16) – Pre-post testing	– Test of vocabulary – Immediate and delayed recall	– Sign differences: Pre-Review > CO > Translation gp – Concurrent Translation showed worst

TABLE A.4.2 *Summary of Studies on Interactive Instruction*

Authors	Sample Characteristics	Grade	Instructional Method(s)	Research Design	Outcome Measures (partial listing)	Results
Blum et al. (1995)	– ELLs with different L1s – Suburban school in Washington metropolitan area – No L1 reading ability	1	Home-based repeated reading with audio-model	Single subject design with replications – n = 5 – Narrative description	– Weekly oral readings: Oral reading fluency, self-monitoring behavior and motivation – Observation surveys: Letter identification, word recognition, other oral reading behaviors	– All students showed improved reading fluency and accuracy over time – Enhanced frequency of and involvement with reading at home
Calderón, Hertz-Lazarowitz, and Slavin (1998)	Hispanic; Spanish-dominant ELLs	2, 3	Bilingual Cooperative, Integrated Reading and Composition (BCIRC)	Btwn (matched) groups: – TR: (BCIRC) n = 129 – CO: Traditional instruction n = 93	– Grade 2: Texas Assessment of Academic Skills (Sp TAAS): reading and writing – Grade 3: Norm-referenced Assessment Program for Texas (Eng NAPT): reading and writing	Grade 2: – TR > CO on rdg and wtg TAAS Grade 3: – TR > CO Eng reading NAPT – TR = CO on Eng language NAPT – 2 yrs of TR > 1 yr of TR > CO – TR > CO on Grade 3 exit criteria to all-English program

(continued)

155

TABLE A.4.2 (*continued*)

Authors	Sample Characteristics	Grade	Instructional Method(s)	Research Design	Outcome Measures (partial listing)	Results
Cohen and Rodriquez (1980)	Hispanic, low SES, urban	1	Group-oriented (interactive) vs. direct, high intensity (HIL) reading instruction	Random assignment to: – TR1: HIL (approx. n = 75) – TR2: interactive group-oriented instruction (approx. n = 75)	– CTBS: reading comprehension subtest	– TR1 > TR2
Doherty et al. (2003)	– Largely Hispanic – Low income – Low-performing rural school in California	3, 4, 5	Comprehensive program using the Five Standards for Effective Pedagogy; emphasis on interactive pedagogy thru IC	Regression analyses to examine results of students in programs with high vs. low conformity to model – n = 266 students; 15 teachers	– SAT-9: Comprehension, language, reading, spelling, vocabulary, overall NCE	– Higher use of Five Standards reliably predicted gains on SAT: Comp, reading, spelling, and vocab

Study	Grade	Participants	Intervention	Design	Measures	Results
Echevarria (1996)	7, 8, 9	– Hispanic ELLs with learning disabilities, metropolitan Los Angeles	Instructional Conversations (IC)	Within subject, alternating treatment design with 5 IC and 5 BR lessons – Assessed fidelity of implementation – n = 5 (n = 3 for some analyses)	– Amount of academic discourse – Utterances (number of): total, self-initiated scripted (scr) & self-initiated non-scripted (non-scr) – Narratives: Structure, number of propositions – Thematic concept: level of conceptualization of theme – Literal recall – Student participation	– IC > BR on academic discourse, total number of utterances, and self-initiated utterances (scr. and non-scr) – IC > BR on concept understanding – IC = BR on narrative structure and propositions – IC = BR on literal recall – High corr btwn IC implementation and student participation ($r = 0.98$)
Fayden (1997)	K	– Native American and Hispanic, rural – Low SES – Limited exposure to books	Shared reading	Within subject design with pre-post-testing – n = 24	– Clay's Reading Strategies – Sand Test: Elementary knowledge of printed material	– Significant improvement on both tests from pre- to post-test

(*continued*)

Authors	Sample Characteristics	Grade	Instructional Method(s)	Research Design	Outcome Measures (partial listing)	Results
Goldenberg (1992)	– Hispanic ELLs in transition from bilingual to English-only instruction	4	Instructional Conversations	Btwn group: – TR: IC lesson on reading about friendship – CO: Basal lesson on reading about friendship	– Literal comp: responses to 10 open-ended, short-answer questions – Conceptual understanding: essay on friendship	– TR = CO on literal comprehension (75% – 80%) – TR > CO on essay: e.g., reference to complex ideas – TR (62%) vs CO (14%)
Klingner and Vaughn (1996)	Hispanic, urban, middle class, with learning disabilities	7, 8	Reciprocal teaching with cross-age tutoring or cooperative learning to promote reading comprehension	Random assignment to: – TR1: Tutorial gp (n – 13) – TR2: Cooperative gp (n = 13) – Pre- post-testing	– Woodcock Johnson: letter-word identification, passage comprehension – Woodcock Language Proficiency Battery (Span) – LAS (Eng and Span)– Gates-MacGinitie Reading comprehension – Interview: reading strategies	– Sign pre- post-test improvement on rdg comp and strategy use for both gps – No sign differences btwn coop and tutor gps (both interactive) – More improvement during teacher-assisted phase than coop or tutoring phase

Klingner and Vaughn (2000)	5	Hispanic, metropolitan school, Southeast United States	Collaborative strategic reading technique and its effects on vocabulary comprehension and on the use of strategies to help one another understand vocab	Within subject design with pre-post-testing – n = 37 – Stats used for vocab results only	– Vocabulary test (researcher-made); stat analysis – Use of reading strategies and helping behaviors during audiotaped cooperative learning group sessions (narrative analysis)	– Sign pre- post-test gains on vocab – Students spent lots of time engaged in academic-related strategic discussion and assisted one another in understanding word meanings, getting the main idea, asking and answering questions, and relating old knowledge to new knowledge
Kucer (1992)	3	Hispanic, bilingual, working class, metropolitan school	– Cloze texts to teach strategies for comprehending unknown words in text	Single-subject design – n = 6 – Narrative description of post-intervention performance	– Videotapes and field notes of lessons: teacher's understanding of lessons – Literacy artifacts: students' use of strategies – Interviews: students' and teachers' retrospective understanding of lessons	– 93% of students' responses during cloze were contextually appropriate – Students used cloze-based strategies as taught, but did not always explicitly understand purpose of instruction in the same way as the teacher intended

(continued)

TABLE A.4.2 (continued)

Authors	Sample Characteristics	Grade	Instructional Method(s)	Research Design	Outcome Measures (partial listing)	Results
Li and Nes (2001)	– Chinese L1 with ESL instruction – Low Eng reading levels – West Texas, urban	1, 2, 3	Audiotaped paired reading	Single-subject design with pre-post-observation – n = 4 – Narrative description	– Oral reading rate and fluency	– Fluency and accuracy increased over 8 mths of intervention
Martinez-Roldan and Lopez-Robertson (2000)	– Latino, Spanish dominant and English dominant – Tucson, Arizona	2	Literature circles	Narrative description of behavior of Span dominant (n = 8) and Eng dominant (n = 14) students during literature circles	– Children's engagement in and benefits from literature-circle discussions	– Young bilingual children can engage in rich discussion of children's literature
Padron (1992)	– Hispanic, bilingual, low income – Suburban, SW	3, 4, 5	Reciprocal teaching and direct instruction in use of cognitive reading strategies	Random assignment to: – TR (2 gps) – CO (2 gps) – See Table A.4.1 for details – Pre-post-testing	– Reading Strategy Questionnaire	– Shift from use of weak to use of strong reading strategies from Grade 3 to 4 – TR gps used more strong strategies and CO gps used more weak strategies

Saunders and Goldenberg (1999)	– Hispanic (Hisp) ELLs – English-proficient students – Low-performing school; low income	4, 5	Instructional Conversations (IC) and Literature Logs (LL)	Btwn group: ELL and Eng proficient students assigned to: – TR1: IC alone – TR2: LL alone – TR3: IC + LL – CO: Regular instruction	– Factual comprehension of written stories – Interpretive comp of stories – Understanding of story theme: explanation and exemplification	– Factual comp: (LL + IC) = IC > LL = CO for both Eng + Hisp gps – Interpretive comp: (LL + IC) = IC > LL = CO for both gps – Theme explanation: – Eng prof students: (LL + IC) = LL = IC > CO – ELL: (LL + IC) > IC = LL = CO – Theme exemplification: (LL + IC) > IC = LL = CO for all gps
Syvanen (1997)	Hispanic, Spanish-dominant, ESL students	4, 5	Cross-age tutoring; 19-week intervention	Within-subject design with pre-post-testing – n = 16	– MMCPC scale: Perception of control of cognitive/social domains by tutors – District reading achievement test – Survey of attitudes toward school	– No sign diff btwn sample's rdg score gains and gains of sample of district students – Pre- to post-test gains in self-control over tutoring process, and attitudes toward reading – No increase in interest in school and reading achievement

TABLE A.4.3 *Summary of Studies on Process Instruction*

Authors	Sample Characteristics	Grade	Instructional Method(s)	Research Design	Outcome Measures (partial list)	Results
Carger (1993)	Hispanic; emergent readers	K	Book-sharing and pretend reading in groups	Single-subject design - n = 3 - Narrative description	- Engagement in reading - Word and idea counts during audiotaped pretend reading sessions	- Children grew in ability to convey meaning with emotion and confidence - Comfort level with reading also increased
de la Luz Reyes (1991)	Hispanic, Span L1, bilingual students, low to middle SES	6	Use of dialogue journals and literature logs to promote writing	Single-subject design - n = 10 - Narrative description	Analysis of literature logs: - Topics and themes, sensitivity to audience - Self-concept and attitudes - Language use (Span vs. Eng) - Length and quality of writing - Spelling and grammar	- ELLs attempted to write in Eng before they had complete control over language - Development of complex ideas and construction of meaning suffered
Gomez, Parker, and Lara-Alecio (1996)	- Hispanic ELLs, low-achieving, southeast Texas	Summer, Pre-6	Free writing vs. structured writing	Random assignment to: - TR: Structured gp. (3 classes) - CO: Free writing (5 classes) - n = 48	Analysis of writing skills: - Micro-level indicators - Analytic ratings - Holistic ratings	TR > CO on analytic and holistic scores, but few stat sign differences

Kuball and Peck (1997)	K	– Hispanic ELLs and Eng L1s, low income, Los Angeles, urban	Whole language	Btwn group design: – Hispanic (n = 8) – English L1 (n = 8) – Pre-post analysis – Narrative description	– Writing Measures: 8 stages of grapho-phonemic skill development 4 stages of composition skills development – Student Questionnaire: self-concept as writers	Writing of ELLs and Eng L1 students improved over 1 year: # students who viewed themselves as writers, ratings of composition skills, grapho-phonemic skills
Kucer (1995)	3	Hispanic, bilingual, literate in Spanish	Use of wall charts to promote use of reading, reader response, spelling, and writing strategies in whole-language classroom	Single-subject design – n = unstated – Narrative description	– Observations of students' use of strategies during reading and writing	– Exposing students explicitly to alternative strategies through wall charts did not ensure they would apply them during rdg and wtg activities – Motivation is also important

(continued)

TABLE A.4.3 (continued)

Authors	Sample Characteristics	Grade	Instructional Method(s)	Research Design	Outcome Measures (partial list)	Results
Kucer and Silva (1999)	– Hispanic, bilingual, working class, metropolitan area	3	Transitional whole language bilingual class	Within subject design with pre-post-testing – n = 26	– Oral reading and story retelling – Story writing and spelling – Field notes and interviews	– Significant gains in reading, based on miscue analysis – No gains in writing
Martinez-Roldan and Lopez-Robertson (2000)	– Latino, Spanish dominant, and English dominant – Tucson, Arizona	2	Literature circles	Narrative description of behavior of Span dominant (n = 8) and Eng dominant (n = 14) students during literature circles	– Children's engagement in and benefits from literature circle discussions	– Young bilingual children can engage in rich discussion of children's literature
Roser, Hoffman, and Farest (1990)	– Hispanic ELLs, low SES, Brownsville, Texas	K, 1, 2	Shared literature	Convenience assignment to: – TR = Shared reading (6 schools) – CO = 6 control schools in district – Narrative description	– Student/teacher reports on their reactions to program – California Test of Basic Skills: Standardized reading test for 2nd grade (no stat analysis)	– TR had greater 1-yr gains than CO (in percentile points): – Language arts: TR = 10.5 pts; CO = 6.3 pts – Reading: TR = 14 pts; CO = 3 pts – Equivalence btwn TR and CO schools was not determined

Study	Grades	Treatment	Measures	Results
Schon, Hopkins, and Davis (1982)	– Hispanic, low SES, Tempe, Arizona	2, 3, 4	Free reading time with variety of L1 (Span) books — Convenience assignment to: – TR: Free reading with variety of Span books (n = 49) – CO: Usual method of instruction – emphasis on Eng reading (n = 44)	– Inter-America Reading Test: reading comp, vocab, speed subtests – Researcher-developed survey: self-concept and attitudes toward reading	– TR = CO on English reading comp, vocabulary + speed – TR > CO on Span reading – Attitudes of TR students improved
Schon, Hopkins, and Vojir (1984)	Study 1: – Hispanic, low SES, school in affluent area of Tempe, Arizona; Study 2: – Hispanic, low SES, school in middle-income area	9–12	Free reading time with high-interest books in Span L1; Study 1: For Eng results: – TR (n = 64): Enriched reading materials and free reading time – CO (n = 47): Other remedial classes; For affective results: TR (n = 44) vs. CO (n = 44); Study 2: – For Eng results: – TR (n = 18) vs. CO (n = 21) – For affective results: TR (n = 33) vs. CO (28)	Study 1: – Metropolitan Reading Test – Measures of attitudes toward reading and self; Study 2: – Nelson Reading Test – Measures of attitudes toward reading and self	Study 1: TR = CO on Eng reading comprehension; Study 2: TR = CO on Eng reading comprehension

TABLE A.4.4 *Summary of Studies on Language of Instruction*

Authors	Sample Characteristics	Grade	Research Design	Outcome Measures (partial list)	Results
Bacon, Kidd, and Seaberg (1982)	Cherokee ELLs	8	Convenience assignment to: – TR: bilingual program in Grades 1–5 (n = 35) – CO: English-only instruction (n = 18)	SRA Achievement Tests: Reading	TR > CO
Burnham-Massey and Piña (1990)	Hispanic, former LEP students, and English L1 students	1–5, 7–12	Convenience assignment to: – TR: Former LEP who had had reading instruction in Span (n = 117) – CO: Eng L1 students (n = 492) – Longitudinal – No statistical comparisons	– CTBS: Reading and language subtests (Gr. 1–5, 7–8) – Grade point averages (Gr. 9–12) – High School Proficiency Tests (Gr. 9–12)	– TR showed steady increase in CTBS reading and language scores from Gr. 1–5 – Grade 5: TR scored at 50%ile in language & 46%ile in reading – Grade 7/8: TR = CO, scored at 45–56%ile on language but 35–41%ile on reading – Grades 9–12: TR = or > CO (percentage students passing test)
Calderon, Hertz-Lazarowitz, and Slavin (1998)	Hispanic, Spanish dominant, low SES, El Paso, Texas	2, 3	Btwn (matched) groups: – TR: Bilingual cooperative, integrated reading and composition (n = 129)	– Texas Assessment of Academic Skills (Spanish) – English norm-referenced Assessment Program for Texas	– TR > CO English reading – TR = CO on English language – 2-yr TR > 1-yr TR > CO

Study	Population		Design	Measures	Results
			– CO: Cooperative learning without bilingual integrated approach (n = 93)		– TR > CO on Grade 3 exit criteria to all-English program
Carlisle and Beeman (2000)	Hispanic, Span at home (60%), Eng at home (28%), both Eng and Span at home (12%), small town in California	1	Convenience assignment to: – TR (n = 19): Spanish instruction – CO (n = 17): English instruction	– Woodcock-Johnson (Span, Eng): reading, listening, writing	– TR = CO on Eng reading – TR > CO on Span reading – Instruction in Span enhanced Span reading – No effect of instruction in Eng on Eng reading
Ferris and Politzer (1981)	– Hispanic, born in Mexico or in United States – TR < CO on SES – TR > CO on Spanish lang	7, 8	Convenience assignment to: – TR (n = 30): Born and educated in Mexico til Grade 3 – CO (n = 30): Born and educated in United States	– Multiple measures of writing skills: holistic, T-units, error analyses	– CO > TR on verb inflection, verb tense, and pro agreement – TR = CO on all other measures
Friedenberg (1990)	Hispanic, former ESL students, Southern Florida	3, 4	Convenience assignment to: – TR (n = 249): reading instruction in Eng and Span – CO (n = 53): reading instruction in English only	Stanford Achievement Test: reading	TR > CO

(continued)

TABLE A.4.4 (*continued*)

Authors	Sample Characteristics	Grade	Research Design	Outcome Measures (partial list)	Results
Fulton-Scott and Calvin (1983)	Hispanic, 3 Southern California urban schools	1, 6	Convenience assignment to: – TR: Bilingual-multicultural – CO1: Integrated ESL – CO2: Non-integrated ESL (n = approx. 10 students per grade level at each school) – Total n = 59, gp n's not specified	– gpa in reading and language – CTBS	– TR > CO1 and CO2: gpa, CTBS
Gersten and Woodward (1995)	Hispanic, TR and CO equivalent on SES, low level of English on entry, 10 schools in El Paso, Texas	4, 5, 6, 7	Convenience assignment to: – TR: Bilingual immersion (n = 111, 5 schools) – CO: Transitional bilingual (n = 117, 5 schools) – TR and CO schools similar characteristics – Longitudinal	ITBS: Language, reading, and vocabulary	– TR > CO in Grades 4, 5, and 6 on language test – TR = CO in Grade 7 on language – TR > CO in Grade 4 – 5 on rdg and gr 5 on vocab – TR = CO in Grade 7 on rdg and vocab – Both TR and CO scored low

Study	Grades	Sample/Design	Measures	Results
Howard, Christian, and Genesee (in press)	3, 4, 5	– Hispanic, primarily low SES – English L1, primarily middle class – 11 two-way immersion sites in United States Btwn group design: – Span (n = 153–162) – Eng (n = 148–167) – n varies by analysis – Longitudinal design	– Cloze reading test in Span and Eng – Narrative writing samples collected 9 times over 3 years	– Span and Eng students showed improvement in Span and Eng reading and writing from Grades 3 to 5 – Exhibited similar growth curves – Eng gp > Span gp on Eng reading and writing measures at all grade levels (sign.)
Lindholm and Aclan (1991)	1–4	– Spanish L1 – English L1 students – 2 schools in Northern California Two-way Spanish immersion group compared to test norms – total n = 249	CTBS: Reading subtest	– Spanish students approached grade level in English reading by Grade 4 – High proficient bilinguals > medium/low proficient bilinguals
Maldonado (1994)	2, 3	Hispanic, learning disabled, inner city, middle and low SES, Houston, Texas Random assignment to: – TR: Integrated bilingual special education (n = 10) vs. – CO: English-only special education – (n = 10) – Pre-post-analysis	CTBS: Reading and language	– CO > TR at pre-test – TR > CO at post-test

(continued)

Authors	Sample Characteristics	Grade	Research Design	Outcome Measures (partial list)	Results
Mortensen (1984)	Hispanic	4, 5, 6	Convenience assignment to: – TR: Bilingual instruction (n = 65) – CO: Eng only (n = 55)	Wisconsin Design Tests for Reading Skills Development	– TR = CO word attack skills – TR > CO comprehension skills
Ramirez (1992) (*See Chapter 5 for greater details of this study*)	Hispanic ELLs	K – 6 longitudinal	Btwn (matched) group: – TR1: English immersion – TR2: Early-exit bilingual – TR3: Late-exit bilingual – Total n = 2,000	CTBS (Eng): Language and reading subtests	– $TR_1 = TR_2$ on lang and reading tests by Grade 6 – Students in all 3 programs increased Eng lang and reading skills at the same rate from K to Grade 1 and from Grade 1 to Grade 3 – Students in late-exit who were given substantial and consistent L1 instruction increased their rate of Eng lang and rdg skills as fast as or faster than norming gp
Saldate, Mishra, and Medina (1985)	Hispanic, low SES, Arizona	1–3	Convenience assignment to: – TR: Bilingual Program (n = 30) – CO: Eng only program (n = 31)	– MAT: Eng or Span (Grade 2) – WRAT: Reading, Eng, or Sp. (Grade 3)	– TR = CO in Grade 2 – TR > CO in Grade 3

TABLE A.4.5. *Summary of Studies of Family Influences*

Authors	Sample Characteristics	Grade	Research Design	Outcome Measures (partial listing)	Results
Blum et al. (1995)	ELLs with diverse L1s, no L1 reading ability, suburban school in metropolitan Washington	1	Single-subject, reversal design ABA with multiple baselines - n = 5 - Narrative description	Weekly oral reading: - Oral reading fluency, self-monitoring behavior, and motivation <u>Marie Clay observation survey:</u> - Letter identification, word recognition, hearing and recording sounds in words, and oral reading behavior	- Use of audio-recordings at home during reading enhanced reading performance - Students expressed preference for audiotape method
Buriel and Cardoza (1988)	1st, 2nd, and 3rd generation Mexican American students, U.S. Southwest	9+	Within-subject design with regression analysis Between-subject: 1st vs. 2nd vs. 3rd generation - n = 103–37 depending on analysis	- Standardized test of reading and vocabulary	- L1 home use was unrelated to reading in 1st generation; modest relationship in 2nd generation; moderate and mixed relationship with 3rd generation - SES unrelated to reading in 1st and 2nd generation and only moderately related in 3rd generation

(continued)

TABLE A.4.5. (*continued*)

Authors	Sample Characteristics	Grade	Research Design	Outcome Measures (partial listing)	Results
Duran and Weffer (1992)	Top 25% of high school grads (talented), Mexican American, large midwestern city	10	Within-subject design with regression analyses – n = 157	– American College Testing: reading subtest – GPA	– Yrs in United States had significant effect on pre-high school reading – Family values did not affect reading ach. directly but did affect ach. through classroom-related behaviors
Hansen (1989)	Mexican American, greater San Francisco, inner city, residential urban, and suburban settings	2, 5	Within-subject design with regression analyses – n = 117	– Stanford Diagnostic Reading Test: comprehension & auditory vocabulary subtests	– Auditory vocabulary grew during summer, but text comprehension did not – Peer language use during summer was related to auditory vocabulary gains
Hughes, Schumm, and Vaughn (1999)	Hispanic parents of learning disabled and average to high average readers	3–5	Btwn group: – parents of LD children (n = 40) – Parents of children with average or above-average reading skills – n = 40	– Types of reading & writing activities at home – Desirability & feasibility of activities – Facilitators & barriers to helping children read at home	– Few differences between parent groups – Most common activity was reading to children or having child read to parents – Parents valued home reading but parents of LD children found it difficult to help them – Most common barrier – lack of communication with school

Study	Population/Context	Grade/Age	Design/Sample	Measures	Findings
Ima and Rumbaut (1989)	Southeast Asian (SE) LEP & FEP ELLs, San Diego school district	7–12	Btwn group: – LEP ELLs – FEP ELLs – n = 239 – Numeric results but no stat analyses	– CTBS: reading, language – GPA	– SES did not distinguish between LEP and FEP SE Asian students – Students whose parents had more education pre-migration scored higher on reading than students whose parents had less education at pre-migration
Jackson and Wen-Hui (1992)	Precocious ELL readers & precocious Eng L1 readers, mixed L1 backgrounds, urban & suburban settings in the Pacific Northwest	K, 1	Btwn group: – Precocious ELL readers (n = 12) – Precocious English L1 readers (n = 12)	– 9 measures of reading: spelling, pseudo-word reading, word reading, oral reading (speed, accuracy); poem reading, silent reading, PIAT reading comprehension (& others)	– The precocious ELL readers were similar to monolingual precocious readers: all frequently had someone read to them, discussing the pictures in the book, pointing out letters and words, and explaining the meanings of words; all also had someone identify numbers for them, and most had been helped to identify letter names, spell words, and understand word meanings – All had attended some kind of pre-school – All of their parents reported that the children read at home at least 2 or 3 times a week

(continued)

TABLE A.4.5. (*continued*)

Authors	Sample Characteristics	Grade	Research Design	Outcome Measures (partial listing)	Results
Kennedy and Park (1994)	Asian and Mexican American (AM), diverse backgrounds	8	Btwn group: – Asian Am (n = 1131) – Mexican American (n = 1952) – Within ethnic group design with regression analyses	– Self-reported English course grades – Standardized reading test scores	– Mex Am: home language use was not related to reading, but SES was; self-control & educational expectations were also significantly related to reading – Asian Am: home language use & SES were related to reading; social psychological variables were also significant
Pucci and Ulanoff (1998)	Hispanic, proficient and less proficient ELL readers, Los Angeles	4	Btwn group: – Proficient readers (n = 12) – Less proficient readers (n = 11) – Stats for cloze test	– Self-report measures of behavior related to reading – Cloze reading test	– Proficient readers had more books in home, enjoyed reading more, & felt they were proficient readers than less proficient readers

Study	Population	Grade	Design	Measures	Findings
Reese et al. (2000)	Latino, low SES, Los Angeles	K–7	Within-subject design – Longitudinal – n = 121 – Path analysis	– Standardized reading test in Grade 7 (CTBS) – Parent interview/survey about family characteristics, demographics, aspirations & expectations, role of parents in education of child, and other factors – Grade at transition to English-only instruction	– Parental SES was significant predictor of English reading – Family literacy practices & grandparents' level of education also predicted students' reading – ELL's success in learning to read Eng did not depend exclusively on L1 input – K. ELLs with greater emergent Spanish literacy and Eng oral proficiency were faster to transition to Eng reading & attained higher levels of English reading proficiency in middle school
Thomas and Collier (2002) *See Table 5 for details*					
Tompkins, Abramson, and Pritchard (1999)	ELLs with different L1s – English L1 students, in low- vs. high-income schools, Central California	3, 4	Btwn group: – low SES schools – high SES schools – total n = 60 – statistical & qualitative analyses	– Journal entries: spelling	– Students in more affluent school used more conventional spelling patterns than students in low SES school

5

Academic Achievement

Kathryn Lindholm-Leary and Graciela Borsato

INTRODUCTION

Academic achievement broadly refers to the communicative (oral, reading, writing), mathematical, science, social science, and thinking skills and competencies that enable a student to succeed in school and society. Because these forms of achievement are difficult to assess, most researchers have relied on a more narrow definition that is largely limited to outcomes on standardized achievement tests. In this chapter, academic achievement refers to content-area achievement as measured in English mathematics, science, or social studies (e.g., history, geography); it does not cover the content areas of English language arts (addressed in Chapter 4), foreign language or other humanities (music, art, theater), or cognition (except as it specifically relates to science or mathematics problem solving). The topic of reading achievement is included if the outcome measure is a standardized test and the study assesses reading and mathematics achievement of one or more educational programs. While many of the studies included in this chapter assess academic achievement by means of standardized achievement tests, others use general measures of school attainment, such as grade point average (GPA), high school drop-out rates, and attitudes toward school and school-related topics.

The academic achievement of ethnic and language minority students has received considerable attention especially as it relates to the underachievement of Hispanics, African Americans, Native Americans, and ELLs. This chapter examines only ELLs and does not consider research on the achievement of Hispanic, Asian-American, or other ethnic minority or immigrant students, except as the samples and results pertain to ELLs. As well, studies that focused only on achievement in Spanish and had no outcome measures in English were excluded.

This corpus of research is summarized in terms of the following themes that were identified from our initial review of these studies:

- Program Issues
- Language Influences on Academic Achievement
- Instructional Issues
- Family and Learner Background Factors
- Assessment Issues

PROGRAM ISSUES

Research on the academic achievement of ELLs consists primarily of evaluations of various program models. Much of this work addresses policy issues relating to the best way to educate ELLs. These studies fall into two distinct groups: (1) evaluation studies (n = 16) that compare student outcomes on standardized tests of mathematics (and often reading) achievement across different program types, usually bilingual versus something else (no program, Structured English Immersion [SEI]/English as a Second Language [ESL], or two different bilingual models); and (2) evaluation studies (n = 8) describing student progress in a particular program type, with outcomes related to standardized achievement tests in mathematics, science, and social studies, GPA, or high school completion/drop out, or various school-related attitudes. Most studies (n = 12) concentrate on students in elementary school. Five studies focused on high school students to determine the influence of participation in a bilingual program during elementary school on their current high school achievement. Studies at the high school level also often examined GPA, high school drop-out or retention rates, and attitudes. There were an additional six longitudinal studies that followed students through elementary school into middle school or high school and one retrospective study.

Comparative Evaluation Studies

The central issue in the debate on the education of ELLs has been whether research demonstrates educational benefits of bilingual or other educational programs specifically designed for ELLs over mainstream English education. Numerous reviews of the research literature have been conducted; some reviews have concluded that bilingual programs are ineffective and others that bilingual education is more effective than English immersion approaches (August and Hakuta, 1997). The comparative evaluation studies reported here were typically conducted to answer the following two policy-related questions: (1) "Is a language education program designed for ELLs better than no specially designed program (i.e., mainstream English)?", and (2) "Which type of program designed for ELLs leads to better academic outcomes?" Some studies addressed only one of these questions and some investigations tackled both. This section summarizes the empirical evidence from these studies according to these two questions; see Table A.5.1 for summaries of the studies.

Question #1: How Effective Are Programs Designed for ELLs in Comparison to Mainstream Programs? Beginning in the 1980s, research was undertaken to address the policy-related question: Is bilingual education as effective as mainstream education in promoting the academic achievement and English language proficiency of ELLs? These studies were designed to compare the academic achievement of ELLs in bilingual education programs with that of their English-speaking peers in English-only programs. In most of these studies, comparison students were similar in their ethnic background (mostly Hispanic; Franco-American in one case) and socioeconomic status (mostly low-income). Results varied according to the grade level of the students in the sample, the type of program they were in, and the language and subject area (reading, mathematics) of assessment. In the aggregate, these studies found that students who had received bilingual instruction performed at grade level usually by the fifth grade, and they scored at least comparable to if not higher than their English-speaking peers or their ELL peers who were in mainstream English classes with no specialized instruction.

As Table A.5.1 shows, there were fifteen studies in this group; five were conducted in the mid-1980s and ten between 1990 and 2002. In this group of studies, a wide range of grades was represented, from Grades 1 to 3 to Grades 7 to 12. In all but six studies (Cazabon, Nicoladis, and Lambert, 1998; de la Garza and Medina, 1985; Gersten and Woodward, 1995; Lindholm, 1991; Ramirez, 1992; Thomas and Collier, 2002), there was little or no description of what bilingual instruction entailed, except to indicate that the curriculum was common across the two programs being compared. Even when the bilingual program was described, the treatment, if any, that the comparison group received was not always clear (Cazabon, Lambert, and Hall, 1993; Lindholm, 1991). It was also unclear in many of these studies how long the students had participated in the bilingual program. For example, in Curiel, Rosenthal, and Richek's (1986) study, students in the bilingual group were in the program for *at least* one year. Thus, these students could have received one, two, three, or possibly more years of bilingual education. Yet, several studies clearly show that the amount of time students participate in a program has a significant impact on their achievement (Curiel et al., 1986; Gersten and Woodward, 1995).

None of these studies used random assignment; three studies matched students according to nonverbal intelligence (Cazabon et al., 1993; Cazabon et al., 1998; Saldate, Mishra, and Medina, 1985), and two for student or other characteristics, such as same school or district, ethnicity, social class, program duration (Medrano, 1988), along with birthplace and education of parents, gender, and family structure (Curiel et al., 1986).

In most investigations, comparison groups did not include students who were individually matched to students in the treatment group. The students in most studies were similar in ethnicity, grade level, and social-class background, except for Burnham-Massey and Piña (1990), who did not specify the backgrounds of the students included in the comparison group. Sample sizes were respectable (subjects per group ranged from forty to five hundred) in all but de la Garza and Medina's (1985), Fulton-Scott and Calvin's (1983), and Saldate et al.'s (1985) (n = 20–31 per group) research. Thirteen of the fifteen studies used standardized achievement test scores in English to assess student outcomes (except Curiel et al., 1986, and Lindholm-Leary and Borsato, 2001).

With respect to reading achievement assessed in English, only one school site in one study reported that bilingually instructed students performed more poorly than English monolingual comparison students (see Table A.5.1). Specifically, Alanis (2000) reported that Grade 5 ELLs in two-way immersion (TWI) programs score significantly lower than EO peers in reading achievement at one school site; at the other school site she examined, however, TWI students performed significantly higher in reading. In four of the remaining studies, bilingually instructed students scored at levels *equivalent* to the English-only comparison groups in reading at the final grade level in which comparisons were made (Burnham-Massey and Piña, 1990; Cazabon et al., 1998; de la Garza and Medina, 1985; Medrano, 1986). In two studies representing three school sites, students who were educated through their first language significantly *outperformed* monolingually educated comparison students in reading (Saldate et al., 1985; Thomas and Collier, 2002).

With respect to mathematics achievement, bilingually instructed students in four of the studies (Alanis, 2000; Cazabon, Nicoladis, and Lambert, 1998; Medrano, 1986; Saldate et al., 1985) and in one school site in each of Alanis' (2000) and Thomas and Collier's (2002, Site #2 in Table 1) investigations scored higher than English mainstream students in English math by the final grade level included in the study. Two studies and one school site in another study reported that students in the bilingual program scored at the same level as comparison group students (Burnham-Massey and Piña, 1990; de la Garza and Medina, 1985; Thomas and Collier, 2002, Site #1). Bilingually instructed students scored significantly lower than their English-only peers in only one school site in one study (Alanis, 2000).

Longitudinal and retrospective studies that have assessed high school students who had been in bilingual programs in elementary school have also yielded results favoring bilingual programs. Burnham-Massey and Piña (1990) report an initial lag in performance on the CTBS reading, language, and mathematics subtests for students in transitional bilingual education (TBE), but found that they caught up to their English-only peers by Grade 5 and surpassed them in mathematics (but scored comparably in reading) by Grades 7 and 8 (see Table A.5.1). By Grade 11, all students who have previously been in TBE passed the high school state-level proficiency subtests. Similar results favoring bilingual programs were obtained in a study by Curiel et al. (1986), who matched Grades 7 to 10 students on several background characteristics: gender, birthplace of mother/father, dual/single-parent family, parental education, and father's occupation. They report that ELLs who had participated in a bilingual program in elementary school had higher GPAs and attendance and a lower high school drop-out rate than EO Hispanic students who had been in an English mainstream program during elementary school. The longer the ELLs had had bilingual instruction, the more positive were their results. Thomas and Collier (2002) and Lindholm-Leary and Borsato (2001) also report lower dropout rates for ELLs who had received bilingual instruction in comparison to ELLs in mainstream English classes.

Only one investigation compared the achievement of ELLs in a bilingual program and ELLs who had had ESL instruction to that of ELLs who had not participated in a specially designed program (i.e., mainstream English-only classes) (Thomas and Collier, 2002). In their large-scale study of four school districts providing specialized instruction to ELLs, Thomas and Collier (2002) found that, by the end of high school, ELLs who had been in mainstream classes and had received no special services scored the lowest in mathematics and reading measured in English and had the highest dropout rates in high school compared to students who had had any other type of special services (SEI/ESL, bilingual, two-way).

These studies have been discussed with respect to student performance in different program types. However, the question remains whether the students achieved at grade level. As Table A.5.1 indicates, the bilingually instructed students scored at least at grade level by the final grade in which they were assessed in English math and reading in five studies (Burnham-Massey and Piña, 1990; Cazabon et al., 1998; de la Garza and Medina, 1985; Fulton-Scott and Calvin, 1983; Medrano, 1986). Students scored average (or close to average) in math but not reading in two studies (Cazabon et al., 1993; Lindholm, 1991). In one evaluation (Thomas and Collier, 2002), student achievement varied by school site and program type, with the bilingually instructed students in the French/English immersion program performing at grade level. At the second school site, ELLs in the TBE program scored at grade level; those in the ESL program scored below grade level; and the mainstream ELLs scored very low. In Gersten and Woodward's (1995) study, the TBE and structured English immersion groups scored below average in language and very low in reading and vocabulary. In five studies (Alanis, 2000; Curiel et al., 1986; Lindholm-Leary and Borsato, 2001; Ramirez, 1992; Saldate et al., 1985), either no achievement data were reported or students' level of performance was not clear.

In the five investigations in which there was information about Spanish achievement, students scored at or above grade level in two studies (de la Garza and Medina, 1985; Thomas and Collier, 2002, Site #2); (slightly) below grade level in two other studies utilizing the same subjects (Cazabon et al., 1993; Cazabon et al., 1998); or slightly below average in reading but slightly above average in math (Lindholm, 1991).

In summary, the question posed in this section can be answered as follows. Programs that are specially designed for ELLs promote at least EQUIVALENT and sometimes HIGHER outcomes than a mainstream EO class. However, if the comparison between a bilingual/ESL/SEI program and no program/English mainstream is made in the early years of a child's education (Grades K-2), it would appear that ELLs in mainstream programs have an advantage. The extant research also clearly shows that by the late elementary grades and particularly in middle and high school grades, ELLs who have received some specialized instruction, particularly first-language instruction, catch up to and sometimes surpass their comparison peers. They score at grade level and are less likely to drop out of high school. ELLs who had not been in any specialized program but participated in mainstream English classes scored the lowest in comparison to students in any other program and ended their schooling with low levels of achievement.

Question #2a: Which Model Leads to Higher Academic Outcomes: Bilingual or ESL or SEI? Ramirez and his colleagues conducted a congressionally mandated four-year longitudinal study of more than two thousand elementary school ELLs with Spanish language backgrounds (Ramirez, Yuen, and Ramey, 1991, reported in Ramirez, 1992). The research question in this federally sponsored project was: "Which of three alternative instructional programs designed to meet the needs of Spanish-speaking LEP students helped them to 'catch-up' to their English-speaking peers?" The three program alternatives were structured English immersion, early-exit (or TBE), and late-exit bilingual programs. Schools representing the three models but not individual students were carefully matched so that the major characteristic that distinguished one program from another was the amount of L1 instruction provided the students. Students were given norm-referenced standardized achievement tests, and the Trajectory Analysis of Matched Percentiles (TAMP) was used to examine the extent to which students closed the gap with English speakers and made growth toward grade-level achievement. Ramirez's study is one of the few studies that described the instructional model and observed the implementation of the model under investigation.

Ramirez (1992) reports that the late-exit bilingual program produced superior outcomes compared to the SEI program, but there were no significant differences between the SEI and early-exit (or TBE) bilingual

approaches. The study concludes that providing almost exclusive instruction in English does not accelerate ELLs' acquisition of English but may
cause them to fall behind; rather, providing ELLs with substantial instruction in Spanish may assist them in catching up to their English-speaking
peers in English reading, language, and math. Ramirez also reports that
the better the implementation of the model, the stronger were the results
favoring primary-language instruction.

Collier (1992) reanalyzed Ramirez's data using normal curve equivalents rather than TAMP analysis and confirmed the results reported by
Ramirez. She reports but does not provide data to show that by the end
of Grade 3, students who received no L1 support were beginning to fall
behind, whereas students who were given some L1 support (early-exit)
kept pace with the norm group, though they were not catching up. Only
the late-exit group was able to make greater growth than the norm group
and achieve at grade level. These students were scoring at the 45th NCE
in English reading and the 51st NCE in English math.

Ten years after the Ramirez and Collier reports, Thomas and Collier
(2002) released the results of a large-scale study with mostly native Spanish-
speaking ELLs. Their sample included four research sites representing
rural and urban school districts and different types of language education program options for ELLs. Data were collected for students who were
identified as ELL in Grade 1 through the highest grade they had reached
by the time the study terminated. The students had to have participated
in the same program for a minimum of four years. Thus, they assembled
longitudinal data for a large sample of ELLs, including two samples of high
school students. Their results revealed that ELLs enrolled in SEI/ESL programs scored lower in mathematics and reading achievement measured
in English and had higher school dropout rates compared to students in
bilingual or two-way programs.

Twenty years earlier, Fulton-Scott and Calvin (1983) had reported similar findings in a small study of students in a bilingual/bicultural program versus a nonintegrated ESL program (ELLs were segregated in ESL
classes) or an integrated ESL program (ELLs received an ESL program
and integrated with their English-speaking peers). Fulton-Scott and Calvin
report that the Grade 6 students who had received bilingual instruction
achieved at a higher level than ELLs who had received ESL, though the
difference was statistically significant only for the comparison between students receiving bilingual instruction versus those receiving nonintegrated
ESL instruction.

In the only study to report contrary findings, Gersten and Woodward
(1995) assessed the achievement of ELLs in Grades 4 to 7 of a TBE program
in comparison to that of ELLs in a SEI program (which they called "bilingual immersion"). The sample included only ELLs who had begun their
respective programs in Grade 1 and continued in the program until they

were eligible for mainstream instruction. This so-called bilingual immersion (structured English immersion) program included four years during which Spanish was used for 30 to 60 minutes per day. Gersten and Woodward reported that "overall, the data show a consistent pattern. In the fourth grade, bilingual immersion [SEI] students demonstrated superior academic performance in all areas assessed. Over time, differences between the two groups decreased" (p. 232). In other words, they found differences in Grade 4 right around the time TBE students were transitioning to English, but those differences diminished across Grades 5 to 7, and by Grade 7 there were no statistically significant differences between the two groups. A comparison of growth by group revealed that the TBE students made more progress (growth of 5.2 NCEs) than the SEI students (growth of 2.4 NCEs), though this difference was not statistically significant. Over the four-year time period of the study, results from Tukey post hoc tests showed significant differences in opposite directions for the two groups: the total language scores of the SEI students decreased, while the scores of the TBE students increased. The vocabulary scores remained constant for the SEI students from Grades 4 to 7 while they increased slightly (3.1 NCEs) from Grades 4 to 7 for the TBE students; this group difference was not statistically significant.

Question #2b: Which Bilingual Model Leads to Higher Academic Outcomes: Early Exit or Late Exit? Several studies have compared the early-exit program model to the late-exit model to determine whether the greater enrichment and longer duration of L1 instruction in late-exit programs have a positive, neutral, or negative effect on student academic achievement. A relevant policy question here is whether one can deliver a short-term program or whether the program must be longer in duration for ELLs to demonstrate positive outcomes. Table A.5.1 provides details about the research methodologies and outcomes of the studies discussed in this section.

While Ramirez (1992), in his four-year longitudinal study, did not specifically report whether late-exit programs yielded higher outcomes than early-exit programs, Collier's (1992) reanalysis of Ramirez's data did show higher achievement on the part of students in late-exit programs compared to early-exit programs. Similarly, Thomas and Collier (2002) report that late-exit (including two-way) bilingual programs promote higher levels of reading and mathematics achievement than early-exit (transitional) programs.

As Table A.5.1 indicates, five studies examined ELLs in two-way programs in comparison to ELLs in early-exit/TBE programs with respect to their performance on standardized tests in English reading and math and their attitudes (Cazabon et al., 1993; Cazabon et al., 1998; Lindholm, 1991; Lindholm-Leary and Borsato, 2001; Thomas and Collier, 2002). At the K-2 grade levels, there was either no difference between early-exit and two-way immersion programs or a difference favoring early-exit programs (Cazabon et al., 1993; Lindholm; 1991). However, these same studies consistently reported standardized test results, attitudes, and enrollment in higher-level math courses favoring two-way programs over early exit/TBE programs by Grade 3 (Cazabon et al., 1993), Grade 5 (Thomas and Collier, 2002, Site #2), and at high school levels (Cazabon et al., 1998; Lindholm-Leary and Borsato, 2001).

Ramirez (1992) examined late-exit programs to determine whether student outcomes were better for programs that used more Spanish in the later grades in comparison to programs that used more English in the later grades. His results showed that students in the school with the greatest use of Spanish and those in the school that used the most English ended Grade 6 with comparable levels of skills in English language and reading. However, with respect to mathematics achievement, Grade 6 ELLs in the two late-exit schools that used more Spanish showed greater gains in achievement than students at the site that had higher levels of English instruction at the later grade levels even though both groups of students had comparable scores in Grade 1. That is, there was a difference in achievement gains when these models were compared with respect to the amount of Spanish instruction in the curriculum. ELLs at the late-exit school that moved abruptly into English instruction (similar to early-exit programs) showed a marked decline in their growth in mathematics relative to the norming population. In contrast, ELLs in the late-exit program (particularly at the site that was most faithful to the late-exit instructional model) showed "continued acceleration in the rate of growth, which is as fast or faster than the norming population. That is, late-exit students appeared to be gaining on students in the general population" (p. 25).

In sum, comparisons of ELLs in different program types indicate that students who received some type of specialized program (TBE, TWI, ESL) scored higher in reading and math than students who received no specialized program in mainstream English classrooms. Also, ELLs who received some specialized program were able to catch up to and, in some studies, surpass the achievement levels of their peers who were educated in English-only mainstream classrooms. This research also indicates that students who participated in programs with longer exposure to L1 instruction (two-way, late-exit) outperformed students who received short-term exposure (early-exit/TBE). If we consider the interim results for Grades K-2 (and sometimes 3), we find that bilingually instructed students either score at lower levels initially than comparison students and perform at similar levels in higher grades, or they score equivalently in grades K-2 and then outperform comparison-group peers in later grades. This pattern of results is also evident for other measures of achievement: GPA, school completion, attitudes toward school, and college preparation. The lower scores in the initial grades may account for the popular *mis*perception that bilingual education is an ineffective means for educating ELLs.

Descriptive Studies

Several studies have examined and described specific forms of bilingual programs; these studies are summarized in Table A.5.2. The program model that has been examined most often is two-way immersion. These studies have all shown that two-way programs were effective in helping ELLs achieve at or above grade-level in their L1 and progress toward grade-level achievement or above in English by middle school. In some of these studies, the focus was on students' motivation and attitudes toward learning (Lambert and Cazabon, 1994; Lindholm-Leary, 2001; Lindholm-Leary and Borsato, 2001). The results from these studies have shown that ELLs were developing positive attitudes toward themselves as learners and toward school. Almost all high school students in two-way programs responded that they had no intention of dropping out; they wanted to attend a four-year college and they planned to attend a four-year college right after high school (Lindholm-Leary and Borsato, 2001).

Seven of these eight studies include results from standardized achievement tests in reading and math (de Jong, 2002; Kirk-Senesac, 2002; Lambert and Cazabon, 1994; Lindholm, 1988; Lindholm-Leary, 2001; Lindholm and Aclan, 1991; Lindholm and Fairchild, 1989) and four included measures of attitudes (Lambert and Cazabon, 1994; Lindholm, 1988; Lindholm-Leary, 2001; Lindholm-Leary and Borsato, 2001). Three of the studies included samples of high school students who had or were currently participating in a two-way program (Kirk-Senesac, 2002; Lindholm-Leary, 2001; Lindholm-Leary and Borsato, 2001). Most of these studies provide a description of the two-way model they were studying. Both 90:10 and 50:50 models of two-way immersion were represented in these studies at both elementary and high school levels.

These studies consistently show that students score very low in English reading in the early grades and progress toward grade-level performance by later elementary or high school. They also show that students who had developed high levels of proficiency in both languages were more successful at closing the achievement gap in reading with the norming group by Grade 4 than students with lower levels of bilingual proficiency (Kirk-Senesac, 2002; Lambert and Cazabon, 1994; Lindholm-Leary, 2001; Lindholm and Aclan, 1991). With respect to math achievement, all studies showed that although the students under evaluation had begun elementary school with low to below average NCEs, they scored average to above average in English math by Grades 4 to 6, depending on the study (de Jong, 2002; Kirk-Senesac, 2002; Lindholm and Aclan, 1991; Lindholm and Fairchild, 1989). The participating students also typically met district or state proficiency standards (de Jong, 2002; Kirk-Senesac, 2002) and scored above district and state averages for ELLs (de Jong, 2002; Lindholm-Leary, 2001).

Three other studies examined students' attitudes (Lambert and Cazabon, 1994; Lindholm-Leary, 2001; Lindholm-Leary and Borsato, 2001). These studies found that ELLs had positive perceptions of their academic competence, bilingualism, and the two-way program itself (Lambert and Cazabon, 1994; Lindholm-Leary, 2001; Lindholm-Leary and Borsato, 2001). Lindholm-Leary and Borsato (2001) found that the majority of ELLs were enrolled in college-bound math courses and only 3 percent in basic math. Further, most of the students felt that they would not drop out of school; they wanted to go to college; they would go to college after high school; and they thought that getting good grades was important. Almost half of the students felt that the two-way program kept them from dropping out of school and that they were academically outperforming their peers who had also started school as ELLs.

The results of these descriptive studies are similar to those presented in the previous section on comparative studies. That is, students who received instruction through their L1 closed the achievement gap with native English speakers and exceeded the performance of their ELL peers in the district (descriptive studies) or in comparison groups (comparative studies). In addition, ELLs demonstrated positive attitudes toward the program, themselves as learners, school, and other cultures and languages.

Other Program Factors

There has been extensive research in mainstream schools on the characteristics of effective schools and programs. These studies demonstrate consistently and conclusively that schools with high quality programs have a cohesive school-wide vision, shared goals that define their expectations for achievement, a clear instructional focus on and commitment to achievement, and high expectations (Berman et al., 1995; Corallo and McDonald, 2002; Gándara, 1995; Goldenberg and Sullivan, 1994; Levine and Lezotte, 1995; Marzano, 2003; Montecel and Cortez, 2002; Reyes, Scribner, and Paredes Scribner, 1999; Slavin and Calderón, 2001; Teddle and Reynolds, 2000; Tikunoff, 1985; U.S. Department of Education, 1998). The importance of these characteristics has been found in studies of mainstream schools (e.g., Levine and Lezotte, 1995; Marzano, 2003), low-performing schools (Corallo and McDonald, 2002; Reyes et al., 1999), and bilingual programs serving ELLs (e.g., Berman et al., 1995; Montecel and Cortez, 2002; Slavin and Calderon, 2001; Tikunoff, 1985).

We identified eleven studies that examined program factors associated with effective schooling for ELLs (Battistich et al., 1997; Berman et al., 1995; Doherty et al., 2003; Fulton-Scott and Calvin, 1983; Lucas et al., 1990;

Mehan et al., 1991; Mehan et al., 1994; Montecel and Cortez, 2002; Ramirez, 1992; Tellez, 1998; Tikunoff, 1985). Two were large-scale federally funded studies (Berman et al., 1995; Tikunoff, 1985) and one was a small-scale study that examined the features common to "exemplary" programs that aimed to promote high achievement among ELLs (Montecel and Cortez, 2002). Yet other studies looked at the importance of school reform (Goldenberg and Sullivan, 1994; Minicucci, 1996) or adherence to standards (Doherty et al., 2003) in promoting academic success among ELLs. Finally, three studies assessed the effects of integration and "untracking" on high school students' achievement (Fulton-Scott and Calvin, 1983; Mehan et al., 1991; Mehan et al., 1994). Aggregating across this corpus of research, programs that were relatively effective shared the following characteristics:

- Educational personnel shared the belief that "all children can learn" (Lucas et al., 1990; Tikunoff, 1985).
- There was a positive school environment; that is, one that was orderly and safe, had a warm and caring community, and facilitated learning (Battistich et al., 1997; Berman et al., 1995; Montecel and Cortez, 2002).
- There was a curriculum that was meaningful and academically challenging, incorporated higher-order thinking (Berman et al., 1995; Doherty et al., 2003; Montecel and Cortez, 2002; Ramirez, 1992; Tikunoff, 1985), was thematically integrated (Montecel and Cortez, 2002), and established a clear alignment with standards and assessment (Doherty et al., 2003; Montecel and Cortez, 2002).
- The program model was grounded in sound theory and best practices associated with an enriched, not remedial, instructional model (e.g., Montecel and Cortez, 2002).
- This enriched model was consistent and sustained over time (Ramirez, 1992). Tellez (1998) examined the program placement of close to eleven thousand ELLs in Grades K-3 and found that one fourth of the students participated in different program types (as many as three different program types in four years). He reported that the greater the assortment of programs in which an individual student participated, the lower was the student's level of achievement. However, he did not provide empirical data to support this claim.
- Teachers in high quality bilingual programs understood theories about bilingualism and second-language development as well as the goals and rationale for the model in which they were teaching (Berman et al., 1995; Montecel and Cortez, 2002).

Fulton-Scott and Calvin (1983) found that bilingual/bicultural and integrated ESL programs in which ELLs were integrated with English-proficient students yielded higher achievement test scores and GPAs than a segregated ESL program that provided limited opportunities for ELLs to interact with English-proficient students. These results are consistent with other studies that have shown that achievement levels of ELLs are higher when they participate in programs that are noncompensatory in nature and that accord them equal status with other students (Berman et al., 1995; Mehan et al., 1991; Mehan et al., 1994; Montecel and Cortez, 2002).

These findings on effective programs for ELLs are consistent with research on effective schools for mainstream students. Both bodies of research show that students, be they mainstream or ELLs, are more academically successful when they attend schools that provide positive learning environments that integrate rather than segregate students and that include a challenging curriculum for all students. Programs serving ELLs are more successful when they are based on sound theory; when teachers understand the program model in which they are teaching and the research-based principles of second-language development that undergird that model; and when students are placed in a consistent and sustained program.

LANGUAGE INFLUENCES ON ACADEMIC ACHIEVEMENT

Previous research on bilingualism, which is not part of the present database, has shown that students with high levels of bilingual proficiency exhibit elevated levels of academic and cognitive functioning in comparison to students with less well-developed bilingual skills (August and Hakuta, 1997). A similar conclusion can be drawn from a review of studies in the present database, which we review in this section. Moreover, it would appear that there is a developmental interconnectedness among language proficiency, literacy, and content skills within and across languages for ELLs.

We identified five studies that examined the influence of oral language proficiency in both L1 and English on math achievement (Fernandez and Nielsen, 1986; Lindholm-Leary, 2001; Lindholm-Leary and Aclan, 1991; Nielsen and Lerner, 1986; Rumberger and Larson, 1998). These studies are consistent in showing that bilingual students with high levels of proficiency in both languages had higher levels of academic achievement than comparison students who were monolingual. For example, Fernandez and Nielsen (1986) used the first wave of the High School and Beyond database (1980), a longitudinal study of U.S. high school seniors and sophomores, to examine the relationship of bilingualism to academic achievement (educational expectations, and vocabulary, reading, and math achievement). They compared the academic performance of Hispanic bilingual (n = 1876), Hispanic English monolingual, Euro-American bilingual, and Euro-American English monolingual students. Proficiency in *both* English and the other language was positively related to achievement for both bilingual groups (Hispanic bilingual and Euro-American bilingual). More specifically, the bilingual Hispanics significantly outperformed their English monolingual

Hispanic peers in achievement. Nielsen and Lerner also found that frequent use of the non-English language was negatively associated with achievement. This finding could be interpreted to mean that the students who frequently used Spanish lacked sufficient proficiency in English to use that language more frequently. If this is true, it would reinforce the link between bilingualism and academic achievement insofar as this latter group of students would be classified as nonproficient bilinguals. Nielsen and Lerner did not define "bilingual" precisely and, indeed, it would appear that it referred to the students' exposure to and not necessarily their proficiency in another language in the home. Nonetheless, this research suggests that advanced levels of proficiency in two languages may confer advantages on academic achievement.

Rumberger and Larson (1998) examined the educational achievement of Grades 7 and 9 Latino students. About 40 percent were identified as current ELLs, 30 percent as monolingual English speakers (EO), and 30 percent as students who had entered school as ELLs with Spanish as their home language but were redesignated as FEP speakers. Their results showed that compared to the EO or ELL students, the FEP students had higher grades and lower transiency rates, were more likely to be on track with their high school credits, and showed greater educational commitment. Particularly noteworthy was the finding that the FEP students were more successful than the monolingual English speakers, despite the fact that the latter had relatively higher social-class background and might have been expected to be more proficient in English.

While most of these studies have reported that bilingual students have higher levels of achievement than monolingual English-speaking students, only one study in our database examined directly the influence of bilingual proficiency on achievement (Lindholm and Aclan, 1991). More specifically, Lindholm and Aclan (1991) examined a group of ELLs in Grades 1 to 4 in two-way immersion programs in California. They categorized the students as low, medium, or high bilinguals on the basis of their oral language proficiency in each language. The results of academic achievement testing revealed significant positive relationships between level of bilingual proficiency and level of achievement in math and reading. Moreover, the students who were classified as "high bilinguals" were able to attain grade-level results in English reading by Grade 4 and in English math by Grade 3. Lindholm-Leary (2001) reported similar findings for English reading, but not math, for Grade 5 ELLs in two-way programs.

Few studies have systematically examined the influence of L1 proficiency or English literacy on content-area achievement. While many of the comparative evaluation studies reviewed herein discuss reading and math achievement in each language, most do not examine the relationships between reading achievement in one language with content achievement in that language or the relationship between content knowledge across languages. Only two U.S.–based studies were identified that address these relationships; both used correlational techniques. Working in two-way immersion programs, Lindholm-Leary (2001) found that reading and math achievement scores were significantly correlated within and across languages: at Grade 6, English reading with English math ($r = 0.81^{**}$), Spanish reading with Spanish math ($r = 0.74^{**}$), and Spanish math with English math ($r = 0.85^{**}$). Moreover, the correlations between math achievement scores across languages increased across grade levels from Grade 1 ($r = 0.53$) to Grade 7 ($r = 0.72$). Garcia-Vazquez et al. (1997) also report significant correlations between English reading and math achievement scores ($r = 0.61$) in Grades 6 to 12 ELLs. Unfortunately, it was not clear in what program these students had been or were currently participating.

INSTRUCTIONAL ISSUES

In contrast to the plethora of research on instructional issues in literacy (see Chapter 4), there is a dearth of empirical research on instructional strategies or approaches to teaching content. Only five studies examined instructional approaches or strategies (Berman et al., 1995; Echevarria, Short, and Powers, 2003; Minicucci, 1996; Montecel and Cortez, 2002; Tikunoff, 1985), including one report on schools with exemplary programs in math and science (Minicucci, 1996). Two other studies, discussed previously, investigated instructional factors that were considered influential in a program's effectiveness (Lindholm-Leary, 2001; Ramirez, 1992). We also include here CREDE technical reports that examined various instructional strategies that could likely have a significant impact on content learning.

Research on mainstream classrooms shows that good instruction is associated with higher outcomes, regardless of the type of educational model that is used (Levine and Lezotte, 1995; Marzano, 2003; Wenglinsky, 2000). The same is clearly evident in studies of ELL or high-risk students as well (Berman et al., 1995; Corallo and McDonald, 2002; Doherty et al., 2003; Echevarria et al., 2003; Goldenberg and Gallimore, 1991; Montecel and Cortez, 2002; Ramirez, 1992; Guerrero and Sloan, 2001). Describing good instruction in programs serving ELLs is complicated because of the constant need to balance the academic and language needs of students with different levels of language proficiency and, sometimes, with different languages and cultural backgrounds. Thus, it is even more important to use a variety of instructional techniques that respond to different learning styles (Berman et al., 1995; Doherty et al., 2003; Montecel and Cortez, 2002) and language proficiency levels (Berman et al., 1995; Echevarria et al., 2003; Montecel and Cortez, 2002). However, which techniques are effective in producing high-level academic outcomes with ELLs is still an open question, as little empirical work has been done on this question.

A number of researchers have begun to address this gap in our knowledge by examining the extent to which incorporating a language-development component into content instruction results in better access to the curriculum and higher achievement (Berman et al., 1995; Echevarria et al., 2003; Minicucci, 1996). Minicucci (1996) found that exemplary schools for ELLs coordinated math/science instruction with language development, thereby providing ELLs with enhanced opportunities to learn and practice science discourse and writing. In a related vein, Short (1994) has discussed the importance of explicit language instruction along with content area instruction. She advocates developing language objectives in addition to content-area objectives for ELLs to provide them access to the core curriculum. Echevarria et al. (2003) report that students who were provided high-quality sheltered instruction, according to the SIOP (Sheltered Instructional Observation Protocol) model, scored significantly higher and made greater gains in English writing than comparable ELLs who had not been exposed to instruction via the SIOP model. While the SIOP model was developed for ESL teachers to use with ELLs, the approach is clearly applicable to language development with ELLs in various language education models.

The promotion of positive interactions between teachers and students is also seen as an important instructional objective. When teachers use positive social and instructional interactions equitably with both ELL and EP students, both groups perform better academically (California State Department of Education, 1982; Doherty et al., 2003). In addition, research suggests that a reciprocal interaction model of teaching is more beneficial to students than the traditional teacher-centered transmission model of teaching (Doherty et al., 2003; Tikunoff, 1985). In the reciprocal interaction approach, teachers participate in genuine dialogue with students and they facilitate rather than control student learning. This model encourages the development of higher-order cognitive skills rather than just factual recall (Berman et al., 1995; Doherty et al., 2003; Tikunoff, 1985).

High-quality exchanges between teachers and students also give ELLs better access to the curriculum (Berman et al., 1995; Doherty et al., 2003; Montecel and Cortez, 2002; Tikunoff, 1985). Minicucci (1996) points out that exemplary math and science programs in California had teachers who were proficient in the language of the students or were trained in second-language acquisition techniques. Stoops Verplaetse highlights this point in a study on content teachers' interactions with ELLs (Stoops Verplaetse, 1998). This study showed that teachers issued more directives to and asked proportionately fewer questions of their ELLs than of their EP students. Moreover, ELLs were asked fewer high-level cognitive and open-ended questions. These results confirm findings from studies of teacher talk in bilingual classrooms by Ramirez (1992) and in two-way classrooms by Lindholm-Leary (2001) that found that teachers used mostly factual recall questions and few higher-order cognitive questions with their students.

Lindholm-Leary (2001) found that teachers produced the highest percentage of higher-order questions when teaching science, though this was not true of math. When teaching math, as compared to science or social studies, teachers used a high percentage of directives. Such interaction patterns do not provide students with opportunities to develop the critical thinking and discourse skills necessary to succeed in math and science.

In a study of the effectiveness of a collaborative reading approach with Grade 5 ELLs, Klingner and Vaughn (2000) stress the importance of cooperative and heterogeneous groupings to promote reading acquisition. They found that students in such collaborative groups spent a considerable amount of time engaged in academic-related strategic discussion (e.g., comprehension checks, elaboration, prompts, feedback). Such grouping strategies afforded students the opportunity to help each other to understand word meanings related to the content area and to relate their current knowledge to previous knowledge. Students who participated in these collaborative groups made statistically significant gains from pre-test to post-test. Unfortunately, this research did not include a control group of students who did not receive the treatment. However, this research is consistent with other research showing that cooperative-learning groups promote higher levels of achievement among ELLs (Calderón and Carreon, 1994; Calderón, Hertz-Lazarowitz, and Slavin, 1998; Calderón, Tinajero, and Hertz-Lazarowitz, 1992) and that cooperative learning is associated with effective programs for ELLs (Berman et al., 1995; Doherty et al., 2003; Montecel and Cortez, 2002).

Research suggests that two other factors promote the educational success of ELLs: technology and materials. More specifically, integrating technology into the curriculum and instruction (Berman et al., 1995; Dixon, 1995) using both languages appears to facilitate student-student interaction and, in some cases, learning. Dixon (1995) reports that ELL and native English-speaking middle-school students could work together effectively on spatial visualization tasks using computers. Moreover, ELLs who received instruction that integrated technology scored higher on tasks measuring the concepts of reflection and rotation and on measures of two-dimensional visualization ability than students who experienced the traditional textbook approach, and they scored at the same level as the EP students. With respect to materials, it appears that using a wide variety of genres of books and many types of materials (visual, audio-visual, and art materials) improves the success of students in bilingual programs (Montecel and Cortez, 2002). While instructional materials have received little empirical attention, August and Hakuta (1997), in reviewing the characteristics of effective schooling for ELLs, found evidence for the importance of instructional materials appropriate to the needs of these students. ELLs need access to specialized materials that make the curriculum comprehensible to them.

FAMILY AND LEARNER BACKGROUND FACTORS

Several learner and family background factors have been found to influence student achievement in content-area classes and on standardized tests. Some studies looked at several different background characteristics and used regression or correlational analyses to assess the relative effects of each (Fernandez and Nielsen, 1986; Hampton, Ekboir, and Rochin, 1995; Nielsen and Lerner, 1986). Other studies selected students with different background characteristics and looked at group differences on measures of achievement (Lindholm-Leary, 2001). Many studies examined immigrants; they did not specifically mention ELLs. The following background characteristics that are related in some way to academic achievement have been examined: socioeconomic status, length of residence or schooling prior to entering schools in the United States, and prior knowledge. Each of these is discussed now.

Socioeconomic Status

An extensive body of research on SES and achievement exists in the mainstream literature (Knapp and Woolverton, 2003). In contrast, there are relatively few empirical studies of SES and its relationship to achievement in ELLs. Previously, we noted that most of the literature on ELLs includes Hispanic students from low-income families. Thus, it is difficult to discern the true effect of SES because of the limited variation in SES among the samples that have been examined (Adams et al., 1994). Notwithstanding this caveat, all studies on ELLs that we reviewed report significant positive relationships between SES and school outcomes:

- Fernandez and Nielsen (1986) found that SES was an important determinant of achievement in Hispanic bilinguals, but less so than for white monolinguals.
- Lindholm-Leary (2001) reported significant SES differences in reading and math achievement for Grade 5 ELLs in two-way immersion programs with free lunch in comparison to those in non-free lunch programs.
- Hampton et al. (1995) report that SES was *the* most significant and dominant predictor of academic performance of 160 Grades 3, 6, and 12 students in rural public schools in California.
- Nielsen and Lerner (1986) report that SES and ability were the strongest determinants of educational expectations among 1,637 Hispanic high school seniors in the High School and Beyond national survey database.

Another measure of SES that has been used in mainstream and ELL research is parental level of education (Knapp and Woolverton, 2003). Adams et al. (1994), using data from the ASPIRA Association Five Cities

High School Dropout Study (Velez and Fernandez, 1991), used GPA as the dependent variable and language proficiency, language dominance, and parental education as predictor variables. They did not find a significant correlation between mother's level of education and student achievement, arguably because there was little variation in mothers' levels of education. Similarly, Lindholm-Leary (2001) found that parental education was not significantly correlated with the Spanish reading and math achievement scores of ELLs. However, parental education level correlated significantly with achievement scores in English reading (NCE = 29 for ≤ high school; NCE = 50 for college) and math (NCE = 45 for ≤ high school; NCE = 53 for college).

Length of Residence in United States and Amount of Schooling Prior to Entering U.S. Schools

Research on length of residence in the United States and prior schooling has yielded some interesting and mixed results. In a study of Hispanic bilingual, Hispanic English monolingual, Euro-American bilingual, and Euro-American English monolingual students, Fernandez and Nielsen (1986) found that the longer (more generations) the family had resided in the United States, the *lower* the students' school achievement. Similarly, Adams et al. (1994) found that more recent immigrants performed at higher levels than second- or third-generation Hispanic students.

There is an increasing body of literature showing that immigrants (Hispanic and Asian subgroups) overall, not necessarily ELLs, achieve at higher levels than second- and later-generation students (Kao and Tienda, 1995; Rumbaut and Portes, 2001). The studies reviewed here concur with this research. Collier (1987) and Duran and Weffer (1992) add further information to this length-of-residence variable.

Duran and Weffer (1992) examined successful Hispanic immigrant high school seniors (those in the top 25 percent of their class) and found that number of years in the United States had a positive correlation with reading achievement. The average number of years in the United States was about nine years for these students, which was measured as the number of years in the United States when they were in Grade 9. As a group, these students performed at grade level, but for each additional year they resided in the United States, they performed 1.3 NCE points higher in reading achievement. Length of residence in the United States was unrelated to math achievement.

In one of the few studies to include ELLs other than Spanish speakers along with a wide range of SES levels, Collier (1987) examined 1,548 ELLs who arrived in the United States at various ages and with a variety of L1 backgrounds to determine how long it took them to reach grade-level achievement in ESL classes. All the students had started school as beginning ELLs and remained in the school system for several years. It is important to point out that students who tested below grade level in their L1 and older students with little or no formal schooling prior to entering the United States were excluded from the study. Collier reported that students who arrived between the ages of eight and eleven were the fastest achievers; students who arrived at ages five to six were projected to require at least two to three more years to reach the level of performance of those who had arrived at ages eight to eleven; and those who arrived between twelve and fifteen years of age were the lowest achievers and did not reach the national average in any subject area except math even after four to five years of residence in the United States. These results are important in demonstrating the significance of L1 literacy skills in promoting achievement in English for students, particularly those who do not arrive until the later stages of their education (ages twelve to fifteen), where the academic language demands are very high.

Both Collier (1987) and Duran and Weffer (1992) show the significance of length of time in the United States. Both, however, only examined students who were successful in school. Unfortunately, Duran and Weffer do not provide enough information about specific length of time in the United States and whether students who arrived at particular age ranges, as suggested by Collier, were more or less successful than others. However, it appears from Duran and Weffer's average age of immigration that their successful students were not newer arrivals in the age category of twelve to fifteen, which Collier found to be the least successful. Regardless, these studies certainly suggest that ELLs who arrive during the high school years without sufficient English language skills do not appear in the most successful groups studied and may appear to have the most difficulty in catching up to grade-level expectations due to the high academic English-language demands.

Prior Knowledge

While cross-language correlations have been studied extensively in literacy domains, they have not been examined in domains related to nonlanguage academic knowledge. However, there is some research on the relationship between achievement in science and prior knowledge (e.g., playing on a seesaw and understanding of levers; riding in a boat and understanding buoyancy). For example, Lee and her colleagues found that prior knowledge and experience (e.g., playing with Legos) provided Hispanic and Haitian ELLs with more knowledge of science concepts (e.g., concept of levers) (Lee and Fradd, 1996; Lee, Fradd, and Sutman, 1995). Lee and Fradd (1996) also found that students with little knowledge of science rarely used any (or appropriate) strategies to solve science problems and to understand scientific concepts. In a related vein, Duran, O'Connor, and Smith (1988) found that ELLs' ability to reason and problem-solve was affected by their ability to call up relevant cognitive schemata.

Assessment Issues

Assessment plays a central role in the education of all students. Tests are intended to measure students' performance in order to identify those who need assistance and to provide feedback on the effectiveness of instructional methods and materials. Tests are also used with increasing frequency to make high-stakes decisions, such as whether a student will move on to the next grade or receive a diploma, which teachers will receive bonuses, and whether schools will be rewarded or penalized (Linn, Baker, and Betebenner, 2002). One of the tenets of the standards-based reform movement is that all children, including ELLs, are expected to attain high standards. In particular, Title I of the Improving America's Schools Act (U.S. Department of Education, 1994) mandates that assessments that determine the yearly performance of each school must provide for the inclusion of limited English proficient (i.e., ELL) students. In addition, the No Child Left Behind Act (U.S. Department of Education, 2001) establishes annual achievement objectives for ELLs and enforces accountability requirements. The rationale for including ELLs in high-stakes tests is to hold them to the same high standards as their peers and to ensure that their needs are not overlooked (Coltrane, 2002). While there has been an increased emphasis on the inclusion of ELLs in high-stakes tests, research on assessment that is pertinent to this population is scarce. Only a few studies have examined this issue that met our inclusion criteria and, as a result, we have expanded the corpus by including research on testing of ELLs published by the national centers associated with educational research (see Appendix A).

A very important question in the assessment domain is whether English language proficiency affects performance on academic achievement tests given in English (August and Hakuta, 1997; Solano-Flores and Trumbull, 2003). If students cannot demonstrate their academic knowledge due to limited proficiency in English, test results are not valid because they reflect students' language skills rather than what they actually know and can do in academic domains. Results from three studies that have addressed this issue suggest that, indeed, language affects achievement test performance.

- Alderman (1982) concluded from his study of high school students in Puerto Rico that there is a risk of underestimating achievement if the test taker is not proficient in the language of the test. Therefore, proficiency in the language of testing is a moderator variable that should be taken into account when assessing academic knowledge.

- Pilkington, Piersel, and Ponterotto (1988) found that, for a group of children with English or Spanish as the home language, the validity of Kindergarten measures in predicting first-grade achievement varied as a function of the predominant language in the home.
- Abedi, Lord, and Hofstetter (1998) found that language-related background variables were good predictors of performance on the National Assessment of Educational Progress (NAEP) math and reading tests. In particular, length of time in the United States was the strongest predictor of students' performance in math – the longer the students had lived in the United States, the higher their performance in math.

Stevens, Butler, and Castellon-Wellington (2000) examined the question of when ELLs are fluent enough to express what they know on a content test in English. In particular, they studied how the language measured on the Language Assessment Scales (LAS) Reading Component, a widely used test of language proficiency, compares to that used on the Iowa Test of Basic Skills (ITBS) Social Studies Test for Grade 7. They found that the ITBS contains content-specific academic language, whereas the LAS Reading contains more generic language, common to everyday contexts. They conclude that the level of language measured by the LAS is not sufficient to indicate students' ability to process the language of the ITBS. Moreover, they found that even though the LAS Reading test has some predictive validity for the purpose of determining readiness to take content assessments, its ability seems limited to predicting that low scores/high scores on the LAS will correspond to low/high scores, respectively, on tests such as the ITBS. In other words, the LAS Reading test lacks fine discriminability.

Several researchers have called into question the appropriateness of using standardized tests as measures of academic achievement for ELLs by pointing out that the norming sample for many commonly used tests seriously underrepresents ELLs, rendering norm-referenced scores on these tests invalid measures of ELLs' knowledge. Abella (1992) found that Grade 5 students who had exited the English for Speakers of Other Languages (ESOL) Program were, according to their grades, performing successfully in school, even though they scored well below the national average on most subtests of the Stanford Achievement Test. In contrast, Davidson (1994) found that the use of The 3-R's (a nationally standardized test normed on English speakers) with ELLs did not represent a serious statistical violation of test norms. At the same time, he went on to argue that multiple measures should be used in order to compensate for the misapplication of norm-referenced tests. Butler et al. (2000) have pointed out that the Stanford 9 (SAT-9) test is not an appropriate measure to assess the academic achievement of ELLs because it was designed to distinguish levels of academic achievement among native English speakers.

Linn et al. (2002) note that the process of establishing proficiency standards for state tests has lacked rigor. Review panels, that typically included teachers and often other interested citizens, reviewed tests and identified cutoff scores that they thought would "correspond to the level of performance expected from a proficient student who is motivated to do well and has had an adequate opportunity to learn the material" (p. 4). They go on to note that the outcome of such a process has led to the establishment of proficiency levels that are so high they are unrealistic. Moreover, when these proficiency standards were developed, the educators who developed them were unaware that the standards would be used to determine Adequate Yearly Progress (AYP) objectives or that sanctions would be imposed if they did not satisfy AYP. From an accountability perspective, a problem arises because the definition of "passing" varies tremendously from state to state. Linn et al. (2002) suggest using "scale scores and monitoring changes in average scores over time in terms of standard deviation units, thereby avoiding the need for performance standards altogether" (p. 16).

Royer and Carlo (1991) have argued that traditional measures of academic achievement should not be used with ELLs because of mismatches between test content on the one hand and educational, cultural, and linguistic experience on the other. They advocate the use of alternative methods to assess ELLs and, in particular, they propose the use of the Sentence Verification Technique (SVT). The SVT consists of reading or listening to a passage and then responding "Yes" or "No" to test sentences depending on whether they correctly reflect the information in the passage. Royer and Carlo found that the reliability and validity of SVT tests are very good. Other researchers, including Valdez-Pierce and O'Malley (1992), have recommended the use of assessment procedures, such as oral interviews, teacher observation checklists, student self-evaluations, and portfolio assessment, that reflect tasks typical of the classroom; these are referred to as *authentic assessment*. Because authentic assessment strategies ask students to show what they can do, it is argued they provide a more accurate measure of what students know, independent of their language skills, than standardized tests.

An important line of research regarding the use of standardized assessments with ELLs concerns test accommodations. Accommodations for ELLs have been defined as "the support provided students for a given test event ... to help [them] access the content in English and better demonstrate what they know" (Butler and Stevens, 1997, p. 5). Abedi (2001) has pointed out that "accommodations are intended to level the playing field, that is, to make language less of a factor, or ideally a non-factor, when measuring performance" (p. 2). Despite the potential importance of test accommodations, empirical studies informing the use of them with ELLs are scarce. Findings from these studies, which are summarized herein, suggest that the language of assessment should match the language of instruction and that modifying test questions to reduce language complexity may help narrow the performance gap between native English speakers and ELLs.

Abedi et al. (1998) randomly assigned Grade 8 ELLs to one of three versions of the NAEP math assessment: original English language, modified English language (the nontechnical language in the original test was made more readily understandable), and original Spanish language. They found that students performed highest on the modified English version, lower on the original English version, and lowest on the original Spanish version. These results suggest that clarifying the language of the test and testing in the language of instruction helps students improve their test performance.

Abedi et al. (2001a) examined the impact of accommodations on the performance of Grade 8 students taking the NAEP mathematics assessment. Five different forms of the test were randomly distributed: original English language (items taken directly from the NAEP test booklet), linguistically simplified English, original English language accompanied with a glossary for the potentially difficult terms, original English language version with extra time to complete the test, and original English language version with a glossary and extra time. Their results indicate that most accommodations helped both ELL and non-ELL students, with the greatest score improvements resulting from the version that included a glossary and allowed extra time. The only accommodation that narrowed the performance gap between ELL and non-ELL students was the simplified English version of the test.

Abedi et al. (2001b) conducted a pilot study of three forms of twenty NAEP items from a Grade 8 science test: original items and no accommodation, original items and customized English language dictionary at the end of the test booklet, and original items accompanied by English glosses and Spanish translation of the glosses in the margins of the test booklet. They found that ELLs performed substantially higher under the accommodated conditions than under the standard conditions, and they did particularly well under the customized dictionary condition. Moreover, the accommodations did not have a significant effect on the scores of the non-ELLs, suggesting that the accommodations did not alter the construct under measurement.

Abedi and Lord (2001) compared the performance of ELLs and proficient speakers of English on math problems from the NAEP tests and examined whether modifying the original items to reduce language complexity would impact student performance. Overall, the ELLs obtained lower scores than the proficient speakers of English. Scores on the linguistically modified version of the test were slightly higher. The language modifications had especially beneficial effects on the results of low-performing students: ELLs benefited more than proficient speakers of English; low SES students benefited more than others; and students in low-level and average math classes benefited more than those in high-level math and algebra classes.

Shepard, Taylor, and Betebenner (1998) found that accommodations consistently raised the relative position of ELLs on the Rhode Island Grade 4 Mathematics Performance Assessment. Accommodations consisted, for the most part, of a change in the conditions of test administration, such as oral reading of the assessment or extended time to complete it.

Castellon-Wellington (2000) investigated the effects of two types of test accommodations: providing extra assessment time and reading items aloud, on the standardized test performance of Grade 7 ELLs. Her results indicated that students did not significantly improve their performance on the Iowa Tests of Basic Skills (ITBS) Social Studies Test as a result of either accommodation, even when given their preferred accommodation.

In summary, both federal and state legislation requires inclusion of all students, including ELLs, in large-scale content assessments. Inclusion of ELLs "signals the commitment of the educational system to support the academic progress of all its students; and it ensures the representativeness of the data reported" (Shepard et al., 1998, p. 1). The use of the same standardized assessments with all students is, however, problematic. Unless the students on whom the test was standardized match closely the students who take the test, the test norms may be inappropriate for the underrepresented students and the resulting scores could be unreliable and possibly invalid (Davidson, 1994). Moreover, the research reviewed here indicates that language proficiency and other background factors (e.g., length of stay in the United States) strongly relate to test performance, indicating additional sources of invalidity. Results from the few studies that have investigated accommodations suggest that the language of assessment should match the language of instruction and that modifying test questions to reduce language complexity may help narrow the performance gap between native English speakers and ELLs.

CONCLUSIONS

Before summarizing the major findings from these studies, it is important to address the question of the generalizability of this body of research. A major methodological limitation concerns the kinds of students who have been evaluated in this body of research. Except for three studies that included Asian language background students and one study with Franco-American students, all study participants were Hispanic low-income students. That most of these students are from low-income backgrounds is important to stress because these findings might not be applicable to Hispanics from families with higher incomes and parental education. A corollary problem concerns the participants in the comparison group who, for many of the studies, were appropriately matched in terms of ethnicity and

SES with those in the intervention group. However, while this is method-ologically sound, it is important to keep in mind that the outcomes for these comparison groups may not reflect the average performance of English-only students in mainstream classrooms.

Another major problem is that the definitions of various program mod-els are often vague. In some cases, bilingual education is clearly defined with respect to amount of instruction time devoted to each language and length of duration of the program (e.g., early-exit or transitional; late-exit or maintenance) (e.g., Ramirez, 1992; Thomas and Collier, 2002). In other cases, it is not clear what specialized instruction the students received in their "bilingual" classroom (Burnham-Massey and Piña, 1990; Curiel et al., 1986; Medrano, 1988; Saldate et al., 1985). In nonbilingual con-texts, sometimes a mainstream English classroom was labeled "structured English immersion" and, in other contexts, structured English immer-sion included specialized instruction for ELLs (Ramirez, 1992). Further, Gersten and Woodward (1995) used the term "bilingual" immersion to refer to English immersion that included daily instruction through Span-ish but was interpreted as English-only instruction when compared to the alternative transitional bilingual education program. Yet, Gersten and Woodward's bilingual immersion was similar to what many have called structured English immersion or just English immersion, while the term bilingual immersion has been used by other authors to refer to two-way (bilingual) immersion education (Lindholm-Leary, 2001; Thomas and Col-lier, 2002). These methodological and definitional differences have added fuel to the debate on the effectiveness of alternative educational programs for ELLs.

Turning to general findings – with respect to program issues, there is strong convergent evidence that the educational success of ELLs is posi-tively related to sustained instruction through the student's first language. In both the descriptive and comparative program evaluation studies, results showed that length of time in the program and time of assessment affect outcomes. Evaluations conducted in the early years of a program (Grades K-3) typically reveal that students in bilingual education scored below grade level (and sometimes very low) and performed either lower than or equivalent to their comparison group peers (i.e., ELL students in mainstream English, SEI/ESL, or EO students in mainstream classrooms). Almost all evaluations of students at the end of elementary school and in middle and high school show that the educational outcomes of bilingually educated students, especially in late-exit and two-way programs, were at least comparable to and usually higher than their comparison peers. There was no study of middle school or high school students that found that bilingually educated students were less successful than comparison-group students. In addition, most long-term studies report that the longer the stu-dents stayed in the program, the more positive were the outcomes. These results hold true whether one examines outcomes in reading or mathematics achievement, GPA, attendance, high school completion, or attitudes toward school and self. Further, in one study (Lindholm-Leary and Borsato, 2001), half of the ELLs attributed their positive attitudes toward staying in school to the two-way program in which they participated.

These findings about the importance of early first-language instruction are also consistent with Collier's (1987) research on immigrant students who arrived in the United States at different ages. More specifically, her findings showed that those students who immigrated after they had received formal schooling in their home country, having already developed strong first-language and academic skills, were more likely to close the gap with native English-speaking U.S. students in English achievement than students who had immigrated at younger ages and were placed in a mainstream English classroom before they had developed a strong conceptual base in any language. One additional important point was exemplified in the research by Tellez (1998), who reported that students who participated in a hodgepodge of different programs performed at the lowest educational levels. In the longitudinal studies discussed here (e.g., Thomas and Collier, 2002), students who received no intervention performed at the lowest levels and had the highest drop-out rates.

Overall, research is consistent in showing that ELLs who received some specialized program (TBE, TWI, or ESL) were able to catch up to and in some studies surpass the achievement levels of their ELL peers and their English-only peers who were educated in English-only mainstream classrooms. These findings indicate further that ELLs who participated in programs that provided extended instruction through the medium of the students' L1 (i.e., two-way immersion and late-exit program) outperformed students who received short-term instruction through their L1 (i.e., early-exit and TBE programs).

Nothwithstanding these positive results, they must be tempered in light of methodological concerns. As noted earlier, only a couple of studies used random assignment of students to treatment and control groups. As Willig (1985) noted, random assignment usually resulted in stronger effect sizes for bilingual over monolingual instruction. Thus, the results summarized here may actually underestimate the true advantages of bilingual instruction. At the same time, and as pointed out in Chapter 4, there are problems associated with random assignment. In addition to ethical issues and generalizability problems associated with random assignment, there is the issue of random assignment of teachers to classrooms. More specifically, unless teachers are randomly assigned as well, a clearly unrealistic possibility, random assignment of students will not provide the methodological clarity that is sought by critics of this body of research. Another shortcoming of this research concerns the lack of precise definitions of program models and inconsistent use of terminology. Programs were often simply labeled "bilingual" or "ESL" without describing what was actually going on in the program. For example, there was no or poor specification of the amount of instruction in each language or the amount of specialized English instruction, the duration of treatment, and the language proficiency of teachers. There is clearly a need for carefully controlled studies that consider what program models work under what conditions and for whom.

The studies reviewed here also indicate that bilingual proficiency and biliteracy are positively related to academic achievement in both languages. More specifically, bilingual Hispanic students had higher achievement scores (Fernandez and Nielsen, 1986; Lindholm-Leary, 2001; Nielsen and Lerner, 1986; Rumberger and Larson, 1998), GPAs, and educational expectations (Fernandez and Nielsen, 1986; Nielsen and Lerner, 1986) than their monolingual English-speaking Hispanic peers. In addition, there were significant positive correlations between Spanish reading and English reading, between English reading and English math, and between Spanish reading and Spanish math, suggesting that there are complex but supportive interdependencies in the language, literacy, and academic development of bilingual students. These results suggest that educational programs for ELLs should seek to develop their full bilingual and biliterate competencies in order to take advantage of these developmental interdependencies. At the same time, it is important to point out that while the research findings reported here are consistent with one another and with previous reviews (August and Hakuta, 1997; see Chapter 3), the actual research base is scant and consists mostly of correlational studies. A systematic program of empirical research is needed to determine how the two languages interact and how and under what conditions content instruction through one language facilitates content acquisition in another language.

Research reviewed here has identified a number of instructional characteristics that are influential in promoting the academic success of ELLs. Many of these characteristics have also been identified in the success of mainstream students, including cooperative learning, integrating technology into the curriculum, high-quality exchanges between teachers and pupils, and responsiveness to different learner styles. What distinguishes research on ELLs from that on mainstream students is the importance of making the curriculum accessible to students who are not fully proficient in English. Indeed, research indicates the importance of incorporating language-development components and sheltering techniques into content instruction.

While research has examined the characteristics of effective content instruction, most of these findings emanate from studies in which the primary focus was not on the instructional characteristics. There is little research into how to make instruction more accessible and meaningful to ELLs in areas considered challenging by native English speakers – that is, science and math. Extant research provides some starting points, but a research program that includes students with different language backgrounds, ages, and previous educational experiences prior to immigrating should be considered in future research. For example, what approaches can assist new immigrant students at the late elementary or high school level to learn content when they have never experienced school in their home country? Collier's (1987) research showing the importance of previous instruction in the country of origin on students' academic success in the United States demonstrates the importance of including this variable. A significant factor to consider in examining such learners is the cognitive overload they experience when learning academic content area through a second language. With the increasing significance of technology in society, research should also include systematic investigation of the impact of computer-assisted instruction for ELLs. Dixon's (1995) research is instructive in demonstrating that technology provides a significant vehicle for successful learning, especially with helpful peers. Finally, research on the influence of peer interactions in promoting content learning in ELLs would provide information on additional contexts in which to help ELLs develop language and content skills, a point that was raised in Chapter 2.

In addition, socioeconomic status, length of residence in the United States, and prior knowledge can be influential factors in ELLs' academic achievement and success in school. Similar to research on mainstream students, research with ELLs found that there is a positive relationship between a student's level of SES and their level of achievement; recent immigrants are more academically successful than second- or third-generation students; and prior knowledge influences academic achievement. The paucity of studies in this area is a significant gap in the empirical literature on learner and family background factors that may inhibit or promote the academic development of ELLs.

As the reviewed research also showed, there are many challenges in assessing the content-area knowledge of ELLs. Test norms may be inappropriate because of differences between ELLs and students in the norming samples; and language proficiency and other background factors may influence test performance. Results from the few studies that have investigated testing accommodations suggest that the language of assessment should match the language of instruction and that modifying test questions to reduce language complexity may help narrow the performance gap between native English speakers and ELLs. Given the high-stakes nature of standardized testing, it is imperative to develop assessment procedures that allow *all* students to demonstrate what they know.

Taken together, these results indicate that ELLs are more successful when they participate in programs that are specially designed to meet their needs (ESL/SEI, bilingual) than in mainstream English classrooms and when the program is consistent throughout the student's education. A program that is enriched, consistent, and provides a challenging curriculum is also endorsed by research on factors associated with effective programs for ELLs.

Much current research suffers from a short-term perspective; only a few studies have examined the long-term results of various program alternatives. Retrospective studies and those that rely wholly on school records, while valuable, provide incomplete information, and certainly cannot address the complex teacher and instructional factors that can affect student outcomes. Indeed, extant research fails to include sufficient information on the specific teacher and instructional factors that are associated with and presumably responsible for successful content learning. Moreover, the oft-asked question, "Which program is best for ELLs?" is overly simplistic because it assumes that only one approach is the best for all students under all circumstances.

References

Abedi, J. 2001. *Assessment and accommodations for English language learners: Issues and recommendations* (Policy Brief 4). Los Angeles: University of California, National Center for Research on Evaluation, Standards, and Student Testing.

Abedi, J., Hofstetter, C., Baker, E., and Lord, C. 2001a. *NAEP Math performance and test accommodations: Interactions with student language background* (CSE Technical Report 536). Los Angeles: University of California, National Center for Research on Evaluation, Standards, and Student Testing.

Abedi, J., and Lord, C. 2001. The language factor in mathematics tests. *Applied Measurement in Education* 14(3), 219–34.

Abedi, J., Lord, C., Boscardin, C. K., Miyoshi, J. 2001b. *The effects of accommodations on the assessment of limited English proficient (LEP) students in the National Assessment of Educational Progress (NAEP)* (CSE Technical Report 537). Los Angeles: University of California, National Center for Research on Evaluation, Standards, and Student Testing.

Abedi, J., Lord, C., and Hofstetter, C. 1998. *Impact of selected background variables on students' NAEP math performance* (CSE Technical Report 478). Los Angeles: University of California, National Center for Research on Evaluation, Standards, and Student Testing.

Abella, R. 1992. Achievement tests and elementary ESOL exit criteria: An evaluation. *Educational Evaluation and Policy Analysis* 14(2), 169–74.

Adams, D., Astone, B., Nunez-Wormack, E. M., and Smodlaka, I. 1994. Predicting the academic achievement of Puerto Rican and Mexican-American ninth-grade students. *Urban Review* 26(1), 1–14.

Alanis, I. 2000. A Texas two-way bilingual program: Its effects on linguistic and academic achievement. *Bilingual Research Journal* 24(3), 225–48.

Alderman, D. L. 1982. Language proficiency as a moderator variable in testing academic aptitude. *Journal of Educational Psychology* 74(4), 580–7.

Aspiazu, G. G., Bauer, S. C., and Spillett, M. 1998. Improving the academic performance of Hispanic youth: A community education model. *Bilingual Research Journal* 22(2–4), 127–47.

August, D., and Hakuta, K. (eds.). 1997. *Improving schooling for language minority children: A research agenda*. Washington, DC: National Academy Press.

Baker, K. A., and de Kanter, A. A. 1981. *Effectiveness of bilingual education: A review of the literature*. Washington, DC: U.S. Department of Education, Office of Planning, Budget and Evaluation.

Battistich, V., Solomon, D., Watson, M., and Schaps, E. 1997. Caring school communities. *Educational Psychology 32*, 137–51.

Berman, P., Minicucci, C., McLaughlin, B., Nelson, B., and Woodworth, K. 1995. *School reform and student diversity: Case studies of exemplary practices for English language learner students*. Santa Cruz, CA: National Center for Research on Cultural Diversity and Second Language Learning, and B. W. Associates.

Burnham-Massey, L., and Piña, M. 1990. Effects of bilingual instruction on English academic achievement of LEP students. *Reading Improvement 27*(2), 129–32.

Butler, F. A., and Stevens, R. 1997. *Accommodation strategies for English language learners on large-scale assessments: Student characteristics and other considerations* (CSE Technical Report 448). Los Angeles: University of California, National Center for Research on Evaluation, Standards, and Student Testing.

Butler, Y. G., Orr, J. E., Bousquet-Gutiérrez, M., and Hakuta, K. 2000. Inadequate conclusions from an inadequate assessment: What can SAT-9 scores tell us about the impact of Proposition 227 in California? *Bilingual Research Journal 24*(1–2), 141–54.

Calderón, M., and Carreon, A. 1994. Educators and students use cooperative learning to become biliterate and bicultural. *Cooperative Learning Magazine, 4*, 6–9.

Calderón, M., Hertz-Lazarowitz, R., and Slavin, R. 1998. Effects of bilingual cooperative integrated reading and composition on students making the transition from Spanish to English. *The Elementary School Journal, 99*, 153–65.

Calderón, M., Tinajero, J., and Hertz-Lazarowitz, R. 1992. Adapting cooperative integrated reading and composition to meet the needs of bilingual students. *Journal of Educational Issues of Language Minority Students 10*, 79–106.

California State Department of Education. 1982. *Basic Principles for the Education of Language Minority Students, An Overview*. Sacramento: Office of Bilingual Bicultural Education.

Castellon-Wellington, M. 2000. *The impact of preference for accommodations: The performance of English language learners on large-scale academic achievement tests* (CSE Technical Report 534). Los Angeles: University of California, National Center for Research on Evaluation, Standards, and Student Testing.

Cazabon, M., Lambert, W., and Hall, G. 1993. *Two-way bilingual education: A progress report on the Amigos Program* (Research Report No. 7). Santa Cruz, CA: National Center for Research on Cultural Diversity and Second Language Learning.

Cazabon, M., Nicoladis, E., and Lambert, W. E. 1998. *Becoming bilingual in the Amigos two-way immersion program* (Research Report No. 3). Santa Cruz, CA: Center for Research on Education, Diversity & Excellence.

Collier, V. P. 1987. Age and rate of acquisition of second language for academic purposes. *TESOL Quarterly 21*(4), 617–41.

1992. A synthesis of studies examining long-term language minority student data on academic achievement. *Bilingual Research Journal 16*(1–2), 187–212.

Coltrane, B. 2002. *English-language learners and high-stakes tests: An overview of the issues*. Washington, DC: Center for Applied Linguistics (ERIC Document Reproduction Service No. EDO-FL-02–07).

Corallo, C., and McDonald, D. H. 2002. *What works with low-performing schools: A review of research.* Charleston, WV: AEL, Regional Educational Laboratory, Region IV Comprehensive Center.

Curiel, H., Rosenthal, J. A., and Richek, H. G. 1986. Impacts of bilingual education on secondary school grades, attendance, retentions and drop-out. *Hispanic Journal of Behavioral Sciences 8*(4), 357–67.

Davidson, F. 1994. Norms appropriacy of achievement tests: Spanish-speaking children and English children's norms. *Language Testing 11*(1), 83–95.

de Jong, E. J. 2002. Effective bilingual education: From theory to academic achievement in a two-way bilingual program. *Bilingual Research Journal 26*(1), 65–84.

de la Garza, J. V., and Medina, M. 1985. Academic achievement as influenced by bilingual instruction for Spanish-dominant Mexican American children. *Hispanic Journal of Behavioral Sciences 7*(3), 247–59.

Dixon, J. K. 1995. Limited English proficiency and spatial visualization in middle school students' construction of the concepts of reflection and rotation. *Bilingual Research Journal 19*(2), 221–47.

Doherty, R. W., Hilberg, R. S., Pinal, A., and Tharp, R. G. 2003. Five standards and student achievement. *NABE Journal of Research and Practice 1*(1), 1–24.

Dulay, H., and Burt, M. 1980. The relative proficiency of limited English proficient students. In J. E. Alatis (ed.), *Current Issues in Bilingual Education* (pp. 181–200). Washington, DC: Georgetown University Press.

Duran, B. J., and Weffer, R. E. 1992. Immigrants' aspirations, high school process, and academic outcomes. *American Educational Research Journal 29*(1), 163–81.

Duran, R. P., O'Connor, C., and Smith, M. 1988. *Methods for assessing reading comprehension skills of language minority students* (Project 2.2 Technical Report). Los Angeles: University of California, Center for Language Education and Research.

Duran, R. P., Revlin, R., and Havill, D. 1995. *Verbal comprehension and reasoning skills of Latino high school students* (Research Report No. 13). Santa Cruz, CA: National Center for Research on Cultural Diversity and Second Language Learning.

Echevarria, J., Short, D., and Powers, K. 2003. School reform and standards-based education: How do teachers help English language learners? Technical report. Santa Cruz, CA: Center for Research on Education, Diversity & Excellence.

Fernandez, R., and Nielsen, F. 1986. Bilingualism and Hispanic scholastic achievement: Some baseline results. *Social Science Research 15*, 43–70.

Fulton-Scott, M. J., and Calvin, A. D. 1983. Bilingual multicultural education vs. integrated and non-integrated ESL instruction. *NABE: The Journal for the National Association for Bilingual Education 7*(3), 1–12.

Gándara, P. 1995. *Over the ivy walls: The educational mobility of low-income Chicanos.* New York: State University of New York Press.

Gándara, P., and Merino, B. 1993. Measuring the outcomes of LEP programs: Test scores, exit rates, and other mythological data. *Educational Evaluation and Policy Analysis 15*(3), 320–38.

García-Vázquez, E., Vázquez, L. A., López, I. C., and Ward, W. 1997. Language proficiency and academic success: Relationships between proficiency in two languages and achievement among Mexican-American students. *Bilingual Research Journal 21*(4), 395–408.

García-Vázquez, E., Vázquez, L. A., López, I. C., & Ward, W. 1999. Language proficiency and academic success: Relationships between proficiency in two languages and achievement among Mexican-American students. *Bilingual Research Journal 21(4)*, 395–408.

Gersten, R., and Woodward, J. 1995. A longitudinal study of transitional and immersion bilingual education programs in one district. *Elementary School Journal 95(3)*, 223–39.

Goldenberg, C. N., and Gallimore, R. 1991. Local knowledge, research knowledge, and educational change: A case study of early Spanish reading improvement. *Educational Researcher 20*, 2–14.

Goldenberg, C. N., and Sullivan, J. 1994. Making change happen in a language-minority school: A search for coherence, (Educational Practice Report #13). Santa Cruz: University of California at Santa Cruz, National Center for Research on Cultural Diversity and Second Language Acquisition.

Guerrero, M., and Sloan, K. 2001. A descriptive analysis of four exemplary K-3 Spanish reading programs in Texas: Are they really exemplary? *Bilingual Research Journal 25*, 253–80.

Hampton, S., Ekboir, J. M., Rochin, R. I. 1995. The performance of Latinos in rural public schools: A comparative analysis of test scores in grades 3, 6, and 12. *Hispanic Journal of Behavioral Sciences 17(4)*, 480–98.

Kao, G., and Tienda, M. 1995. Optimism and achievement: The educational performance of immigrant youth. *Social Science Quarterly 76*, 1–19.

Kirk-Senesac, B. V. 2002. Two-way bilingual immersion: A portrait of quality schooling. *Bilingual Research Journal 26(1)*, 85–101.

Klingner, J., and Vaughn, S. 2000. The helping behaviors of fifth graders while using collaborative strategic reading during ESL content classes. *TESOL Quarterly 34(1)*, 69–98.

Knapp, M. S., and Woolverton, S. 2003. Social class and schooling. In J. Banks and C. A. McGee Banks (eds.), *Handbook of research on multicultural education, 2nd Edition* (pp. 548–69). New York: Jossey Bass.

Lambert, W. E., and Cazabon, M. 1994. *Students' view of the Amigos program* (Research Report No. 11). Santa Cruz, CA: National Center for Research on Cultural Diversity and Second Language Learning.

Lee, O., and Fradd, S. H. 1996. Literacy skills in science learning among linguistically diverse students. *Science Education 80(6)*, 651–71.

Lee, O., Fradd, S. H., and Sutman, F. X. 1995. Science knowledge and cognitive strategy use among culturally and linguistically diverse students. *Journal of Research in Science Teaching 32(8)*, 797–816.

Levine, D. U., and Lezotte, L. W. 1995. Effective schools research. In J. A. Banks and C. A. Mcgee Banks (eds.), *Handbook of research on multicultural education* (pp. 525–47). New York: Macmillan.

Lindholm, K. J. 1988. *The Edison elementary school bilingual immersion program: Student progress after one year of implementation*. Technical Report No. 9 of the Center for Language Education and Research, UCLA.

———. 1991. Theoretical assumptions and empirical evidence for academic achievement in two languages. *Hispanic Journal of Behavioral Sciences 13(1)*, 3–17.

Lindholm, K. J., and Aclan, Z. 1991. Bilingual proficiency as a bridge to academic achievement: Results from bilingual/immersion programs. *Journal of Education 173(2)*, 99–113.

Lindholm, K., and Fairchild, H. 1989. *Evaluation of an "exemplary" bilingual immersion program* (Technical Report TR13). Los Angeles, CA: University of California, Center for Language Education and Research (ERIC Document Reproduction Service No. ED 307 820).

Lindholm-Leary, K. J. 2001. *Dual language education*. Avon, UK: Multilingual Matters.

Lindholm-Leary, K. J., and Borsato, G. 2001. *Impact of two-way bilingual elementary programs on students' attitudes toward school and college*. Santa Cruz, CA: Center for Research on Education, Diversity & Excellence.

Linn, R. L., Baker, E. L., and Betebenner, D. W. 2002. Accountability systems: Implications of requirements of the No Child Left Behind Act of 2001. *Educational Researcher 31*(2), 3–16.

Lucas, T., Henze, R., and Donato, R. 1990. Promoting the success of Latino language-minority students: An exploratory study of six high schools. *Harvard Educational Review 60*(3), 315–40.

Marzano, R. J. 2003. *What works in schools: Translating research into action*. Alexandria, VA: Association for Supervision and Curriculum Development.

Medrano, M. F. 1986. Evaluating the long-term effects of a bilingual education program: A study of Mexican-American students. *Journal of Educational Equity and Leadership 6*(2), 129–38.

1988. The effects of bilingual education on reading and mathematics achievement: A longitudinal case study. *Equity and Excellence 23*(4), 17–19.

Mehan, H., Datnow, A., Bratton, E., Tellez, C., Friedlaender, D., and Ngo, T. 1991. *Untracking and college enrollment* (Research Report No. 4). Santa Cruz, CA: Center for Research on Education, Diversity & Excellence.

Mehan, H., Hubbard, L., Lintz, A., and Villanueva, I. 1994. *Tracking untracking: The consequences of placing low track students in high track classes* (Research Report No. 10). Santa Cruz, CA: National Center for Research on Cultural Diversity and Second Language Learning.

Minicucci, C. 1996. *Learning science and English: How school reform advances scientific learning for limited English proficient middle school students* (Educational Practice Report No. 17). Santa Cruz, CA: National Center for Research on Cultural Diversity and Second Language Learning.

Montecel, M. R., and Cortez, J. D. 2002. Successful bilingual education programs: Development and the dissemination of criteria to identify promising and exemplary practices in bilingual education at the national level. *Bilingual Research Journal 26*, 1–22.

Nielsen, F., and Lerner, S. 1986. Language skills and school achievement of bilingual Hispanics. *Social Science Research 15*, 209–40.

Pilkington, C. L., Piersel, W. C., and Ponterotto, J. G. 1988. Home language as a predictor of first-grade achievement for Anglo- and Mexican-American children. *Contemporary Educational Psychology 13*, 1–14.

Ramirez, J. D. 1992. Longitudinal study of structured English immersion strategy, early-exit and late-exit transitional bilingual education program for language-minority children (Executive Summary). *Bilingual Research Journal 16*(1–2), 1–62.

Ramirez, J. D., Yuen, S. D., Ramey, D. R. 1991. *Longitudinal study of structured English immersion strategy, early-exit and late-exit transitional bilingual education programs for language-minority children* (Final report to the U.S. Department of Education). San Mateo, CA: Aguirre International.

Reyes, P., Scribner, J. D., and Paredes Scribner, A. (eds.). 1999. *Lessons from high-performing Hispanic schools: Creating learning communities.* New York: Teachers College Press.

Rosnow, R. L., Rosenthal, R., and Rubin, D. B. 2000. Computing contrasts, effect sizes, and counternulls on other people's published data: General procedures for research consumers. *Psychological Methods 1*, 331–40.

Royer, J. M., and Carlo, M. S. 1991. Assessing the language acquisition progress of limited English proficient students: Problems and a new alternative. *Applied Measurement in Education 4*(2), 85–113.

Rumbaut, R., and Portes, A. 2001. *Ethnicities: Children of immigrants in America.* Berkeley, CA: University of California Press.

Rumberger, R. W., and Larson, K. A. 1998. Toward explaining differences in educational achievement among Mexican-American language-minority students. *Sociology of Education 71*(1), 68–92.

Saldate, M., Shitala, S. P., and Medina, M. 1985. Bilingual instruction and academic achievement: A longitudinal study. *Journal of Instructional Psychology 12*(1), 24–30.

Shepard, L., Taylor, G., and Betebenner, D. 1998. *Inclusion of limited-English-proficient students in Rhode Island's grade 4 mathematics performance assessment* (CSE Technical Report 486). Los Angeles: University of California, National Center for Research on Evaluation, Standards, and Student Testing.

Short, D. J. 1994. The challenge of social studies for limited-English-proficient students. *Social Education 58*(1), 36–8.

Slavin, R. E., and Calderón, M. 2001. *Effective programs for Latino students.* Mahwah, NJ: Lawrence Erlbaum Associates.

Solano-Flores, G., and Trumbull, E. 2003. Examining language in context: The need for new research and practice paradigms in the testing of English-language learners. *Educational Researcher 32*(2), 3–13.

Stevens, R. A., Butler, F. A., Castellon-Wellington, M. 2000. *Academic language and content assessment: Measuring the progress of English language learners (ELLs)* (CSE Technical Report 552). Los Angeles: University of California, National Center for Research on Evaluation, Standards, and Student Testing.

Stoops Verplaetse, L. 1998. How content teachers interact with English language learners. *TESOL Journal 7*(5), 24–8.

Teddle, C., and Reynolds, D. 2000. *The international handbook of school effectiveness research.* London: Falmer Press.

Tellez, K. 1998. Class placement of elementary school emerging bilingual students. *Bilingual Research Journal 22*(2–4), 279–95.

Thomas, W. P., and Collier, V. P. 2002. *A national study of school effectiveness for language minority students' long-term academic achievement.* Santa Cruz, CA: Center for Research on Education, Diversity & Excellence.

Tikunoff, W. 1985. *Applying significant bilingual instructional features in the classroom.* Rosslyn, VA: National Clearinghouse for Bilingual Education (ERIC Document Reproduction Service No. ED 338 106).

Troike, R. C. 1978. Research evidence for the effectiveness of bilingual education. *NABE Journal* (3), 13–24.

U.S. Department of Education. 1994. *Improving America's Schools Act*. Washington, DC: U.S. Government Printing Office.

1998. *Turning around low-performing schools: A guide for state and local leaders*. Washington, DC: Author.

2001. No Child Left Behind Act. Washington, DC: U.S. Government Printing Office.

Valdez-Pierce, L., O'Malley, J. M. 1992. *Performance and portfolio assessment for language minority students*. NCBE Program Information Guide Series. Washington, DC: National Clearinghouse for Bilingual Education.

Velez, W., and Fernandez, R. R. 1991. The ASPIRA Association school retention study. *Equity and Excellence* 25(1), 55–61.

Wenglinsky, H. 2000. *How teaching matters: Bringing the classroom back into discussions of teacher quality*. Princeton, NJ: Educational Testing Service.

Willig, A. C. 1985. A meta-analysis of selected studies on the effectiveness of bilingual education. *Review of Educational Research* 55(3), 269–318.

TABLE A.5.1. *Comparative Evaluation Studies*

Authors	Sample Characteristics	Grades	Program	Research Design	Outcome Measures[a]	Results[b,c]
Alanis (2000)	Hispanic, low SES, Participate = 3 yrs	5	Two-way (50:50)	Btwn group: - TR: ELL TWI (n = 56) - CO: Non-ELL EO (n = 80) - Norms	- TAAS: Eng, Read, and Math (type of score not clear)	School 1: Read and Math: 2-way < non-ELL in EO School 2: Read: TWI ELL > non-ELL in EO class Math: TWI ELL > non-ELL in EO class
Burnham-Massey and Piña (1990)		1–12	Bilingual (type not specified)	Btwn group: - TR: Bil (n = 115) - CO: Non-ELL EO (n = 492) - Norms - Longitudinal	- CTBS: Read, Lang, and Math (NCEs) - High school proficiency measures: Read, Write, Eng, and Math - No statistical analyses run	Grade 5: - Students in Bil scored at/above grade-level (NCEs = 48–52) - Grades 1–5, grow 12–16 NCEs - Read, Lang, Math: Bil = EO Grades 7–8: - Read: Bil = EO (NCEs = 42–45) - Lang: Bil (NCEs = 48–53) = EO (NCEs = 47–48) - Math: Bil (NCEs = 56–57) = EO (NCEs = 52–54) Grade 12: - GPA and high school proficiency tests: All students in Bil program passed high school prof. measures in Read, Write, Eng, and Math - At grade level

Study	Population	Grades	Program type	Design/comparison	Measures	Findings
Cazabon et al. (1993)	Hispanic, low SES, matched on nonverbal intelligence	1–3	Two-way (50:50)	Btwn group: – TR: TWI (n = 76) – CO: TBE (n = 70) – Longitudinal	– Student attitudes – District test of lang skills – CAT grade equivalent (GE) scores in Eng Read and Math – CTBS Español: Read and Math	Grade 3 in most recent cohort: – Eng Read: TWI (2.9) = TBE (2.1) – Eng Math: TWI (3.9) = TBE (2.7) – Span Read: TWI (3.1) = TBE (3.6) – Span Math: TWI (3.3) = TBE (3.0) – TWI slightly above grade level and TBE below grade level in Eng read and math – Positive attitudes
Cazabon et al. (1998)	Hispanic, low-SES	4–8	Two-way (50:50)	Btwn group: – TR: TWI (n = 250) – CO: Non-ELL EO (n = 212) – Longitudinal	– CAT grade equivalent: Eng, Read and Math SABE grade equivalent: Spanish, Read and Math – ANCOVA (Raven as covariate)	– Read: TWI = EO Grades 4–8 – Math: TWI > EO Grades 4–5***; TWI = EO Grades 6–8 – Span Read: TWI = TBE Grades 4–7 – Span Math: TWI = TBE Grades 4, 6–7; TWI > TBE Grade 5*** Grade 8: – At grade level in Eng read and math – Below grade level in Sp read and math
Collier (1992) Re-analysis of Ramirez (1992)	Hispanic, low SES	K-6	Bilingual (early and late)	Btwn group: – TR1 = Early exit – TR2 = Late exit – n = Subset of Ramirez's 2,000 students – Norms	– CTBS: Eng Read and Math (NCE gains over time) – No statistical analyses reported	After 2 years (K–1): – No difference by program Upper elem grades, late-exit students: –Scored at 51st NCE in English math and 45th NCE in English reading – Reports other groups scored lower, but no scores provided

(continued)

TABLE A.5.1 (continued)

Authors	Sample Characteristics	Grades	Program	Research Design	Outcome Measures[a]	Results[b,c]
Curiel (1986)	Hispanic, low SES, Matched: Gender, family structure, parent birthplace and education	7–10	Bilingual (type not specified)	Btwn group: – TR: Bil (n = 86) – CO: non-ELL EO (n = 90)	– GPA – Attendance – Retention – High school graduation	Dropout rate: – Bil (24%) < non-Bil (43%)** Retention: – Bil (5%) < non-Bil (15%)* – Students in Bil education had significantly higher GPAs and lower school drop-outs the longer they had participated in the Bil program
de la Garza and Medina (1985)	Hispanic, low SES, Program partic = 3 yrs	1–3	Bilingual (type not specified)	Btwn group: – TR: Bil (n = 24) – CO: non-ELL EO (n = 118) – Norms – Longitudinal	– SAT: Eng – CAT: Eng – CTBS Español: Read and Math – Raw scores transformed to T-scores	By Grade 3: – Students at grade level (T scores = 48–53) – Read voc: Bil > EO* – Read: Bil = EO – Math computation: Bil = EO – Math concepts: Bil = EO – Grade level in Eng and Span, Read and Math
Fulton-Scott and Calvin (1983)	Hispanic, low SES	1, 6	Bilingual (type not specified)	Btwn group: – Bil: (n = 20) – Integrated ESL: (n = 20) – Non-integrated ESL: (n = 20)	– CTBS grade-equivalent: Eng (assume total score, but not clear) – Grade point average: Read, Lang, and Math	By Grade 6: – CTBS: Bil (6.9) > Non-int (4.9)* Bil (6.9) > Integ (6.0)* Integ (6.0) = Non-int (4.9) – Read GPA: Bil (4.7) > Non-int (2.9)* Bil (4.7) > Integ (3.5)* Integ (3.5) = Non-int (2.9)

| Gersten and Woodward (1995) | Hispanic, low SES, Program partic = 4 yrs | 4–7 | Transitional (early exit) and Structured English Immersion (30–90 min/day of Span) | Btwn group: - TR: TBE (n = 117) - CO: SEI (n = 111) - Longitudinal | - ITBS NCE: Eng, read, lang, and vocab - OLDM (Eng score used as covariate) - Rate of entry into mainstream classes - Attitudes | - Lang GPA: Bil (4.6) > Non-int (2.9)* Bil (4.6) > Integ (3.7)* Integ (3.7) = Non-int (2.9) - Math GPA: Bil (4.7) > Non-int (2.8)* Bil (4.7) = Integ (4.1) Integ (4.1) > Non-int (2.8)* - Bilingual at grade level |

Grades 4–6:
- TBE < SEI
Grade 6:
- Both groups scored low:
- Lang Bil (39.2) < SEI (43.2)*
- Vocab Bil (25.9) = SEI (27.7)
- Read Bil (32.8) = SEI (33.6)

Grade 7:
- SEI = Bil
- Lang Bil (43.2) < SEI (44.4)
- Vocab Bil (33.5) = SEI (34.7)
- Read Bil (27.9) = SEI (28.6)
- SEI students significantly more likely to enter mainstream (99%) than Bil (65%)***
- No difference in students' attitudes
- By Grade 7, students scored low in Vocabulary and Read, close to grade level in Lang

(continued)

TABLE A.5.1 (*continued*)

Authors	Sample Characteristics	Grades	Program	Research Design	Outcome Measures[a]	Results[b,c]
Lindholm (1991)	Hispanic, low-SES	2–3	Two-way (90:10)	Btwn group: – TR: TWI (n = 168) All ELLs – CO: TBE (n = 118)	– CTBS NCE: Eng, Read and Math – T-tests & ANOVAs: Determine group differences in Read and Math	By Grade 3: – ELLs scored low in Eng Read (NCE = 27) – Slightly below average in Eng Math (NCE = 42) – Below average (NCE = 42) in Span Read – Above average in Span Math (NCE = 60) – Comparing ELLs in TWI vs. TBE–no significant differences in Grade 3
Lindholm-Leary and Borsato (2001)	Hispanic, low SES	9–12	Two-way (90:10)	Btwn group: – TR: TWI grads, previously in TWI in elementary (n = 142) – CO: non-TWI (n = 17)	– Attitudes – GPA – Enrollment in Math courses – ANOVAs & χ^2: determine group differences	– Positive attitudes related to school and academic competence; motivated; college prep behaviors; enrolled in higher-level math courses (TWI students) – Comparing non-TWI to TWI students, TWI students like school more** are more prepared for 4-year college*: know more about entrance requirements**, attend college info*, and enrolled in higher-level math courses*

Study	Population	Grade	Program	Design	Measures	Findings
Medrano (1986)	Hispanic, low SES	7–9	Bilingual (type not specified)	Btwn group: - TR: BE (n = 179) - CO: non-ELL EO (n = 108) - Retrospective	- CTBS scaled scores: Eng	Grade 6: - Read: Bil (691) = EO (697) - Math: Bil (704) > EO (699)* - Grade level in Eng Read and Math
Ramirez (1992) Large Congress-mandated study	Hispanic, low SES	K–4 or K–6	Transitional (early exit and late exit) and Structured English Immersion	- n = 2,000 students, -Longitudinal (Students not matched, but programs matched for key programmatic characteristics)	- CTBS: Eng Read, Lang Arts, and Math - Trajectory Analysis of Matched Percentile (TAMP): comparison of growth to norming pop.	- After 2 years, students do equally well in Eng Read and Math - Bilingual education helps ELLs catch up to Eng-speaking peers in Eng Read, Lang Arts, and Math - ELLs in Eng mainstream fall behind
Saldate et al. (1985)	Matched-Hispanic, low SES, PPVT	1–3	Bilingual (type not specified)	Btwn group: - TR: Bil (n = 31) - CO: non-EL EO (n = 31) - Longitudinal	- WRAT: Eng and Span for Grade 3 (type of score unknown)	Grade 3: - Eng Read: Bil > EO* - Eng Spell: Bil = EO - Eng Math: Bil > EO* - Span Read: Bil > EO* - Span Spell: Bil > EO* - Span Math: Bil > EO*
Thomas and Collier (2002)	SITE #1 Rural: Mostly Franco-Am, low SES, ELLs have some academic prof in Eng	4–7	French/ English 1-way	Btwn group: - TR: ELL Bilingual Immersion / BI (n = 47) - CO: ELL MainEO (n = 39) - Longitudinal	- Various tests (ITBS, CTBS, Stanford 9, Terra Nova) NCE: Eng Read and Math 4 NCEs gps is sign, 4 small btw, 6 moderate, 10 large	BI vs MainEO: - Read BI (56) > MainEO (48) - Lang BI (59) > MainEO (51) - Math BI (55) > MainEO (52) - Grade level in Eng Read and Math

(continued)

TABLE A.5.1 (*continued*)

Authors	Sample Characteristics	Grades	Program	Research Design	Outcome Measures[a]	Results[b,c]
Thomas and Collier (2002)	SITE #2 Large Urban: Hispanic, low SES	2–11	Transitional (early exit) and ESL	Btwn group: – TR: ELL TBE (n = 3,333) – CO: ELL ESL (n = 3,655) – CO: ELL MainEO (n = 1,599) – CO: EO MainEO (n = 103,887)	– Stanford 9 NCE: Eng, Read and Math – APRENDA 2 NCE: Spanish, Read and Math – Drop-out rate 4 NCEs between groups is significant, 4 NCEs small, 6 NCEs moderate, 10 NCEs very large	Grade 5 with min 4 years in program-longitudinal: – Eng Read: TWI (51)> DBE (41) and TBE (41) DBE (41) = TBE (41) – Eng Math: TWI (59)> DBE (51) and TBE (50) DBE (51) = TBE (50) – Span Read: TWI (65)> DBE (56) and TBE (57) DBE (56) = TBE (57) – Span Math: TWI (63)> DBE (54) and TBE (56) DBE (54) = TBE (56) Grade 11 – Cross-sectional: – Read: EO (49) = TBE (47) > ESL (40) > MainEO (25) – Math: EO (46) = TBE (44) > MainEO (34)

| Thomas and Collier (2002) | SITE #3 Mid-sized urban: Hisp, low SES | 8–11 | ESL Content Instruction | – TR: ESL Content (n = 141) – Longitudinal | – ITBS NCEs | ESL (41) > MainEO (34) Dropout rate: Bil/ESL and EO (3%) < MainEO (4.6%)
 – TBE close to grade level in Read and Math
 – ESL slightly below grade level in both Read and Math
 – Main EO very low in Read and low in Math
 Grade 8:
 – Read and Write (NCE = 36–38)
 – Math and Science (NCE = 41–49)
 Grade 11:
 – Read and Write (NCE = 37–47)
 – Math and Science (NCE = 44–48)
 – Gr 11, below grade in Read, near grade other content |

[a] Uses norm-referenced standardized achievement test unless noted otherwise.

[b] The =, >, and < signs and probabilities (* $p < 0.05$, ** $p < 0.01$; *** $p < 0.001$) note the original determination of group differences; = is used if group differences are not significant in the original statistical analyses.

[c] If there are multiple years of data provided in the research article, the results are presented for the most recent data.

TABLE A.5.2. *Descriptive Studies of Two-Way Immersion Programs*

Authors	Sample Characteristics	Grades	Program	Research Design	Outcome Measures	Results
De Jong (2002)	Hispanic, low SES	5	Two-way (50:50)	Within group: – n = 95 – Descriptive	– SAT NCE: Eng, Read and Math – Mass. State Curriculum Content Frameworks (scaled scores)	By Grade 5: – Students (above) average in Math (NCEs = 43–73) – Below grade level in Read (NCEs = 38–43) – Students passed state measure of proficiency in Lang Arts, Mathematics, Science and technology
Kirk-Senesac (2002)	Hispanic, low SES, Partip = min 5 years	3–8	Two-way (80:20)	Within group: – n = 24 – Longitudinal – Descriptive	– Illinois Standards Achievement Test (ISAT): Read, Write, Math, Social Science, and Science – Illinois Goal Assessment Program (IGAP): Read, Write, Math, Social Science, and Science – GE scores	– Read and Math Grade 3–8: At grade level in Read & Math – On state assessments, most students (81–88%) met the standards in Read and Write; 2/3 in Math and Science; 1/2 in Social Science – Pass rates significantly higher than those for the district and state for ELLs
Lambert and Cazabon (1994)	Hispanic, low SES	4–6	Two-way (50:50)	Within group: – n = 32 – Longitudinal – Descriptive	– Student attitudes – CAT grade equivalent scores: Eng, Read – Raven Progressive Matrices test of non-verbal abstract reasoning	– Most students have positive attitudes toward school, TWI program, and other languages and cultures By Grade 6: – Students at grade level in Read – Average in a measure of abstract reasoning

Lindholm (1988)	Hispanic, low SES	K–1	Two-way (90:10)	Within group: – n = 73 – Descriptive	– CTBS NCE: Eng scores – Student attitudes	Grade 1: – Slightly below average in Read and Math – Expected levels of academic competence (attitudes), similar to other Eng speakers
Lindholm and Aclan (1991)	Hispanic, low SES	1–4	Two-way (90:10 and 50:50)	Within group: – n = 249 students (n = 159 ELL) in 2 schools – Correlational	– CTBS-U NCE: Eng	Grades 1–2: – Very low in Read (NCEs of 16–31) – Moderately low in Math (NCEs of 26–44) By Grade 4: – Almost average in Read (NCEs of 42–53) and Math (NCEs of 46–54) – Students with high levels of bilingual proficiency scored at grade level in Read and Math (NCEs of 53–54)
Lindholm and Fairchild (1989)	Hispanic, low SES	K–6	Two-way (90:10)	Within group: – n = 78 – Descriptive – Longitudinal	– CTBS NCE: Eng	Grade 6: – Average in Math (NCE of 56) – Slightly below average in Read (NCE of 43)

(continued)

221

Authors	Sample Characteristics	Grades	Program	Research Design	Outcome Measures	Results
Lindholm-Leary (2001)	Hispanic, low SES, urban, suburban and rural	K–8	Two-way (90:10 and 50:50)	Within group: – n = 8,000 students in 18 schools – Descriptive and correlational – Longitudinal – Stats	– Various norm-referenced standardized achievement tests: Eng, Read, Lang and Math	Read & Lang: – Students begin at 22nd NCE; make significant progress (43rd NCE)–not reach the 50th NCE by Grade 7 Math: – Two-way students in 50:50 score average and those in 90:10 approach average by Grade 5 – Positive cross-cultural and lang attitudes, and perceived scholastic competence
Lindholm-Leary and Borsato (2001) Cited in Table 1	Hispanic, low SES	9–12	Two-way (90:10)	Within group: – n = 142 – Descriptive	– Student attitudes – Drop-out rates – GPA – Course placement in Math	– Positive attitudes toward school, want college degree, enrolled in college-bound Math courses, and won't drop out – 42% felt TWI program kept them from dropping out

6

Conclusions and Future Directions

Fred Genesee, Kathryn Lindholm-Leary,
William M. Saunders, and Donna Christian

In Chapters 2 through 5, we presented research findings and methodological issues specific to each domain of learning. In this chapter, we turn to common trends in the research findings reviewed in Chapters 2 through 5 and then go on to identify directions for future research.

COMMON TRENDS

Role of ELLs' First Language

The first notable trend is the influential role that ELLs' native language plays in their educational achievement. Maintenance and development of ELLs' L1 is influential in all domains we examined: oral language, literacy, and academic achievement. The influence of the L1 was evident in studies that examined planned instructional or programmatic interventions (Chapter 5) and those that examined unconscious, implicit processes that are implicated in literacy and oral language development (in Chapters 2 and 3; for example, when ELLs draw on their knowledge of cognates in the L1 when decoding words in the L2 or the transfer of reading comprehension strategies from the L1 to the L2). In citing evidence in support of maintaining and using ELLs' L1, we do not deny the critical importance of English for educational achievement. We noted in Chapters 2 and 4 that there is an important link between L2 exposure and proficiency and the development of literacy skills in English. However, the importance of ELLs' L1 raises an educational challenge. How can the developmental complementarity between L1 and L2 be used to their educational benefit at a time when legislation in some states disfavors instruction through the medium of languages other than English? Equally important, how can the L1 be maintained when most ELLs, in those states and others, are in fact enrolled in programs where English is the sole language of instruction? There is a need to explore noninstructional uses of ELLs' L1 in order to determine how it can continue to develop and benefit their literacy and academic development. For example, the use of the L1 could be promoted in family and community contexts by having parents read to children or children read to parents in the L1; by providing after-school programs for students where the L1 is used for literacy or academic purposes; or by ensuring that L1 books and videos are stocked in public libraries. The effectiveness of such extracurricular interventions warrants empirical investigation to determine their impact on ELLs' educational success.

Developmental Links between First and Second Language

A second major trend to emerge from this collection of studies concerns the nature of the developmental links between L1 and L2 in the education of ELLs. Under one hypothesis, it might be expected that high levels of general L1 proficiency would be related to high levels of L2 oral language, reading and writing, and academic achievement. However, a careful reading of the relevant research indicates that specific aspects of L1 ability (e.g., understanding of paradigmatic word associations, the ability to provide formal definitions of words, knowledge of L1–L2 cognates) are more influential in L2 development, especially in domains related to L2 literacy and academic achievement. A similar pattern was found for the developmental relationship between L2 oral ability and L2 literacy. We, and others (e.g., Cummins, 2000) have characterized these critical aspects of L1/L2 oral ability in various ways: sometimes as components of L1/L2 oral proficiency that are related to academic purposes; sometimes as oral language that serves higher order cognitive processes; and sometimes as thorough or deep understanding of language in contrast to surface-level proficiency or understanding. The true nature of these critical features of L1 and L2 oral proficiency is clearly an important direction for future research. Although we lack complete understanding of the precise nature of these skills, it is clear that educators should adopt differentiated and complex views of L1 and L2 development and their interrelationship if they are to optimize ELLs' development of language for academic purposes. We have sufficient knowledge at this time to devise strategic and focused language teaching/learning interventions that could enhance the educational outcomes of ELLs.

Instructional Approaches

Third, interactive learning environments that provide carefully planned direct instruction of target language skills, as needed, are likely to be most effective. Moreover, language skills that are linked to literacy and academic domains should be the target of such instruction. Home-based interventions or bilingual instruction in school that focus on L1 language development should emphasize language skills implicated in higher order cognitive processes and language for literacy and academic purposes. There is considerable transfer of these kinds of L1 language skills to the L2 and these are the skills that are associated with achievement in literacy and academic domains. More specifically, for example, ELLs can benefit from knowing that there are certain words in the L1 that have the same form as words in the L2 and that some of these words also share meaning. Even in English-only school settings, emphasis on English for academic purposes is likely to have the greatest payoff in student achievement. An emphasis on language for literacy and academic purposes, be it the L1 or L2, does not mean that language skills for day-to-day communication should be neglected. However, development of language skills for day-to-day communication is insufficient to promote high levels of literacy and academic achievement in school.

Subgroup Differences

A fourth finding to emerge from our analyses of this corpus of studies is the significance of differences among subpopulations of ELLs. The importance of differences between students was indicated in research on family and community variables as well as in research on crosslinguistic and cross-modal aspects of literacy development. Differences among subpopulations of ELL students was evident in multiple ways – in their learning strategies, their transfer of skills from the L1 to the L2, their motivations, and the influence of L1 use at home on achievement in school, among others. These kinds of differences were found in first versus later generations of Hispanic ELLs, in ELLs from low versus those from more advantaged socioeconomic backgrounds, and in ELLs with Hispanic versus Asian cultural backgrounds. Other neglected but important sources of difference are age or grade level upon entry to U.S. schools, capacity to learn (i.e., students with typical capacities for learning versus those with impaired capacities), and language typology. Student diversity warrants increased attention in future research, especially at the current time when accountability, and especially standards-based accountability, risks overshadowing pedagogical issues linked to diversity.

Time

Finally, time emerged as a significant factor in student learning. There are two aspects of time that are important: duration and consistency. The effects of duration were most evident in program evaluation studies. Evaluations of educational programs for ELLs who were in the program for a relatively short period of time produced results, in some cases, that differed sharply from evaluations that were conducted after the students had participated in the program for some time. Later evaluations produced more positive outcomes than early evaluations. It makes pedagogical and developmental sense that time is important because learning takes time and is cumulative. As a result, the true effects of educational programs are likely to be evident only after some time.

Consistency, another dimension of time, matters. Consistency of educational experience affords students developmentally coherent opportunities to learn. Programs that plan for coherence across grade levels and developmental stages yield more positive student outcomes than programs that do not. In fact, evaluation studies have shown that students exposed to a variety of different approaches perform poorly in comparison to students who have had consistent exposure to the same program over time. This is yet another reason why educators need comprehensive frameworks for planning instruction over time, as noted previously. We return to a discussion of the importance of development in planning research on ELLs in the next section. Continuous, coherent, and developmentally appropriate educational interventions are absolutely critical if ELLs are to achieve their full potential in school.

FUTURE DIRECTIONS

There is an overarching need for sustained, programmatic research that aims to build and test models of effective teaching and successful learning in school settings with ELLs. This calls for research whose primary goal is theory development. Shavelson and Towne (2002) have made a similar recommendation in the National Research Council report on *Scientific Research in Education* (see "Scientific Principle 2: Link Research to Relevant Theory"; Executive Summary, p. 7). Single studies with an immediate applied orientation lack generalizability and, thus, applicability to other educational settings. Widespread application of research findings to the benefit of large numbers of ELLs is more likely to come from sustained research efforts whose primary aim is a full and in-depth understanding of an issue than from one or two isolated studies on a specific topic. Applied research consisting of single studies is not as useful as theory-driven research in identifying the needs of ELLs across the United States. Support for theory-driven research with extended time frames calls for funding agencies and research institutes to support research activities without an emphasis on immediate application. It also calls for political authorities, in their policies and funding initiatives, to balance "improving education immediately" with "expanding our understanding" so that education can be improved over the long run. The latter requires time and material resources.

At the same time, consumers of educational research need to appreciate that findings about "best practices" do not necessarily mean "single best practice." Policymakers and the public at large must come to understand that there is not just one way to teach ELLs effectively. To the contrary, there are alternative ways to achieve satisfactory oral language, reading and writing, and academic outcomes for ELLs. Indeed, it is highly unlikely that a single instructional approach or method is likely to be effective for all ELLs given the diversity of backgrounds, resources, and challenges they bring to the learning environment, often within a single classroom. Educators need to be able to make use of alternative instructional approaches to promote the development of all ELLs under diverse and changing circumstances. Indeed, it is likely that equal outcomes can be achieved through the effective application of alternative methods. The important point here from a research perspective is that research designs that compare one method against another may be useful to answer some types of questions, but other designs may be needed when it is unreasonable to expect that there is one best or single answer. The challenge facing educational researchers is to identify the successful methods in terms of the circumstances and learners for which they are successful. To do this, researchers must apply a diversity of comparison points.

In general, the complexities of the educational enterprise call for varied and multiple research designs, including case studies, ethnographies, and classic experimental and quasi-experimental designs. In the field of monolingual language acquisition, for example, case studies and ethnographies have played critical roles in early theory development; Brown's case studies of Adam, Eve, and Sara (Brown, 1976) and Heath's ethnography of language and literacy development in children from minority backgrounds (Heath, 1983) are classic examples. Likewise, in the field of bilingualism, Leopold's monumental case study of his daughter, Hildegaard, was instrumental in launching research on bilingual acquisition and is still widely cited for its findings (Leopold, 1949). The case study approach is particularly useful during the initial stages of investigation into new issues or as a way of developing new theories. At the same time, more controlled experimental and quasi-experimental designs are essential if we are to expand exploratory investigations in systematic ways, to acquire in-depth understanding of particular issues, and to test the generalizability of alternative theoretical possibilities. Experimental and quasi-experimental designs are an important way of testing educational theory; they are required to systematically examine, refine, and elaborate theoretical possibilities and to test applications. In short, it is unlikely that a single research design or methodology will be able to address the full complexity and range of issues faced by educators working with ELLs. As Shavelson and Towne (2002) note: "... scientific claims are significantly strengthened when they are subject to testing by multiple methods.... Particular research designs and methods are suited for specific kinds of investigations and questions but can rarely illuminate all the questions and issues in a line of inquiry" (p. 7, Executive Summary).

We offer suggestions for future research in the following sections under three main headings: (1) Developmental Research, (2) Learners, and (3) Classrooms. We end with a recommendation for follow-up state-of-the-art reviews.

Developmental Research

Research on the oral language, literacy, and academic achievement of ELLs is fundamentally about learners' "development" in educational settings – how student competencies change over time and the maturational, socio-cultural, and pedagogical factors that facilitate or impede change. Truly longitudinal research on teaching and learning in settings with ELLs would be of significant benefit to the education community because it would yield insights about the complexities of the educational development of ELLs. Much of the research reviewed in this volume has examined learners at a single grade level or different learners at several grade levels (see, however, Howard, Christian, and Genesee, 2003; Reese et al., 2000). As a result, we have scant understanding of the actual developmental changes that ELLs go through during the acquisition of oral language, reading and writing, and academic skills from beginning level to mature, advanced levels. Research that focuses on ELLs at specific grades can give the impression that what is true for one age group is equally true for another and what works at one stage of development works at another. We need longitudinal research designs to test the extent to which this is really true. Lacking solid longitudinal research, we risk exposing students at different stages of development to ineffective learning environments.

Investigating the developmental changes that the same learners go through from grade to grade would contribute to our understanding of the role of specific maturational, sociocultural, and pedagogical influences on achievement and how these change and interact as learners mature and engage in school and community life. Since development is dynamic, a different combination of learner and instructional factors will probably account for learning at different grade levels. For example, it is likely that different components of oral and written language play important roles in learning to read and write at different stages of acquisition. We know from research on monolingual literacy acquisition that while phonological awareness plays a significant facilitating role in early stages of reading acquisition and, in particular, decoding, its importance diminishes in later stages. Likewise, when it comes to instruction, it is likely that specific instructional approaches and/or techniques will be differentially beneficial when learners are beginning to learn to read and write in comparison to when they have attained relatively advanced levels of skill at reading and writing. An understanding of these developmental changes can provide a solid basis for curriculum design and instructional intervention. There is a critical need for research on the development of writing skills. This was by far the most neglected domain of development and yet is, arguably, the most challenging since it draws on all other skills – oral language, reading, academic, and cognitive.

In the same vein, future research on the co-development of oral language, literacy, and academic skills is critical if we are to understand the developmental interdependencies of these interrelated skills and if we are to design educational initiatives that facilitate their co-development. There is a particularly strong need for research that examines the links between oral language and literacy development on the one hand and between oral language development and academic achievement on the other hand. We also need to know whether the same interdependencies in oral and written language characterize achievement in different academic subjects. We have much to learn about the level and kinds of oral language and literacy skills necessary to promote grade-appropriate academic achievement by ELLs and whether these depend on the nature of the subject matter – mathematics versus science versus social studies, for example. We also need to understand better the differential role of oral language and literacy (whether in L1 or L2) in fostering academic achievement at different grade levels as academic subject matter becomes more abstract, complex, and arguably language-dependent. This is an especially important issue in the education of ELLs who enter American schools in middle or high school and particularly in the case of students who have not had the benefit of prior education.

There are challenges to conducting developmental research in real school settings. This can be illustrated in the program of research initiated by Saunders and Goldenberg, a CREDE study designed to test, over time, the independent and combined effects of several instructional components within a successful transitional bilingual education program in southern California (see Saunders, 1999). During the study, legislation was passed in California that led to the demise of many bilingual programs so that the programs targeted in the study changed. While some of the intended research was completed (see Saunders and Goldenberg, 1999; and Saunders and Goldenberg, 2001), the longitudinal aspect of the project, although critical for investigating the success of students' transition, was not completed. Thus, while researchers and funding agencies should plan for sustained, longitudinal research, they should also be prepared for disruptions in their efforts that are brought about by circumstances beyond their control.

Learners

As we noted earlier, the lion's share of research attention has been on ELLs from Hispanic backgrounds. There is a need for research on the development of learners from other major ethnolinguistic groups in the

United States. Students of Vietnamese, Hmong, Cantonese, and Korean background need to be examined because they are the next most populous groups of minority students in the United States (Kindler, 2002). Including different ethnolinguistic groups is particularly important in research on the influence of instructional and noninstructional factors in order to determine if the same constellation of instructional and family/community influences accounts for learning when students come from different SES and language backgrounds. Research by Steinberg, Dornbusch, and Brown (1992) has shown that the particular constellation of factors that accounts for successful learning is different for Asian American, African American, and Hispanic high school students. Replication and extension of this line of research, including factors that are pertinent to ELLs specifically, would be useful. There is also a pressing need for additional research on ELLs in higher grades and on ELLs who enter the U.S. educational system in middle or high school, particularly those with little or no prior schooling. The learning demands on these students are especially challenging, and educators need more research on these particular students if they are to respond effectively to their needs.

We need to expand our understanding of English oral-language development in ELLs. English is both a goal of educational instruction and a means to achieving other goals and, in particular, academic excellence. Yet, of all the research domains we examined, oral-language development received the least empirical attention. We need research that describes the developmental course of oral-language proficiency in ELLs from different language/cultural backgrounds and in ELLs who enter the United States at different ages with different amounts of prior education and exposure to English. Moreover, as noted previously, we need empirical evidence of the relationship between oral-language development and academic achievement; for example, what oral-language skills are needed to succeed in mastering academic subjects and how do these change over time?

Additional research on ELLs with impaired capacities for language and/or academic learning is also needed if we are to address the needs of *all* ELLs, those with typical ability to learn as well as those with various disabilities. Future research would benefit from more detailed documentation of students' specific impairments. In this regard, researchers must be careful to differentiate students with endogenous impairments from those who are simply delayed in their language learning and/or academic achievement because of their second-language status. Current published research has shown little sensitivity to these confounding possibilities. There is also a serious need for research on the incidence and nature of impairment among ELLs and on the validity of assessment methods used to identify such students. Future research into the nature and extent of impairment in ELLs in comparison to monolingual English-speaking learners would be particularly useful because it would indicate whether ELLs who have learning/language impairments suffer from the same kinds of impairments and to the same extent as monolingual learners. This, in turn, would have considerable implications for the identification and education of ELLs with atypical capacities to learn. Regardless of ELLs' particular ethnolinguistic group membership or learning capacity, future research on ELLs must provide much greater detail about their linguistic, educational, and family backgrounds.

It would also be useful to conduct research on different groups of ELLs in the same studies. This would make it possible to ascertain how the oral language, literacy, and academic development of various groups differ and this, in turn, would help us to begin to identify which instructional interventions are appropriate in each case. For example, students may be (1) truly monolingual ELLs, (2) have relatively advanced levels of proficiency in both the L1 and the L2, (3) have stronger L1 than L2 skills, or (4) vice versa, have stronger L2 than L1 skills. A fundamental question within this domain of research is how the linguistic, cognitive, and educational development of students is influenced by their status as monolingual learners, proficient bilingual learners, or second-language learners. Addressing this fundamental question requires careful and detailed information about ELLs' language status.

Classrooms

The recommendations for future research in this section focus on classroom contexts. Our review revealed considerable research on alternative instructional approaches/strategies for teaching literacy to ELLs and a number of important general conclusions emerged from that review. As we noted in Chapter 4, educators need more than an array of specific methods or activities that they can draw on when planning literacy or academic subjects. They need comprehensive frameworks for selecting, sequencing, and delivering instruction over the course of an entire year and from grade to grade. Two frameworks that provide such guidance are the Five Standards for Effective Pedagogy (Tharp et al., 2000) and the SIOP model for integrating language and content instruction (Echevarria, Vogt, and Short, 2000). Taken together, these two frameworks provide tools for planning education that can incorporate a variety of instructional approaches to ensure that the learning environment is meaningful, coherent, and individualized. While both frameworks enjoy some empirical support (see Echevarria, Short, and Powers, 2003; and Tharp et al., 2000), extension of this work would serve to expand our understanding of the scope of their effectiveness. Neither framework is prescriptive but lends itself to variation and modification. Future research on specific variations of the Five Standards and SIOP models, alone or in combination, with students from different language backgrounds, at different ages/stages of development, and for different subject matter would help us refine our understanding of the conditions under which they work well.

Classrooms vary significantly from one another with respect to number of students, language and cultural backgrounds of students, SES, and prior literacy training, to mention some obvious dimensions of variation. Moreover, classrooms with ELLs often change as students enter and leave. With the exception of Lindholm's research on the effectiveness of two-way immersion programs in classrooms with different ethnolinguistic compositions (Lindholm-Leary, 2001), we have little understanding of how classroom composition affects teaching and learning or of how teachers cope with classrooms with different compositions of students. Some pressing questions arise: What is the nature of oral-language use, both teachers' and students', in classrooms with students whose mastery of oral English is limited? How can the oral-language development of ELLs be promoted in classrooms with learners with varied levels of English proficiency? How can instruction through English be delivered to ensure comprehension and mastery of academic material in classrooms with learners who have different learning needs? How does change in student composition over the course of the school year influence student interactions and learning? Future research is called for that focuses on the classroom as the unit of analysis in order to better understand the social and intellectual dynamics of classrooms and how to design instruction that is effective in different classroom contexts.

In a related vein, classrooms and the schools in which they are located do not exist in a vacuum. They are part of larger, more complex, and changing communities. Educators often remark on the relationship between the school and the community and the efforts they make to bring about collaboration between schools and communities. Future research with the community as the unit of analysis would help move us beyond impressionistic speculation to empirically grounded knowledge. Some fundamental questions arise: Does the ethnolinguistic composition of the community affect the expectations and goals of the community vis-à-vis their children's education and, by extension, the role of their children's teachers? What can or should teachers do in response to communities that might differ from mainstream Anglo-American communities? What can and should communities do to facilitate their child's education in mainstream schools?

While issues concerning teachers and professional development are dealt with in volume (details in this), we also believe that attention needs to be paid to teachers, including their levels and kinds of professional development, their understanding of different instructional and assessment approaches, their knowledge and application of second-language acquisition theory, and the processes that are required to ensure that new teachers acquire competence in using new approaches.

Future Reviews

In closing, our final recommendation is that systematic reviews of research findings on the oral language, reading and writing, and academic development of ELLs be undertaken on a periodic and regular basis. This would permit researchers and educators to take stock of current research on the education of ELLs and of our progress in investigating issues critical to planning effective education for these learners. In addition, there is a need for considerably more support of research on the education of ELL students. The statistics are clear – ELLs will constitute an ever-expanding and, thus, important portion of the school-age population. Effective education for ELLs means planning for their and the nation's future.

References

Brown, R. 1976. *A first language*. Harmondsworth, UK: Penguin.

Echevarria, J., Short, D., and Powers, K. 2003. *School Reform and Standards-Based Education: How do Teachers Help English Language Learners?* Technical Report. Santa Cruz: Center for Research on Education, Diversity & Excellence.

Echevarria, J., Vogt, M. E., and Short, D. J. 2000. *Making content comprehensible for english language learners: The SIOP model*. Needham Heights, MA: Allyn & Bacon.

Heath, S. B. 1983. *Ways with Words*. New York: Cambridge University Press.

Howard, E. R., Christian, D., and Genesee, F. 2003. *The development of bilingualism and biliteracy from grade 3 to 5: A summary of findings from the CAL/CREDE study of two-way immersion education*. Santa Cruz, CA, and Washington, DC: Center for Research on Education, Diversity & Excellence.

Kindler, A. L. 2002. *Survey of the states' limited English proficient students and available educational programs and services: 2000–2001 summary report*. Washington, DC: National Clearinghouse for English Language Acquisition & Language Instruction Educational Programs.

Leopold, W. 1949. *Speech development of a bilingual child: Volume 3*. New York: AMS Press.

Lindholm-Leary, K. J. 2001. *Dual language education*. Clevedon, UK: Multilingual Matters.

Reese, L., Garnier, H., Gallimore, R., and Goldenberg, C. 2000. Longitudinal analysis of the antecedents of emergent Spanish literacy and middle-school English reading achievement of Spanish-speaking students. *American Educational Research Journal* 37(3): 633–62.

Saunders, W. 1999. Improving literacy achievement for English learners in transitional bilingual programs. *Educational Research and Evaluation* 5(4), 345–81.

Saunders, W., and Goldenberg, C. 1999. The effects of instructional conversations and literature logs on limited- and fluent-English proficient students' story comprehension and thematic understanding. *The Elementary School Journal* 99(4), 277–301.

2001. Strengthening the transition in transitional bilingual education. In D. Christian and F. Genesee (eds.), *Bilingual education*. Alexandria, VA: Teachers of English to Speakers of Other Languages, Inc.

Shavelson, R. J., and Towne, L. 2002. *Scientific research in education*. Committee on Scientific Principles for Education Research. Washington, DC: National Academies Press. http://www.nap.edu/execusumm/0309082919.html

Steinberg, L., Dornbusch, S. M., and Brown, B. B. 1992. Ethnic differences in adolescent achievement. *American Psychologist* 47(6), 723–9.

Tharp, R. G., Estrada, P., Dalton, S. S., and Yamauchi, L. 2000. *Teaching transformed: Achieving excellence, fairness, inclusion and harmony*. Boulder, CO: Westview Press.

Appendix A

Definitions of Abbreviations in Research Summary Tables

%ile	percentile
ach	achievement
AM	American
assign	assignment
bil	bilingual
BINL	Basic Inventory of Natural Language
BOLT	Bahia Bay Oral Language Test
BR	basal reader
BSM	Bilingual Syntax Measure
btwn	between
CAT	California Achievement Tests
CO	Control Group
cog	cognitive
comp	comprehension
coop	cooperative
corr	correlation
CTBS	California Test of Basic Skills
def	definition(s)
diff	difference
dom	dominant
SABE	Spanish Assessment of Basic English
ELL	English language learner
Eng	English
EO	English only
ESL	English as a second language learner or program
FEP	fully English proficient; fluent English proficient
FLS	Functional Language Survey
GE	grade equivalent (score)
gp(s)	group(s)
GPA	grade point average

gr	grade
grads	graduates
hi	high
Hisp	hispanic
IC	Instructional Conversations
Integ	Integrated classroom
IPT	Idea Proficiency Test
ITBS	Iowa Test of Basic Skills
K	kindergarten
L1	first/native language
L2	second language
lang	language
LAB	Language Assessment Battery
LAS-O	Language Assessment Scales-Oral
LEP	limited English proficient
LD	learning disabled
MainEO	Mainstream English only classroom
MANOVA	multivariate analysis of variance
Mass	Massachusetts
Max	maximum
med	medium
multi	multiple
n	sample size
NCE	normal curve equivalent
non-int	non-integrated classroom
NSST	Northwest Syntax Screening Test
obs	observations
partic	participation; participants
PIAT	Peabody Individual Achievement Test
PPVT(-R)	Peabody Picture Vocabulary Test (Revised)
pro	pronoun
prof	proficient/proficiency
pt	point
r	coefficient of correlation
rdg	reading
rdg comp	reading comprehension
RSQ	Reading Strategy Questionnaire
SAT	Stanford Achievement Tests
SE	special education
SES	socio-economic status
sig, sign	significant/significantly
Sp, Span	Spanish
SOLOM	Student Oral Language Observation Matrix
SRA	Science Research Associates

stats	statistical
SW	southwest
TAAS	Texas Assessment of Academic Skills
TABE	Texas Association for Bilingual Education
TR	Treatment Group
TVIP-H	Test de vocabulairio en Imagenese Peabody- Adaptación Hispanoamericana
Voc/vocab	vocabulary
wk	week
WLPB-R	Woodcock Language Proficiency Battery-Revised
WRAT	Wide Range Achievement Test
wtg	writing
yr	year

Index

CPSIA information can be obtained at www.ICGtesting.com
Printed in the USA
BVOW07s0307280714

360590BV00001B/3/P